Bruce Logan provides us with a valuable and extended reflection upon many decades of cultural upheaval. *Pilgrim* is a beautifully written memoir, the product of hard-won insight, and full of wisdom and wit.

— **Rex Ahdar**
Emeritus Professor of Law
University of Otago

Pilgrim has helped me appreciate living with hope and purpose in a world that otherwise seems dominated by grotesque perversions, which we are told we must not only endure but also celebrate and subscribe to. I frequently reacted with 'aha' or 'yes, of course' as Logan elegantly plots the recent way-markers on the road to what could be the terminal decline of civilisation. There is a very satisfying precision in the explanations, which are delivered in an enticing story, rich with literary allusion.

— **Simon Tomey**
Business Consultant, UK

In this brilliant book, Bruce Logan describes the path we have taken to our current cultural state. He weaves the strands of long experience, observation, and wide reading and learning to explain our broken relationship with our origins and the moral base that sustained us for so long. It is an account that has application across Western civilisation. Completely accessible. It can and should be read by everyone.

— **Forrest Capie**
Professor Emeritus
City University of London

"Who would true valour see? Let him come hither . . ." Bruce Logan does just this in *Pilgrim*, his absorbing memoir of almost nine decades of experience as a husband, father, grandfather, teacher, researcher, writer, and perspicacious commentator. Having lived in many places around the world and witnessed unprecedented cultural change, Bruce carefully weaves anecdote and observation with profound spiritual and philosophical wisdom. The result is a beautifully compiled and compelling narrative that avoids the trap of sentimentality or nostalgia, issuing a timely warning about the choices facing Western civilisation.

— **Rev. Dr. Michael Reid**

Historian

Bruce Logan's *Pilgrim* demonstrates acuity, humility, and the clarity of an octogenarian who recognises what is at stake in the 'culture wars' and dares to name the culprits. His fascinating and beautifully written account paints the trajectory of how Western civilisation has arrived where it has. Significantly, his analysis contextualises the New Zealand experience and is a 'must-read' for anyone who finds him/herself navigating the consequences of a vortex of subjectivism where everything is true and nothing is true. The reader, however, is not left without hope. Logan's commentary is replete with allusions from a rich and bountiful canon of literature, theology, and philosophy, and points to a culture that can recover and find its 'true north': this requires a rejection of the counterfeit narratives and a return to the one true and eternal Author.

— **Desirée Williamson-Lay**

Leadership and Communication Consultant

Using the metaphor of pilgrimage, Bruce looks back over eighty years to document the social, religious, and cultural changes that have taken place during his lifetime. The eternal celestial city, once the destination for all pilgrims, has been replaced by a vanishing utopia, civilisation replaced by culture, moral authority removed from religion and transferred to the political sphere. Written with clarity, laced with irony and humour, a must-read for all who seek to understand the people and events that have shaped the days in which we live.

— **Brendan McNeill**
Entrepreneur and Investor

In *Pilgrim*, Bruce Logan frames his experiences as a pilgrimage toward Truth. Bruce convincingly argues that from the period of vibrant hope of post-war New Zealand to the fragmented present, there has been a progressive erosion of objective Truth, Judeo-Christian values, and belief in the human dignity gifted by a benevolent Creator, which has inevitably culminated in a society that has become morally adrift and intellectually confused. Bruce lays down a compelling challenge, a *wero,* a heartfelt call to rediscover the transcendent Truths that once anchored our young nation. He urges us to critically re-examine the divisive emerging ideologies that seek to shape the future of New Zealand against the canon of transcendent Truth and reclaim hope and meaning for humanity in an age of uncertainty.

— **Peter Juriss**
Educator

Which embedded beliefs lie behind your current approach to life? Behind our societal approach also? Not a small topic. But it's an epic one, and Kiwi octogenarian Bruce Logan is not afraid of it. Why do we need faith in something bigger, more awesome, more sublime? Who gets to choose what a 'good society' means? If free speech is a going concern, should this ordered freedom be universal? But is it? Bruce grasps his right to this freedom and truly has the courage of his convictions.

Don't dismiss his hard-won findings until you've taken a deep dive into the schools of thought he references. Bruce's scholarship and wisdom both underscore the importance of examining where we've collectively been, to see where we're logically headed.

— **Liesl Johnstone**
Journalist

Pilgrim

WILD SIDE PUBLISHING
Auckland, New Zealand
www.wildsidepublishing.com

ISBN Softcover 978-1-991299-86-4
ISBN EPub 978-1-991299-85-7

Typeset in Garamond Pro and Raleway.
Cover art by Rafferty Stuart.

Cataloguing in Publishing Data
   Title: Pilgrim: Multiculturalism, diversity and civil religion in New Zealand today
   Author: Bruce Logan
   Subjects: Culture and society; Cultural anthropology; Historic perspectives on contemporary issues; Contemporary New Zealand; New Zealand political landscape; Philosophy; Popular apologetics; Christian apologetics; Cultural Marxism; Multiculturalism in New Zealand; Church and state; Education reform; Human rights; Human sexuality; Diversity, equity and inclusion; Civil religion; Cultural relativism.

A copy of this title is held at the National Library of New Zealand.

Pilgrim

MULTICULTURALISM,
DIVERSITY AND CIVIL RELIGION
IN NEW ZEALAND TODAY

BRUCE LOGAN

To my wife, Mary, for her patience and generosity, and to my daughters, Alexis and Harriet, for their encouragement.

Ring the bells that still can ring
Forget your perfect offering
There is a crack, a crack in everything.
That's how the light gets in.

       — Leonard Cohen. Anthem. 1992.

I've often heard it said, a preacher
might learn with a comedian for a teacher.

     — Johann Wolfgang von Goethe, Faust, Part One.

Contents

I The Complaint in Brief   1

II Multiculturalism! What's That?   14

III What's Been Going On?   40

IV The Tricky Trinity: Identity, Politics and Therapy   91

V DIE, The Enemy of Character   108

VI When Rights Are Wrong   130

VII Sex Is a Big Deal   160

VIII Civil Religion   188

IX Education and Civil Religion   241

X In Case You Missed It   268

Books Worth Reading   285

Glossary of Key Words and Concepts   291

I

The Complaint in Brief

. . . But man, proud man,
Dress'd in a little brief authority,
Most ignorant of what he's most assured—
His glassy essence—like an angry ape.
Plays such fantastic tricks before high heaven
As makes the angels weep; who, with our spleens
Would all themselves laugh mortal.

Isabella in *Measure for Measure*. II.ii. 117-125

The temptation to tell lies would be too great, to try to justify one's self-centred folly. Hence, this is neither an autobiography nor a definitive examination of aspiration or folly. It's about being given a life long enough to be suspicious of human vanity, indeed, one's own vanity. Observations, one hopes, prove to be insightful but never self-important. Risking the accusation of nostalgia, it's what this beleaguered but hopeful octogenarian thinks he has discovered as he travels the road that increasingly reminds him of his mortality.

There was a time when I declared life a tragicomedy, a perverse comfort. Now that I'm older, pilgrimage is a better description. It's softer, and the pilgrim, forever realistic, on the way to the celestial city, is less likely to be tempted by cynicism. Tragicomedy tends to erode the comfort of hope, and without hope, the purpose of the journey gets lost.

Without conceding too much to the equity-loving levellers, there is a sense that we all need to know there is a prize at the end of the road. Some might be foolish enough to think they deserve it, and it might be that accusations of dementia will arise. I've been told examples are legion. However, this octogenarian, all eighty-seven years of him, doesn't have dementia—well, not yet. But the once-upon-a-time civilisation he has loved, shared, criticised, and enjoyed is well advanced in what looks like a prodigal forgetfulness. Around nearly every curve in the road, regulation-intoxicated bureaucrats undermine the confident freedom he took for granted in his youth. Indeed, civilisation's dementia is so advanced that the old signposts, defaced by graffiti, are becoming almost impossible to read. The relief of a satisfying conversation is not easily found. It's like what happened when the Tower of Babel came down: a lot of chatter but not much communication. It has become evident to this grandfather that any society that has lost its belief in the permanent reality of objective value has an immediate problem with moral and intellectual confidence.[1]

◆ ◆ ◆

Being an octogenarian has its downside; that's obvious. Well, there's some good news; it has benefits as well. Experience can sharpen the mind, and the 'lust of the flesh' doesn't consume all of one's energy. So, he tries to ignore the hastily painted signposts that would seduce him into scampering down the highway of forgetfulness. And it would be down; pilgrims worthy of the name travel only on the road that leads to the Celestial City. And that's the point: the Celestial City is real. By the grace of God, he would never drink from the water of Lethe, the sign-writers' favourite tipple. Keeping off the road that would take him to oblivion is not easy. The temptation is to shut his eyes and forget everything he has learned to love.

I remember watching an old western, considered a classic by many, with two of my grandsons one evening. We had been talking about movies, as you do with your grandsons. They asked me what movies I liked when I was their age. We watched one of my favourites, 'High Noon' (1952), starring Grace Kelly and Gary Cooper. And dear me, it was from another age, but the kids loved it.[2] It was worth watching for the opening scene alone. We shared a common delight in the victory of justice and the hero's vindication. It's a good story, and that evening it crossed the generations. The theme song, by Tex Ritter, is the perfect voice for a Western ballad and is unforgettable. *"Do not forsake me, Oh my darling, on this, our wedding day . . . If I'm a man, I must be brave."* Sure, it was in black and white and technologically a bit primitive, but the attractive power of masculine courage captured my grandsons' imagination. Even the word 'coward' turned up. I'm not sure we're allowed to use that word anymore. I went to YouTube and looked at the comments on the movie. Repeatedly, they were from a gratified father or grandfather watching the film with his children or grandchildren. Small beer, you might say, but I think not. The story reinforced the virtue that we shared and loved. I'm told young men and women, too, want to be courageous, although they may express their courage in different ways, as they very clearly did in the movie. And the kids picked up on that without any suggestion from me. I was thankful for the privilege and responsibility. Now, nearly two decades later, we can still talk about it. All good stories can cross generations; that's the point.

Attempting to make sense of the far-reaching religious and cultural changes in New Zealand over the last eight decades could prove foolhardy. Nevertheless, this pilgrim does know where he's going and where he's been. Doubtlessly, he will encounter the rolling eyes of post-modernity's recent innovations, middle-aged adolescents, and other young liberals, not to mention the older ones decorating our universities. Despite their fantasy, the Celestial City will not be replaced by Utopia either now or in the promised distant future.

Of course, I won't be able to avoid the rolling eyes and the accusations of nostalgia and naivety. I don't even want to. There's no way around it; many things I used to think true and good are no longer considered good or true; at the very least, they are under suspicion. My realisation of that makeover has been coming slowly, almost innocently at first, with an unthreatening frivolousness. But it has become more than just the self-serving, even comical adolescent scepticism that *Sportin' Life* displays in Gershwin's Porgy and Bess (1959). *"The t'ings dat yo' li'ble to read in da Bible, it ain't necessarily so." Sportin' Life* and his playmates were of their time, more wannabe tempters than philosophers, more the mocking voice in the school playground than the voice of a convincing sceptic.

Inevitably, we have moved on. History has been declared unnecessary; tradition is hidden under a shroud, and we must pretend to tolerate the intolerable. Yet, despite the appearance of confidence invested in that charade, we are afflicted by what I can only describe as a widespread spiritual ennui. I'm surrounded by lies I must believe.

I am engulfed daily in an ideology that tells me the science defending it is settled and, at last, it knows how human beings should live. Equity, a reconstructed notion of equality, is one of the romantic doctrines the state-supported ideologues would have me believe, absorb, and put into practice. Somehow or other, along with everyone else, I must be persuaded that social and economic outcomes should be the same for everyone. A tautology rolls over me. Justice is equity, and equity is justice. Contemporary human rights theory will liberate the oppressed.

In self-defence, just before I'm accused of self-serving nostalgia, I recall what Socrates allegedly said about young people: *"They love luxury, have bad manners, gobble up food, and terrorise their teachers."* Criticising youth can be a satisfying sport for the aged, although I suspect that criticising tradition has become an even more enjoyable sport for the young. Maybe Socrates was right. And, by the way, he confessed to having a poor memory, unlike this pilgrim. Masculine, as he certainly was, described himself as a *"midwife"* to his ideas; a woman, Diotima, was his teacher. His past didn't limit him, and neither does mine. Nor do I yearn to possess the future. It's not self-indulgent, bad-mannered kids I'm worried about. My concern is the vacuous rhetoric of diversity and inclusion we would pass on to our children, seducing them into thinking they have a moral foundation by which to live. I have nine grandchildren, not all equally lovable, but I love them all. I am anxious about their future.

If we are guilty as a nation, it's not to be found in a failure to take racism or sexism seriously, or whatever other *'ism'* there might be. The past is there to shed light on the present. It doesn't help when we try to interpret the past with minds convinced by DIE (diversity, inclusion, and equity) propaganda. (I've given the widespread use of DEI my particular spin because it will end not only in tears but with the suicide of Western civilisation.) My concern is the failure to pass on what we know, or once knew to be true, to our children. A nation that fails with its children fails everywhere. Parents still love their children, but we have lost our collective sense of duty and loving responsibility towards the next generation. Loss of confidence is causing us to believe all kinds of nonsense. For example, rights have become disconnected from their duties; fact and opinion are frequently conflated, while social justice theory has reduced life to a struggle between the oppressor and the oppressed. We are only succeeding in making the next generation more anxious.[3]

◆ ◆ ◆

This is a story of one who still believes that truth is discoverable and that tolerance is about holding one's nose and getting on with it. It's not a unique story. Thousands of older New Zealanders share the journey, although 'pilgrimage' might not be at the front of their minds. They remain sojourners, nevertheless. Religious beliefs, private and public morality, politics, civil society, and technology have evolved so rapidly that it has been challenging to keep up. So, this is about one New Zealander's attempt to come to terms with all that and explain why he talks of a 'pilgrimage'. Not entirely from slate to the Internet, but just about. For the information of younger readers, slate was what children used to write on in class as recently as the mid-nineteenth century. Some older readers might remember that in *Anne of Green Gables,* Anne whacked Gilbert Blythe over the head with a slate for calling her *"Carrots"* and tugging her red hair. Not the best start for somebody who would later become Anne's husband. But that's what happened back then. Pulling a girl's hair was a clumsy, masculine attempt to be noticed. Now, as they say, the Internet would go viral.

An octogenarian can easily be out of step in a society that would make its doctrine of inclusion compulsory. Still, there's much more going on here than the grumpiness of an old man lost in what passes for justice in our latter-day world of 'diversity, inclusion, and equity'. The foundation of my world has been plundered. I say 'plundered' deliberately. The crown jewels have been stolen, and the thief plans to replace them with counterfeit versions. Not only would he replace the original with the counterfeit, but the unrepentant thief would insist the counterfeit is more valuable.

I first gained insight into the theft, although I didn't fully understand it then, during a conference of English teachers in my first year as the head of the English department in a rapidly growing school. The main address was given by someone considered a guru on *The New English,* which I talk about later. Anyway, I thought what he said was gobbledygook. I dared say so to some of my colleagues and was rapidly put in my place. They were convinced they were replacing error with a new kind of truth. It took me a while to see that the counterfeit was a chameleon with pretensions of permanence. Variously, cultural relativism, critical theory, anti-race theory, queer theory, identity politics, something called cancel culture, and another something called virtue signalling would come to underpin the cultic identity politics of magisterial multiculturalism. King Charles III, bless him, still calls it by its original name, 'political correctness', in his disenchantment with the contemporary Church of England.[4] The present popular name is, of course, 'woke.' I'm not sure whether that description is gaining or losing popularity. Whatever we call it, it's a slippery beast, taking on different identities to disguise its religious pretensions as it captures the culture.

Unenlightened by any sense of irony, we have drifted into what appears to be the unintelligible servility of self-imposed conformity in the name of diversity. It's a bit like kids protesting about school uniforms, as they submit to the restrictions of prevailing fashion. Having misunderstood the civilisation that knew how to tolerate legitimate protest, protestors infected by amnesia have become an instrument to undermine the civilisation that nurses them. The protesters cannot consider that civilisation will have its revenge. But vengeance it will have, I fear.

So, *feeling* safe, rather than *being* safe, is a big deal. That's unsurprising; the counterfeit copies fudge the gap between fantasy and reality. Indeed, in that crazy all-inclusive part of life we now call politics, an illiberal elite in the universities, a poorly educated MSM, and confused politicians insist on everyone submitting to their fantasy. At the same time, old 'proles' like me cling haphazardly to a fuzzy realism. I don't think it's just my octogenarian imagination, but a new *enfant terrible*, 'psychological safety,' with a trigger warning for snowflakes,[5] has become necessary to preserve that ubiquitous fantasy of self-esteeming identity. We think less and feel more. The sentimentalists make up the new hegemony.

By psychological safety, I mean that a belief in the sovereignty of self-asserting tribal identity is so self-evidently a good thing and deeply embedded that it must be that we can live in our own selected sanctuaries and control the fulfilment of our fantasies. It's unlikely that the safe space refugee could ever come to grips with Hamlet's dilemma of self-examination:

> "Whether 'tis nobler in the mind to suffer
> The slings and arrows of outrageous fortune,
> Or to take arms against a sea of troubles,
> And by opposing end them." (III. I)

The safety spacers would probably think that Hamlet is advocating for protest. The anguish of prevaricating nobility is a concept that just might be lost to them.

◆ ◆ ◆

I don't think that my childhood during the immediate post-World War II years was an aberration; neither physical nor psychological security was ever an issue for my friends or me. We're all boomers now; we were too young to have comprehended the horrors of the War. We wouldn't have understood the conceptual machinery of a 'safe space' even if someone had brought it to our attention. In the 1950s, a young boy, freckles or not, had good reason to be safe and feel safe. So, too, did girls, for that matter. Family life had its problems; it always has, and family life in the 1950s in southern New Zealand was far from perfect. However, it still had enough power to shape our identity and meaning. Although published in 1947, very few parents at the time read Carle C. Zimmerman's seminal *Family and Civilization*. Perhaps that didn't matter; they would have thought his conclusions were common sense. One needs to take anecdotal evidence with a grain of salt, but I suspect that family abuse has increased rather than decreased.

Reading comics about *Superman* or the *Phantom* was far from social media. Every Tuesday, I would buy *The Champion*, a publication praising the heroic, from fighter pilots to fourth form (Year 9) rebels. We even read books. Pornography addiction—what's that? Drugs? Well, there's aspirin. The weekly *Girls Crystal* is even further away. Even the name sounds like it's from another planet. The so-called 'Long March through the Institutions' might have entered Antonio Gramsci's Italian Marxist mind, although it was still a mere shibboleth rising from the dark halls of the Frankfurt School, not yet ferreting its way into the United States. Heroism was still possible and desirable. Stories for boys tended to be almost entirely about the importance of choosing between good and evil. Indeed, there was a heaven to gain and a hell to avoid. I remember it well because I was one of those boys. Heaven might have come with a price for the hero, but it was always possible. That was the point.

If we were afraid of anything, it might have been the smelly, eccentric peddler plying the suburb on his overloaded bike. We imagined his sleaze without understanding. He would take our photographs with his 'Baby Brownie' and try to sell them to our parents for a shilling (ten cents). I still have a picture he took of me flashing my pocketknife at the world. Pocket knives were a big deal for little boys in those days. Flashing my pocketknife, I ruled the world. In 2025, such a display would indicate, without any doubt, that I was on the road to a life of violence.

So, if you were to ask me what the difference is between then and now, I would have to say—Hope. We had it in spades, as they say. Even in our early teens, we were still unworldly, laughing at the strange man who hung around our dressing shed after we had a cold shower following rugby practice. Hot water had been invented, but it hadn't made its way into our showers. Anyway, cold showers are good for you. We weren't afraid or even indignant. We knew what perverts were, or thought we did.

Perhaps we were somewhat overconfident in our unthreatened identity. Racial identity, for example, was a non-issue. The best player on the team was a Māori and nearly made the All Blacks. He remained a close friend, and we always kept in touch when we found ourselves in the same city, until he died. The Great Depression was a distant memory, and the War had faded into the background. There was no reason to fear the future—quite the opposite. And when the Cold War did eventually invade our psyches, particularly during the Cuban Crisis in the early 1960s, hope remained to dilute our fear. At least we were nearly all in it together; now it would seem we're in nothing together. Membership in one of the ever-increasing number of tribes is the bottom line. John Lennon's *Imagine* has become the anthem of tribal and global unity.

Now I know the blight on society, which we now call domestic violence, existed in the 50s and 60s. Doubtless, some women stayed in abusive marriages because the social climate made it difficult or even impossible to leave. Family life was not all beer and skittles, as we used to say. Nevertheless, the impact of pervasive single parenthood on what we have come to call the mental health of children was yet to come. And just in case I am misunderstood, this is not a condemnation of the individual single parent because many battle to do their very best under challenging circumstances. I have firsthand experience with that through one of my daughters. She has done and continues to do a sterling job. Many successful men and women are fulsome in their praise of a single parent, usually the mother. Nevertheless, it is a criticism of a society that encourages single parenthood by failing to accept that marriage and the natural family contribute to moral integrity, mental health, and national unity. Perhaps because of that failure, we fail to realise that the family is the critical institution of civil society.

◆ ◆ ◆

It's evident to this octogenarian that we are losing any credible conviction about what it means to be human—if we have not already lost it. Many of us no longer believe that any dignity we might have left was given to us by our Creator. It comes as no surprise to me that a gathering shadow of confused identity chills the post-modern mind. I won't admit it's my age, and I certainly agree with what Carl R. Trueman says in *The Desecration of Man (First Things, January 2024)*: *"With no God-given human nature and no God-ordained human end, the question 'What is man?' is easily answered. He is nothing much; his nature, too, is disenchanted."*

It's this creeping paralysis of moral and intellectual unity that concerns me. Any insight we might have about the human condition is distorted by an overwhelming but unstable materialism, even if Richard Dawkins calls it the *"truth of secular humanism."* And here's the rub: Richard Dawkins, for example, discusses secular humanism as though it were a thing, a philosophically and morally neutral state of being that one achieves by being a rational and reasonable human being. And Dawkins is not alone in his presumption that a neutral secular humanism exists. Indeed, it is one of the great miscalculations of our time.

Having grown up in a Christianised civilisation, the so-called secular humanists think that objectivity is the product of their rationality, whereas, in contrast, it depends on the order intrinsic to God's creation. For example, scientific method relies on a belief in that order; it is not the creator of order. Scientific method cannot give rise to scientific method any more than subjectivity can provide neutral objectivity. The presumed assertion that cultural relativism (CR) is the foundation on which we must all stand, is the Devil's confidence trick, reinforced by the over-reaching descendants of *Giant Despair* from *Doubting Castle* in Bunyan's *The Pilgrim's Progress*. Most recently, the apostles of DIE would proselytise with astonishing confidence from their contemporary taxpaid faculties in the institutions of Pharisaic Retreat.

Notes:

1. See Glossary for explanation of the term 'objective value'.

2. *High Noon* is readily available on YouTube. Well worth a watch with your children.

3. Haidt, Jonathan. *The Anxious Generation*. Penguin Books. 2025.

4. *Daily Express*. Nov. 1, 2024.

5. I take this term "Snowflakes" from Michael Rectenwald's *Springtime for Snowflakes*. New English Review Press. 2018.

II

Multiculturalism! What's That?

Queen of this universe!
Do not believe those rigid threats of death.
Ye shall not die.
Ye shall be as Gods,
Knowing both good and evil as they know.
John Milton. *Paradise Lost*. Book 9. 684-688

I was living in Australia in 1972 when I first heard the term 'multiculturalism' introduced into conversation. A trendy academic friend believed that Australians weren't taking the culture of immigrants seriously enough. The policy of assimilation, reinforced by a self-assured Australian society, had to go. I only partially understood the claim, but she spoke with such conviction that it was difficult to believe she might be guilty of wishful thinking or just wrong. We were yet to be seduced by the ubiquitous politics of 'identity,' and I was not yet educated about what would become known as the '*Long March through the Institutions.*' Indeed, it would become a very long march attempting to undermine any vision I might have had of the good and the beautiful. Eventually, the contrast between the 'Long March' and its revision of the good and beautiful would encourage me to view, without embarrassment, my long life as a pilgrimage replete with the joy of a grateful heart. A pilgrimage is not a march. By the simplest definition, a pilgrim wanders and struggles on the way home but never marches. Soldiers march, as my law professor friend, Rex Ahdar, reminded me.

◆ ◆ ◆

The immediate catalyst for my Australian friend's outburst, which seemed reasonable enough then, was the arrival in Australia during the 1950s and 1960s of over half a million mainly Greek and Italian immigrants. Australia's population in 1950 was eight million. Older readers might recall John O'Grady's 1957 novel, *They're a Weird Mob*, or the 1966 film adaptation. The problem I realised much later was that my friend and I had a superficial grasp of the meaning of 'culture.' We certainly had no idea of the difference between the easily recognisable, tangible, and sometimes stereotypical norms of 'surface culture' and what I eventually understood as 'deep culture.'

Indeed, it wasn't until I became acquainted with Harold Turner, one of New Zealand's insightful theologians, in the mid-1980s, that I understood the difference.[1] With the best will in the world, we were blundering into areas of human meaning that we didn't understand. But we were young and idealistic enough to think we could change the world. A dangerous belief at any time, particularly in the mind of a politician, as my voluble Australian friend turned out to be.

Neither of us anticipated that 'culture' would become a neutering catch-all term to replace 'civilisation.' A pejorative vocabulary of self-righteous deceit lurked in the wings, preparing to colonise our minds. Indeed, Western civilisation would come to be 'Eurocentric,' 'sexist,' 'hegemonic,' 'colonialist,' 'systemically racist,' 'homophobic,' and inexplicably 'transphobic,' quite beyond redemption.

It was beyond our imagination that a ubiquitous and dogmatic ideology, with its insistence on the equality of all cultures, would compel everyone to be convinced of its commandeering 'truth,' promising new freedom. I had no reason to suspect that the moral authority underpinning civil society would be removed from religious tradition and surrendered to the political. I'm sure my academic friend didn't either. We had no idea of the struggle that lay ahead.

Despite latter-day disclaimers, we grew up in a society that respected tolerance; we didn't talk about it much, but it was a virtue that carried intimations of prudence and courage. It seems to me that tolerance, most recently, has come to be a bit like sex: talk is compensation for action. Anyway, we put up with things we disagreed with, and as I said, we held our noses and got on with it. Most of us still shared our thoughts on what we thought was right or wrong. Perhaps we were naïve, with limited experience, but not narrow-minded; however, I suspect that difference passed us by. The music teacher at my high school was probably a functioning alcoholic, but everyone put up with him, even if he did turn up sometimes under the weather. He was amusing and somewhat vulnerable in a way that adolescent boys can understand vulnerability. We liked him; he did a good job. We thought he was somewhat anti-establishment, and we were convinced that he was an excellent musician. Eccentrics were fascinating, even romantic figures. Looking back, we were more prepared to tolerate differences than the 'inclusionists' are today. Suspicion of difference was more the consequence of simple prejudice than imposed doctrine. We didn't delight in all differences. Of course, some were more acceptable. We were kids. The abstractions of an overreaching ideology had not yet arrived to threaten the naivety of our shared humanity.

I've often wondered about that pleasure in difference, wondering if it's realistic. I think it is. Immigrants were still a novelty, but we weren't expected to embrace an ideology demanding respect for doctrinaire difference. We were confident in our shoes, and any difference wasn't threatening, although our limited horizon hardly encouraged a broad mind. When I was ten or eleven, I recall speaking to a few Dutch immigrants and refugees from Indonesia and telling one of them that he had an accent. He smiled and told me I had one, too. I denied it, of course. Nevertheless, he was fascinating, a novelty to be enjoyed. In 1970, I recall meeting a friendly and talkative black man in a Montreal bar. 'People of Colour' was a phrase yet to be invented. We both had some time on our hands. He was from Nigeria, and I told him I was from New Zealand, but he had no idea where New Zealand was. Everything we learned about each other was a novelty. I loved the chat, and it made my afternoon. Alas, it was before the days of e-mail, and we lost touch.

How could we have imagined that cultural relativism, and what was to become multicultural dogma, would turn our enjoyment of difference into a command not to notice it? The education informed by natural discernment would be overwhelmed by the doctrine of discrimination. Years later, the intrusion of cultural relativism would make it less likely to take advantage of the chance of a Montreal meeting. Intimations of racial tension would have got in the way. I had no idea that multiculturalism would come to inform the derivative morality of cultural relativism and to demand not tolerance but an affirmation of what we once thought intolerable. It took some years to comprehend that the ideology would prove to be fraught with an inherent contradiction—that multiculturalism could only be mastered by acting as a parasite on the civilisation from which it was born. My pilgrimage was to teach me that equity, sometimes referred to as social justice, is the sinister offspring of cultural relativism. Equity, which demands equal outcomes for everyone, differs vastly from the traditional notion of equality under the law and the belief in equal opportunity we once took for granted.

I had no idea that human dignity would cease to be a gift from our Creator and instead be declared a right bestowed by one's tribe and confirmed by an overreaching state: Everyone, perhaps even octogenarians, must be protected by a levelling of talent, temperament, and proportional representation in every aspect of political life. Everyone must have the same prize. As early as 1996, British writer Melanie Phillips was discerning this in her excellent *All Must Have Prizes*. Her book remains as enlightening as it was when I read it a year after its publication. *"Ideas have consequences,"* a young friend of mine used to say. Equality of outcomes is a logical consequence when cultural relativism becomes the foundation of our civilisation. Indeed, the word 'civilisation' has all but disappeared from our vocabulary.

By 1987, a passionate acolyte of cultural relativism was a dog with a bone, at least in California. On January 15 of that year, five hundred protesting students led by Jesse Jackson chanted outside Stanford University's main gate, *"Hey hey, ho ho, Western civ has got to go."* The

University's introductory humanities programme, 'Western Culture,' lacked diversity. It is no longer Western civilisation, just Western culture, where prizes are unevenly distributed. Astonishingly, the academics and the university administrators, either out of timidity or a shared ideology, seemed more than willing to appease the youthful protesters. A replacement programme, *Cultures, Ideas, and Values,* which included the study of texts on race, class, and gender, was hastily put together. Other universities followed in the United States. Eventually, the entire English-speaking world became a multicultural society, enlightened by the new Stanford programme. Still, slow off the mark, it took me some years to realise that 'diversity' was no longer a mere synonym for variety; that it was to become the received doctrine underpinning aspiration and salvation.

According to the Stanford students, hegemonic Western civilisation lacked diversity, and such *"inequity"* had to be remedied. Everyone had to accept what was to become multiculturalism's vision of the world: a servile assortment of different races and unfamiliar cultures living under its self-righteous version of quixotic folly, but without the comedy. In the 1980s, I didn't anticipate that tolerance in the context of cultural relativism would become so intolerant; perhaps I should have. Had I done so, I might have warned one of my daughters, who began her university studies in 1989. But then, that was some year—the Berlin Wall fell, and demonstrations in Tiananmen Square ended in massacre.

Although many students might not have heard of Jean-Jacques Rousseau, they were seduced by his ideas, which had become elevated to a creed. In his 1755 *Discourse on the Origin of Inequality among Men,* he said, *"equality which nature established among men"* had to be restored, and *"the inequality which they have instituted among themselves"* had to go. And, closer to home, there was the impact of Herbert Marcuse's *"repressive tolerance"*—a pernicious doctrine yet to infect nearly every university campus.

◆ ◆ ◆

The chanting Stanford students might not have wanted all classes, races, and tribes to have equal opportunities and outcomes in every endeavour. It's unlikely they had thought through the consequences of their demands. The world was not like their privileged Californian belief in the reality of fantasy. People live where apparent variables cannot be changed, nor do they necessarily want them changed. Although I'm sure they would have denied it, the students enjoyed the uniformity of supervised thought and conscience to camouflage their pretensions. In any case, that's what they got. Historical revisionism: the child just out of the womb, not yet bold or strong enough to bring about the obfuscation of scientific method, causing it to collapse into its counterfeit, scientism. The historical subtleties of the human condition were beyond the students. Perhaps not a wilful blindness, but unlike Gustav Mahler, they didn't understand that *"Tradition is not the worship of ashes, but the preservation of fire."* Growing up in California failed to convince them that life is not for the faint of heart.

Newly married, my first experience of California was in 1968. At first, I sensed something in the air that wasn't foreign to me: the pervasive atmosphere of hope. The world was a great place, and it could only get better. Los Angeles was vibrant, exciting, and good-natured. I had heard, attributed to Horace Greeley, *"Go West, young man."* Pioneering and hopefulness are always a happy couple. But I didn't know that Hope was seeking a new mistress under the covers. I didn't understand the cause of the hope I had experienced as a child and thought I felt in California. I knew almost nothing of what was happening in Paris, the revolt of the disenchanted entitled. I might have heard of Jean-Paul Sartre, a strange phenomenon called *Existentialism,* and the gossip around his affair with Simone de Beauvoir.

Two years later, when I became a graduate student, I was to encounter Albert Camus' 1942 novel *L'Étranger* and other absurdist and existential works. The nihilism and disillusionment of the main character, Meursault, and his rebellion against traditional morality defied my comprehension. In 1968, I wasn't aware of either nihilism or disillusionment, the questioning of meaning in an indifferent universe. Of course, as time has passed, I now understand why the European spiritual ennui after the Second World War took on an entirely different character in the United States. American optimism encouraged young people to believe they could change the world. They were secure and safe, unlike much of Europe, which was suffering the consequences of the Second World War.

That civilisation grows out of the religion that orders its morality seems to have dodged the Stanford students, academics, and administrators. On the other hand, perhaps the academics understood only too well what they wanted, as did Rousseau and his influential acolyte, Herbert Marcuse, who sought a replacement overarching narrative: *the transcendent has to be replaced; the material world is all there is. Naturalism must black out belief in God the Creator.* Whatever the case, it's unlikely that the Stanford students had thought through the consequences of their demands for the liberation they imagined would come with the imperative of diversity.

I can assert, with some insight, that the students didn't understand the culture's deep religious foundation and binding nature. They were blind to the mythology, theology, and history that had given rise to Western civilisation's philosophy and its theology of the human body and its destiny. Any belief in the value of a literary canon was to become anathema. Notably, the biblical declaration of human dignity could no longer serve as the basis for any theory of civil society or ideas of political authority. I was to learn that traditional literature, art, and music were to lose their power to redefine and humanise. Any distinction between high and low culture would be wiped from the slate.

Indeed, the Stanford students would never have thought that their demand for diversity could only happen in a Christian-dependent civilisation, that they were victims of an ungrounded altruism severed from its roots. It took me a while, but I gradually realised they were lightweight imitators of the nineteenth-century utilitarians who believed that Christian morality could be retained without God. Of course, they didn't think like that, but that's what they were doing. They would find their way to a workable, inclusive morality with sufficient passion. Now, approaching the second quarter of the twenty-first century, the folly of that belief should be evident to all of us. In nearly every Western country, almost every social indicator is in decline. The sensible thing would seem to be that we should ask why.

◆ ◆ ◆

In 1969-1970, conscious of our privilege, I lived with my wife, Mary, in an apartment block for postgraduate students in Toronto. The animus of the Stanford students' protesting spirit was still to come. Accusations of racism and colonialism had not yet 'matured', if one can use that word in such a context. Nevertheless, protest, given much of its 'rage' by the war in Vietnam and the unpopular draft by lottery, was to become a rite of passage. Toronto became a sanctuary for draft dodgers. One stayed with us for a few days. Although we were still young, we couldn't fail to notice our guest's remarkable lack of knowledge about the world. Of course, I still didn't understand it, but 1968 and 1969 were pivotal years heralding what was to come. It was midsummer—July 20, 1969—when Apollo 11 landed on the moon. At a party that lasted much of the day and most of the night, we watched Neil Armstrong walk on the moon and proclaim, *"That's one small step for a man, one giant leap for mankind."* We thought it wonderful; it seemed to match the spirit of the time. Richard Nixon had been in the White House for only six months; *Watergate* was yet to come, and optimism ran high.

A month later, there was Woodstock. Many of the students in our block travelled south, and when it became a free-for-all after the fences were taken down, news spread quickly; nearly all of us followed suit. Looking back, the whole thing seems so poignant. Of course, all the chatter about peace and love was always somewhat pathetic, but it didn't seem so then. Perhaps I was missing something, but I could never get excited about Jimi Hendrix's music. Crosby, Stills, Nash, and Young were more appealing. Despite the rain and inadequate sanitation, I suspect our flowering of hope as kids in the 1950s gave Woodstock its passion. Alas, it was a fantasy that evolved into a nightmare, transforming the human landscape into something more pedestrian than we ever imagined.

Looking back, I now understand that I was somewhat intimidated during the first few months of my graduate studies. In my class, thirteen of us, the whole class, had managed to secure a Province of Ontario graduate scholarship. That's why we were there. It seemed to me at the time that all the others were very bright. They were from illustrious places like Oxford, Harvard, Montreal's McGill, and less exotic places like Cardiff. The Cardiff graduate became a frequent squash-playing opponent, even if he did have the odd habit of wearing unwashed socks around his neck to cure his frequent colds. The lean and hungry-looking Oxford aesthete was the most intimidating. He knew so much more than the rest of us and delivered his knowledge with what looked like disdain. He spoke with authority on Samuel Beckett, Sartre, and Camus, as well as 'the absurd', Existentialism, and the Frankfurt School. I later realised that he was a progressive relativist in embryo—the "very perfect model of the modern cultural relativist".

◆ ◆ ◆

Slowly, the dogma of multiculturalism, lurking unformulated in the demands of Stanford students, has become the story that shapes us—not because it is understood, but because it isn't. It might be helpful to note that there are at least two distinct approaches to engaging with multiculturalism. One is to see the arrival of legal immigrants into a host nation as an educator of the host nation. In the Australian case, new interesting habits, different food, a distinct fashion sense, more stimulating conversation, European-style café street action, and even the fascination of hearing foreign languages spoken were stimulating. Viewed this way, multiculturalism is an enriching phenomenon that helps us appreciate and enjoy the differences of others. By the mid-1970s, those multicultural delights had reached Brisbane, a large country town where I lived with my wife and firstborn daughter. Visiting an Italian or Greek restaurant on a warm Queensland evening was enjoyable, although it had lost its novelty. Maybe I was seduced by all the fallen blue Jacaranda flowers sparkling on the moist grass in New Farm Park. Perhaps the perfume of the frangipani just outside our bedroom window gave rise to a feeling of relaxed well-being. Warm evenings and youthful optimism are a heady mix.

The second way to view multiculturalism is to accept it as the foundational ideology underpinning human rights legislation. Forget the theological verities and historical events that shaped Western civilisation, and go along with the mind-numbing assertion that all cultures are equal. I don't think there was any way I could have understood in 1974 that the Greek/Italian multicultural "enrichment" was a simplified microcosm, a canary in the mine, of what was to become the overwhelming ideology that would eventually control us all. I was almost as ignorant as the Stanford students. Anyway, the differences between Greek, Italian, and Australian cultures were not that significant at a deep level. The 'romance of the primitive' was yet to come.[2]

◆ ◆ ◆

If all cultures are equal, how do we know each culture's uniqueness so we might experience the pleasure of affirming the new tolerance? Cultural relativism, I have discovered, rests on nothing more than ideological assertion. It's just as much a product of the 'hegemonic business', to use Gramsci's pejorative neologism, which describes the so-called 'Eurocentrism' it despises. The cultural relativist presumes it's possible, even desirable, to step outside traditional religion and culture and condemn it while approving all other faiths and cultures. On what grounds does the relativist criticise the culture, more accurately the religion, that gave rise to any idea of dignity he or she possesses? They repeat Marx's erroneous 'Scientific Socialism.' They would sit in judgement of Western civilisation, although it was that civilisation that gave them the tools for criticism. It's like trying to take one boot off and then wondering why you walk funny. The presumption of moral neutrality is a fantasy born out of vanity and envy. It's a variation of the temptation in the Garden, as it encourages us to believe that we can discern the difference between right and wrong without Divine guidance.

I have learned to believe that the diversity fantasy is a reductionist and counterfeit replacement for the first two of the Ten Commandments, the summation of the Law, as Jesus said. *"Love God with all your heart, mind, and strength, and your neighbour as yourself"* is not the moral imperative of the progressive multiculturalist mind, despite all the hype around kindness. Perhaps I should have noticed how the psychological theory of self-esteem gradually replaced the biblical foundation of human dignity, which gave heart, contented confidence, and power to the moral concept of self-respect. The theory of self-esteem, which emerged in the 1970s to challenge the notion of discipline in schools and the home, encourages us to discover ourselves by exploring the human psyche and looking inward rather than outward to the permanence of traditional virtue. In our way, it might seem we have caught up with Alexander Pope's (1688-1744) *Essay on Man, "Know then thyself. Presume not God to scan. The proper study of mankind is man."* Pope goes on to say that man is . . .

> *"A being darkly wise, and rudely great:*
> *Born but to die, and reas'ning but to err . . .*
> *Chaos of thought and passion, all confused . . .*
> *Sole judge of truth, in endless error hurl'd:*
> *The glory, jest, and riddle of the world!"*

The human imagination, *"Great lord of all things, yet a prey to all,"* always searching for its identity, has undergone a subtle and profound transformation. Self-examination has lost its critical power. The humility that comes with the *gentle contemplation of the world's riddle,* the mystery of existence, continues to fade from our consciousness. Such an impoverished imagination ensures that neither you nor I are humble sinners confronting the possibility of death every day and needing redemption; instead, we are self-defining, unsuspecting, imitation Prometheans whose meaning is found in the satisfaction of desire. We're all adolescents now. I suspect that the poignancy of the struggle between vision and temptation is beyond the levelling of multicultural theory. The Sublime is undoubtedly beyond it. Ah! The sublime, what's that? That sense of mystery, necessary to a satisfying understanding of the human condition, has evaporated into the poison of subjectivism.

So, what is wrong with the second view of multiculturalism, and what does it look like to this octogenarian? First, it is a bold, bare-faced lie, if I may be pardoned, a cliche. It is sustained neither by reason nor history; it is the creation of ideologues presuming the title of intellectual. It presupposes that cultures share the dignity possessed by men and women created in God's image, while it denies the source of that dignity. And it's the denial of the source that gives multiculturalism its energy and animus against Christianity. It appears to uphold justice and respect for differences when it insists on imposing uniformity and its version of justice. And that imposition is not open to examination, because it's the emperor without clothes. The real Prometheus is let loose among us.

Looking back, I can now see the first evidence of the shift in our grasp on identity: the replacement of sinners by victims. It is almost impossible to overestimate the profound significance of this shift in our understanding of what it means to be human. If you are not a sinner who has offended a holy God, then you are a victim of someone else's oppression or maybe nature's savagery. In what else might one find the cause of suffering? One's whole life is spent learning to come to terms with that oppression and savagery without the knowledge of what one is even doing. The ancients did better. They came to grips with fate by appeasing the gods. The modern pagan, the redesigned tribal member, must come to terms with his or her victimhood by declaring it an injustice awaiting a political solution.

American philosopher Peter Kreeft comments on the difference between Jean-Paul Sartre and Saint Augustine in one of his *World on Fire* lectures. I thought it helpful. Kreft sees Augustine as the *"most converted"* and Sartre as the most *"unconverted."* Augustine is the archetypal believer, and Sartre is the archetypal unbeliever. He points out that no idea defines the difference between Augustine and Sartre better than their idea of God. Augustine is sure that there is an eternal God and, therefore, an eternal truth. Sartre is equally confident that there is no eternal truth and no eternal mind. There is no God. Kreft explores the reasons for the conflict of visions and their consequences. Unfortunately, it would take too long to explore Kreft's compelling points. I make the simple point that belief or unbelief in God is foundational to understanding who we are. Alas, discussing the issue in New Zealand seems embarrassing, particularly when we talk of Jesus Christ.

The multicultural mind has no antenna to understand that the world is *"out of joint,"* like Hamlet's Denmark. It has no idea that nature and the human mind have *"been groaning as in the pains of childbirth up to the present time. Not only so, but we, ourselves who have the first fruits of the Spirit, groan inwardly as we wait eagerly for our adoption to sonship, the redemption of our bodies."* [3] The old idea of original sin has been rejected and replaced by faith in man's reach for Arcadia. A reach that grows shorter and shorter as I approach my eighty-seventh year.

From the mid-1970s to the 1990s, I wrote several articles for the *New Zealand Herald* and other newspapers, which gave me a modest profile. One evening, towards the end of 1988, I was on a television programme with Russell Marshall, then Minister of Education, and others. I think I was there because I was a conservative noise within the Post Primary Teachers' Association (PPTA). The evening's issue was the abolition of corporal punishment in schools. I had never used it, and probably most teachers favoured abolition. Whatever the case, I suggested on the programme that many teachers didn't favour its abolition. I thought I was stating a fact. I hadn't realised that a new censoriousness, inhibiting criticism, was beginning to enter the progressive mind. In the context of the new definition, even apparent support for physical punishment was violence. Not in my wildest dreams did I expect that even mild invective, imagined or real, would be eventually considered violence.

A few weeks later, I attended the PPTA's annual general meeting, alongside other members of the PPTA Executive and several hundred teachers. The meeting opened with three Executive members displaying a remit on the screen for discussion. Putting remits on the screen by members of the Executive for general discussion was standard practice. The first one up claimed I should be censured and apologise for what I had said on television because the abolition of corporal punishment was PPTA policy. Pointing out that not every PPTA member agreed with the policy was not allowed. At first, I thought it was a joke, but it wasn't. It was a bit of a buzz for a time, but eventually, it came to nothing. It might just have been one of the first indications of the forthcoming transformative cancel culture: the desire to silence dissenting opinions and observations. The green shoots of progressive authoritarianism were poking out above the soil.

I had no idea what was happening; my country was mutating. With all its messiness, the morality of flesh and blood was replaced by the abstractions of bureaucratic puritanism, although that, I suspect, gives puritanism a bad name. It was just a matter of discovering which political category one belonged to—or, more to the point, which category of victimhood required the most protection. Indeed, choosing which political category of the disadvantaged one belonged to became imperative. Perceived disadvantage became an advantage. Of course, it was because, with the decline of moral agency, victimhood had to replace the status of the sinner. Such an outcome, by necessity, had to rejig entirely our understanding of freedom. I had been taught to believe that the individual's morality was formed by religion, culture, and family. And it was not within the state's role to take on that responsibility.

As I have already suggested, the most penetrating consequence of the transformation was the loss of any concept of sin. We were trainee Beelzebubs, in that pride, once the besetting sin that plagued us all from Adam to the Alphabet people, became a virtue; our liberated transformation insists we be proud of our newly discovered faux humility. Recently, two children raised the Pride flag (note the capital P) at a local primary school. An approving photograph of them in the Education Gazette (July 2022) has the caption, *"Akonga at Beckenham Te Kura o Puroto raise the Pride flag at their school."* Having dissolved the strands of the traditional ties that bind, the acid of pride has been transformed into the elixir of life we must all drink. Learn to love yourself; that's the trick.

The imperfectly understood old belief taught a permanent, eternal law that transcended human subjectivity, revealing God's character. Its acceptance and practice weren't without warts, but Western civilisation, as I have said, was fitfully ordered by that revelation. I don't think it's unreasonable to claim that the Common Law only makes sense in that context. Indeed, without it, the idea of respect for the individual, intrinsic to common law, is seriously compromised, if not lost entirely. Sovereignty is the bewitching issue. Who's the boss? What should guide us?—the presumed purity of human desire, the rational liberal mind, or the biblical vision of the Transcendent?

Without excuse or embarrassment, multicultural dogma exchanges the sovereignty of God for the sovereignty of Man[4] by assuming the superiority of naturalism, that nature is all there is, over any claim to permanent and transcendent truth. And that creates a huge problem. Naturalism, or more accurately, its contemporary swollen imposter, multiculturalism, presumes its moral neutrality. Despite that presumption, or perhaps because of it, it lacks the desire and the means to assess its presuppositions or judge its internal tension or conflict. However, it does presume to judge any philosophy or religion that would deny its sovereignty. That's why its primary weapon must be hate speech legislation. Unbelievers cannot be permitted to draw attention to the flaws of multiculturalism.

For more information on this topic, refer to the chapter on civil religion. Inevitably, subjectivism takes on the authority of a natural religion. Multiculturalism would replace the Christian theology of the person as the glue of civil society. However, in doing so, it retains the worst aspects of the prejudice and vindictiveness of, for example, the seventeenth century's theological wars.

◆ ◆ ◆

Of course, the seventeenth-century civil war in England will not be at the forefront of the progressive twenty-first-century mind. From one perspective, it was a period of violence caused by self-righteous religious convictions. For some people, it was a period of sensitive conscience. Religious conviction has that capacity, depending on our perception of its source, to make us wise or vindictive. Oliver Cromwell, convinced as he was about the relationship between religion and government, did not quickly come to the execution of Charles I. Regicide remains a serious business, as it was then and still is. Because the religious debate and the first waves of nationhood were so intense, I suspect it helped bring English literature to one of its high points. The seeds were already there with Shakespeare and his contemporaries. Milton's epic *Paradise Lost* and *Paradise Regained* followed. Bunyan's *Pilgrim's Progress*, with its exploration of sin and merciful salvation, captured the theological intensity of the Puritan spirit in an accessible manner. Whatever the case, England, from Shakespeare to Milton, was discovering its national identity and who should oversee and protect it. However, I am not claiming that Western civilisation is Christianity in action. It certainly isn't. It would not prove to be the Kingdom of God. Nevertheless, our appreciation of the created individual's uniqueness and understanding of freedom has arisen from their roots in the Bible. Multiculturalism is a pretender that will not give rise to a flowering of literature or meaningful political insight. The parasite has no life if it cannot feed off its host.

The increasingly mindless vandalism of protests on the streets is revealing. Protests are only rational if one obeys a higher law than the one the protester finds anathema. Otherwise, it's just a battle over who holds the correct opinion. The Puritans, for example, were quite sure that in their opposition to the divine right of kings, they were being obedient to a higher law. Indeed, the foundation of their protest was their belief that they were faithful to that higher law. "*Lex Rex*" (the law is King), said Samuel Rutherford in 1584. By 'King,' Rutherford meant the law revealed and sustained by the God who created it, providing all men and women with a legal foundation for dignity. It would have surprised the Stanford students if someone had told them that the legitimate foundation for protest was already understood by the second half of the seventeenth century. Drawing on the book of Romans in the New Testament and the works of Thomas Aquinas and others, Samuel Rutherford argued that everyone, including the king, is subject to the rule of law—God's Law. An immoral government can legitimately be overthrown. Indeed, to oppose an immoral government is to honour God; one must be sure of the ground on which one stands.

The irony inherent in the Stanford students' call to 'righteous protest' in the 1980s is lost on them and their devotees. They failed to comprehend that the civilisation that permitted reasonable and peaceful protest was the one they wanted to destroy. If law, which defines right from wrong, is a mere human invention, 'might is right.' Such a law offers no basis for assuming the equality of all citizens it governs or the sovereignty of diversity. The unaided human imagination cannot give us a universal concept of human dignity. It must give rise to tyranny, the violence accompanying it, and the violence employed to eliminate it. Of course, as I have intimated, like any other pilgrim, all the above came to me slowly. It took a while to realise that multiculturalism fails to bring about the harmony it seeks because it is a radical simplification of the way we live, ignoring individual human uniqueness. It is not so much about respecting differences as about flattening them. It demands that we not only hold all cultures and, ultimately, all groups as equal, but also that the state determines and enforces such equality as new groups assert their identities and fight for their rights.

There is another, perhaps even more profound problem. By asserting that all cultures and religions are equal, cultural relativism, with its avant-garde of multiculturalism, cannot confront an overreaching religion without denying its flawed ideology. Claiming the authority of cultural relativism, it denies its authority. For example, such a loss of confidence is a problem in Europe right now as it confronts a resurgent Islam, particularly in France. The issues with Islam are real. From 2008 until the COVID hysteria killed it, I spent several months every summer, except one, with my wife in a town seldom visited by tourists in the South of France. Social change during that time was remarkable. Immigration was encouraged, and most of the new immigrants were Muslim. The mayor wanted the old part of the town gentrified, and one partial solution was to make the property accessible to immigrants by substantially subsidising the gentrification. The subsidy was so generous that even New Zealanders living in the town could receive a thirty percent subsidy for roof repairs.

◆ ◆ ◆

It's always been a common French practice for people to go for a cigarette and a cup of coffee in one of the local cafés before work; maybe without the cigarette these days. Men and women would frequently chat with friends at that time of day. However, as time passed, young Muslim men, often unemployed, started meeting in the same cafés. Difficulties arose when many women thought they were being leered at or embarrassed by the men. When she came to stay with us from New Zealand, one of my daughters noticed it within the first week or two. I could see it, so I had no difficulty believing my daughter or the other women. The result was that fewer women felt at ease about attending the cafés, and tensions increased. Raising a rational complaint was almost impossible in an atmosphere of pervasive multiculturalism. Some claimed that café profits were reduced, and gossip and resentment likely exacerbated the issue.

Such an outcome serves as a poignant reminder of the consequences of imposing cultural relativism on society. It lacks the rational resources to prevent misunderstanding and eventually cope, in the case of France, with the increasing demand for Sharia law, one of the country's most significant social and political issues. Multiculturalism is unable to defend itself, or anyone else, against an aggressive religion that rejects cultural relativism's 'blasphemy.' As multiculturalism embeds itself in the nation it governs, it fails to protect that nation's traditional culture that gave it its first breath. The insistence intrinsic to Islam is that it be recognised as an absolute religion and, consequently, the cultural dictator. Multiculturalism undermines confidence by attempting to provide an ethic that encompasses everybody, but not everyone wants to be included. I remember the response in our village to the Nice terror attack when a rampaging truck killed 84 people and injured 434 in July 2016. At the service in the village square, we sang the Marseillaise loudly and discussed liberty, equality, and brotherhood at length. Still, not one of the speakers mentioned the identity and source of the terrorist. Everyone knew, of course, and said so in private conversation, but the cult of multiculturalism had silenced all of us.

Michel Houellebecq's best-selling satirical 2015 novel, *Submission,* explores one likely outcome: François is a bored middle-aged lecturer at the Sorbonne, an expert on the nineteenth-century decadent writer Joris-Karl Huysmans. François doesn't quite reach the dizzy heights of Huysmans, but he does watch porn, sleep with his students and eat poorly. To make the best possible spin of it, he's a politically naïve, over-sexed hedonist. Around him, France's new Islamic party enters an alliance with the Socialists to stop the political right from assuming power. The Le Pen dynasty is not mentioned in the book, but must be in every reader's mind. The Coalition sweeps to power, heralding dramatic changes. Although spiritual lethargy and cultural carelessness may hinder the bloodshed of revolution, the outcome remains revolutionary nonetheless. The Sorbonne is privatised, and François is made redundant because only Muslims are allowed to teach there. Women are required to wear a veil, and gender equality is replaced by polygamy. Many of François' academic colleagues convert to Islam to get good jobs and enter arranged marriages with attractive younger wives. The desire for comfort overwhelms the inconvenience of moral conviction. The novel leaves us wondering what François will do.

Just a little addendum to the café story: The communist mayor who supported Muslim immigration was replaced by another who supported the National Rally, which does not support Muslim immigration. A friend who still lives in the town tells me that the declining presence of Muslim men in the cafés has brought the women back. She thought many had gone to either Marseille or Toulon to find employment.

◆ ◆ ◆

The inability, or perhaps unwillingness, of the police in Rotherham (UK) to attend to the continuing abuse and sexual grooming of young girls is another example of multiculturalism's inherent flaws. *"For decades, organised gangs of abusers preyed on children in their homes and in local institutions with impunity while authorities turned a blind eye."* The Telegraph (13/01/2025). Scared of being accused of Islamophobia or racism, the police and authorities refused to act because the abusers were nearly all of Pakistani origin. Police reports, for example, from 2003 and 2006, were found to be entirely inaccurate. *"The police proved deeply uncomfortable about the ethnicity of suspects, and those attempting to raise concerns were warned that passing on information could violate the human rights of those suspected."* There is, of course, no ultimate excuse for terrible abuse. However, multicultural theory has made it more challenging to bring offenders to justice. Seemingly on another planet, I was taught that modern democratic society had developed a way of life that encouraged governments to enforce the law without revolution or bloodshed. There was a time when we talked about civil society with some confidence. We understood the institutions and their interconnectedness. Each institution, including families, churches, charities, clubs, professional associations, schools, and universities, had its area of responsibility and independence from the state. All this has been swamped by multiculturalism, and by the way, lost to the Stanford students of the seventies.

With their immature appreciation of Christianity, multiculturalists lack the imagination to realise that the law above human law, the law of God, is not a collection of suggested moral demands. It is the revelation of God's character, and it is His character that defines the permanence of objective value, incidentally giving rise to scientific method because God has created an ordered world. Such a law gives us a high view of human purpose and meaning. The apostles of cultural relativism, continuing to be unaware of the cultural foundation on which they stand, must continue to deny the sovereignty of God, which means an endless reinterpretation of their understanding of truth and moral behaviour. Society lapses into a kind of *"designer tribalism"* [5] that mistakes security for liberty. All of us must find his or her safe space. The state's primary function is to keep cognitive dissonance to a level that sustains identity politics. It's a by-the-seat-of-our-worn-out-pants affair. The contemporary Pilgrim is the forbidden Pilgrim.

Notes:

1. Rev. Dr. Harold Turner is respected internationally for his original contributions to the study of New Religious Movements. His extensive work, which mapped out a new field, gave rise to the Gospel and Cultures Trust, later *Deepsight Trust*. His work is archived at the University of Birmingham, England.

2. Lines, William J. *Romancing the Primitive*. Quadrant Books. 2023.

3. Romans 8:22-23

4. Doubtless, some will claim the generic use of the term 'man' here is offensive. Nevertheless, good reasons support its use in this context. The so-called battle between Mankind and God has a long history, and it is in consideration of that history that 'man' is used.

5. See Roger Sandall. *The Culture Cult: Designer Tribalism and Other Essays*. Westview. 2001. Introduction.

III

What's Been Going On?

Why do the nations rage
and the peoples plot in vain?
The kings of the earth set themselves,
and the rulers take counsel together,
against the Lord and against his
Anointed saying,
"Let us burst their bonds apart
and cast away their cords from us."

Psalm 2:1-3

I know that nostalgia infected by regret might be an old man's affliction. Nevertheless, it does not need to lead one astray. Looked at with some historical knowledge, New Zealand in the 1950s, 1960s, and even the 1970s can look remarkably innocent despite its flaws. The changes have been so dramatic that some would have the country change its name, not only as a response to the change but also as a catalyst for further change. Of course, change is inevitable, and not all changes have been bad. We might be kinder than we used to be, although the motivation behind that kindness may be suspect. Technological advancement is a mixed blessing, but we embrace it. I would have had great trouble writing this book without a computer. We live longer, and we might even be healthier, but mental health statistics that encourage us to be neurotic are ignored. We're certainly taller and maybe stronger. Rugby players are faster and stronger. Without modern medications and surgery, I would be blind and probably dead. Homeowners have more goodies to put in their houses, and their children have a more comprehensive range of occupations and professions. We can travel a great deal more. Tertiary education, probably too much of it, is available at a considerable cost and increasing debt to anyone who wants to take advantage of it. Many courses are not worth taking, but that's another story.

There are weighty issues that give substance to my apparent nostalgia. For example, historical perspective, literary insight, a commitment to scientific method, and, most importantly, a liberal education concerned with character no longer form the foundation for education. *"Wither has fled the visionary gleam? Where is it now, the glory and the dream?"* said Wordsworth, lamenting the descent of his imaginative power from youth to old age. I lament with Wordsworth, but for more than he had to endure. It's not only that I regret the loss of the traditional stories that fired my childhood's imagination, but even more discouraging, my country has lost its raison d'être. What now gives flight to the youthful imagination? *The visionary gleam, the glory, and the dream* still had historical and contemporary content in the 1950s and '60s. Nationhood and even patriotism were still meaningful. Perhaps they still are, but in a very different way; maybe on the sports field. It's not evident to everyone, but it is to me, that multicultural theory has transformed the way we look at our history. In the 1950s and 1960s, we instinctively understood G. K. Chesterton's *Democracy of the Dead,* even if we hadn't been told about it. We had not yet come to believe that we must deny tradition, that everything that had gone before needed a complete moral, psychological, and political reset, let alone an economic one. I recall coming across Chesterton's statement:

> *"Tradition means giving votes to the most obscure of all classes, our ancestors. It is the democracy of the dead. Tradition refuses to submit to the small and arrogant oligarchy of those who merely happen to be walking about."*[1]

He encourages us not to neglect a good man's opinion, perhaps not even a bad man's opinion. Octogenarians know we must be sensitive to tradition if we are to value goodness and democracy. A widespread denial of tradition guarantees the wilderness. Deny where you came from, and you'll not know where to go.

Alas, C.S. Lewis' version of chronological snobbery infecting the Stanford students of the eighties was to swamp the fading visionary imagination their compromised parents might once have had. Their embryonic demand for 'diversity,' embracing only the authority of the present, would have eclipsed recognition. Perhaps they hadn't thought it through, but they were, nevertheless, anticipating the cult of equalising tribal identity under the shibboleth of equity, one of the pseudo-trinitarian goddesses yet to rise from the swamp.

It took a while, but it slowly seeped into my mind that social justice theory sustained by an expanding number of human rights was to be the regulator of a new vision of identity and alleged opportunity. I must thank the 'American Treasure,' Thomas Sowell, for confirming that insight. His *Discrimination and Disparities* alongside *A Conflict of Visions* were a revelation to me. And as time has passed, that revelation has proven to be more insightful than I imagined. The insights from those texts have been reinforced recently by his *Social Justice Fallacies,* which is replete with devastating documentation. Alas, the spreading cult of subjectivism doesn't yield to documentation readily. But more of that later.

It seems that it has happened without our conscious knowledge, but good character is no longer the first requirement of a responsible citizen. The idea that self-respect fosters a particular kind of moral toughness, as exemplified in what we used to call character, has largely faded. The virtuous citizen now accepts and affirms the identity claims of others, but that moral action is a political act rather than an act of conscience. Perhaps that's what I was referring to when I suggested a suspicious motive behind kindness. Another way of putting it is that the political conscience overwhelms the private conscience with political dogma, which encourages hypocrisy. Self-censorship was motivated by fear of ridicule rather than respect for others. We were seduced into doubting our own grasp on reality. A new term has been invented to describe it: Gaslighting.'

Men and women are equal, but only equal insofar as the state says. And as those of us who have read Orwell's *Animal Farm* know, some are more equal than others. The difference between the equality we inherit under transcendent law and the equity we share by state fiat was to become, if not unrecognisable, certainly unspeakable. I am who I am, and that's the end of it. But perhaps not. There is an overarching irony that should cause us to think. At a time when we are being told ad nauseam to be tolerant and inclusive in our diversity, a deconstructed political replacement of the biblical commandment, "Love one another," I wonder why more of us suffer from mental health problems than ever? Indeed, 'mental health' appears to have become a catchall term for a range of actual or apparent ailments, from loss of self-esteem and a failure to have one's identity recognised to the consequences of severe trauma and addiction.[2] We are told that therapy is not only the medication for personal trauma but also the answer to the human predicament. Any inhibitory notion of discipline or delayed gratification seems to have faded into the woodwork. Indeed, therapy is the only means by which we can come to understand and solve our problems. Salvation is not initially discovered through an admission of guilt but instead in realising one's apparent victimhood. Guilt before an omniscient, holy God is merely an imagined psychological issue, probably pathological. Relief cannot come from repentance, forgiveness, and redemption. Relief comes when the human creature discovers and expresses his or her true self, or even 'their' true self, in defiance of grammar and God.

There was a time when most of us knew that good mental health, although we didn't call it that, was a consequence of thinking of others, and that much bad mental health was a consequence of preoccupation with the self. It has occurred to me, somewhat belatedly, that the recommended plunge into oneself to discover who one is, smells like, sounds like, and looks like the unsuspected fusion of hedonism and Gnosticism. That one can possess a particular kind of knowledge inaccessible to others by exploring the mysteries of one's psyche reveals an ominous grasp at deity. The claim that one's identity is an inviolate private truth beyond criticism is hubris gone mad. The plunge into oneself to discover the truth about oneself and the world can only be terrifying.

Now, it might be difficult for someone born after, let's say, 1990, to understand just how absurd the contemporary politics of identity sound to an octogenarian. Social deconstruction without any clear vision of what the new structure should be made of or look like resembles the kind of hallucination that one gets from eating magic mushrooms. At best, identity politics can only leave us wallowing in the *Slough of Despond*. It's as though everyone is as far from reality as the Mad Hatter in *Alice in Wonderland*. They follow the Queen of Hearts, who thought the verdict should come before the evidence. Having chopped everything down, the mushroom eaters will not know where to begin. Any signpost they erect will point in any imaginable direction.

School Daze

In my final year of school, 1956, it was still a common practice for most single-sex state secondary schools in New Zealand to sing hymns and recite the Lord's Prayer during daily assemblies. And my daughters tell me that they prayed the Lord's Prayer in their schools in the nineteen-eighties; one integrated and the other private. They were activities initiated but not enforced by the old 'narrative,' as we call it. However, the new narrative, hostile to the old, is just as religious and undoubtedly more authoritarian in imposing itself on our psyches, as it is enforced by the state and its education system rather than taught by the family and supported by the local school. We should not be unaware that a new education system has been set up to reorder how we think about the world. Forget about the Stanford students. We have the Ministry of Education's *Common*

Practice Model: Pedagogical Approaches for Literacy, Communications and Maths. It is replete with the pseudo-Marxist terminology of critical theory. At the outset, it has this to say about what it calls 'critical maths' . . .

> *"A critical maths pedagogical approach uses maths to develop critical awareness about wider social, political, ideological, and economic issues. Critical maths recognises the importance of understanding, interpreting, and addressing issues of power, social justice and equity in the community and in the wider world. Akonga (students) are encouraged to interrogate dominant discourses and assumptions, including that maths is benign, neutral, and culture free."*

. . . and critical literacy,

> *"Critical Literacy recognises that texts are socially constructed and not neutral. It involves interrogating and constructing texts. Critical literacy is more than critical thinking. It involves identifying how texts position readers by analysing inclusion, exclusion and representation. At the heart of critical literacy is an understanding of the relationship between language and power. Texts may be oral, visual, gestural, spatial, or multi-modal. This includes digital literacy."*

Neither of the Ministry's critical pedagogies has much to do with education in any traditional sense. They speak like and have the intention of revolutionary propaganda. Sure, the Coalition

Government has promised us reform. And let us hope we get it. But are they sufficiently up with the play to deliver? Very few Members of Parliament seem to understand what it means to have a conservative mind. Is anyone in the Ministry of Education immune to the poison of subjectivism implanted in their minds by the diversity cult? I see no sign that any political party in New Zealand understands the ideological forces of destruction given to them by cultural relativism. I see no Heracles on the horizon to slay Hydra, the fearful master. I'm not holding my breath while waiting for a bureaucratic change of heart. There will be tinkering around the edges, no doubt. I'm not convinced that anyone among the Ministry's bureaucrats understands what combining tradition and progress means. Without a coherent philosophy that understands the conservative instinct, revolution will always trump reform.

Perhaps I can discern some hope on the horizon. The Minister of Education, Erica Stanford, says she is committed to a "knowledge-rich curriculum." One can only hope she understands what she says and realises just how difficult it will be to recover from the imposition of the culture cult. It's difficult to be confident in a minister who seems unable to discern the difference between equity and equality. In a recent video on YouTube entitled, "How colonisers went from learning te Reo Māori to trying to exterminate it," Professor Elizabeth Rata, a New Zealand curriculum expert, points to a comment made by the sociolinguist, Dr Vini Olsen-Reeder: "Once the Pakeha government was established here, the desire grew to exterminate the Māori people."

This kind of nonsense is now preached by a small and noisy minority, sustained by the overriding cultural relativism. Will the prospect of a 'knowledge-rich' curriculum overcome the deep-seated inclination towards cultural relativism? One hopes so. The updated 'Year 7-13 English Learning Area Content Draft' might help us return to an appreciation of good literature and its place in our tradition. Whatever the case, if it ever does, it will take several years to bite.

◆ ◆ ◆

In the 1960s and '70s, I was a Soren Kierkegaard fan, misleadingly called the father of Existentialism. I must mention his 1846 essay, *The Present Age*, in which he identified two kinds of revolution. The first one we all recognise. It's bloody, passionate, and tumultuous, wanting to overthrow everything in the name of Utopia. The French Revolution of the eighteenth century and the Russian and Chinese Revolutions of the twentieth century are dramatic examples. It should be evident to most of us that in 2025, we are participating in a different kind of revolution from the first one Kierkegaard identifies. It's bloodless, so far, with a holy passion that would swamp traditional significance and meaning. And yet, there's more. Vacuous concepts of identity are being puffed up to support what is becoming a revival of an old religion sold to us as something new.

So, it is hardly surprising that an overwhelming issue of our time spins around, seducing us into an acceptance of identity politics. As I have suggested in the introduction, throughout the 1950s and into the 1990s, a human being was still a creature created male and female in God's image. It's not that everyone thought about it, but it still shaped the way that nearly all of us saw the world. We didn't need to be subjected to aggressive academic and media propaganda and, more recently, commercial activism that would self-righteously support the ideology of individual self-levelling autonomy, a belief in the "freedom" of emotional power, and the essential goodness of human desire. In Wellington, government bureaucrats, with neither perception nor embarrassment, impersonate New Testament Pharisees. They write curricula replete with vacuous neologisms that would reorder the way we think about the world, recent Coalition reforms notwithstanding. Unwilling to do what we used to think God told us to do, the Pharisaic bureaucrats would have God do what they demand—for our own good, of course. *The Conversion Practices Prohibition Legislation* of 2022 is an excellent example of bureaucratic and, indeed, Parliamentary overreach. With remarkable incoherence, it assumes that homosexuality is biologically determined while sexual identity is a social construction, and that both should be given the same legal protection.

It wasn't until we were well into the 1980s that I began to understand that democracy sustained by common law, the free market, freedom of religious belief and expression, and freedom of speech were all under deliberate and structured threat. I certainly didn't appreciate that the grinding down of orthodox Christian belief had been gathering momentum since the First World War in nearly every Western country. Neither did I know that, for most of the twentieth century, the Western world was undergoing a simmering spiritual and intellectual ferment and the consequent erosion of confidence in Western civilisation. Now, in the twenty-first century, that erosion is a landslide.

Had I understood that the deconstructors (as I like to call them) were at work in the early 1960s when I was a young man at university, I might have become a wiser and better student. However, I was living in New Zealand then, and the deconstructors arrived later than they did in the USA, UK, or France, although, as I have now discovered, they proceeded more quickly. When I returned to New Zealand's heartland, the King Country, in the mid-1970s, after a decade away, the country was on the cusp of change, gathering momentum since the First World War in nearly every Western nation. However, it must be said that the present conflict aroused by critical race theory had not quite arrived. My daughter began school in Taumarunui, where she was the only blonde child. I can't remember it being an issue of any kind. Nearly everyone living on our street was Māori. I can't remember that being an issue either.

◆ ◆ ◆

To understand the erosion of traditional virtues and their decreasing influence in the classroom, I turned to the Romantics of the eighteenth century. I didn't know enough about what was going on. First, Jean-Jacques Rousseau (1712-1778) wrote and said a great deal but lived out very little of either. Although his contribution to the writing of the *Encyclopédistes* was relatively small, they supported his revolutionary spirit, even if some occasionally attacked his ideas. Diderot, Voltaire, Baron de Montesquieu, and Boucher d'Argis come to mind. Here is something from Rousseau that anticipates the unravelling of Western civilisation:

"Man is born free, and everywhere he is in chains" is the original simplistic lie, explained by Nietzsche and promulgated by Marx.

"Man will never be free until the last king is strangled by the entrails of the last priest." Marxism before Marx. *"Only passions, great passions, can elevate the soul to great things."* Such romantic nonsense can only collapse into the authority of subjectivism. The beginnings of a cult that would 'romance the primitive.'

"What wisdom can you find that is greater than kindness?" This is sentimental codswallop, a deconstruction of traditional biblical morality. Rousseau was anything but kind to his children. That the Stanford students were Rousseau's unsuspecting devotees should be obvious. In his 1988 book *Intellectuals*, the historian Paul Johnson considers Rousseau, with considerable justification, to be the first modern intellectual and the most influential person who would shape the world to his own image. Johnson raises the interesting question of how morally justified it is for Rousseau to advise others when his private life does not align with his declared public principles. He treats his wives, mistresses, and children badly and displays little respect for the truth. What Johnson said is worth quoting at some length.

> *"Older men like Voltaire started the work of demolishing the altars and enthroning reason . . . Rousseau was the first to combine all the salient characteristics of the modern Promethean: the assertion of his right to reject the existing order in its entirety; confidence in his capacity to refashion it from the bottom in accordance with principles of his own devising; belief that this could be achieved by the political process; and, not least, recognition of the huge part instinct, intuition, and impulse play in human conduct. He believed he had a unique love for humanity and had been endowed with unprecedented gifts and insights to increase its felicity. An astonishing number of people, in his own day and since, have taken him at his own valuation."* [3]

Rousseau was not the first to presume that an Arcadian substitute for Heaven might be reached without God, but he gave the fantasy a massive shot in the arm. Whatever the case, his life was a contradiction between his words and his actions. He was a hypocrite, preaching virtue and practising vice. It is not unreasonable to suspect he was entirely devoted to his glorification, which he presented as empathy for others.

In *The Devil's Pleasure Palace*, a book I thoroughly enjoyed, Michael Walsh claims that *"Rousseau conflated himself and his own needs, wants, desires, and hopes with those of all humanity."*[4] The poison of subjectivism was entirely in control of his mind and psyche.

M. De Voltaire had this to say in a polite but deliciously satirical letter to Rousseau about his *Discourse on the Origins and Basis of Inequality among Men*:

> *"I have received your new book against the human race, and thank you for it . . . No one has ever employed so much intellect to persuade men to be beasts. In reading your work one is seized with a desire to walk on all fours. However, as I have lost that habit for more than sixty years, I feel, unfortunately, that it is impossible for me to resume it . . ."*[5]

At the very least, Voltaire had a better sense of humour than Rousseau. His *Candide,* flawed as it is, is much more fun than Rousseau's *Emile*. The vainglorious Promethean vanity at home in Rousseau's psyche was only to gather speed and influence. We could also explore Friedrich Nietzsche's critique of the *'English flatheads'*.[6] George Eliot and John Stuart Mill believed they could maintain Christian morality without God. Even more remarkable, a contemporary follow-up, Richard Dawkins, the atheist extraordinaire, is quite happy to be called a cultural Christian. [7] To speak American . . . he's a freeloader. It would be a little excessive to call him a grifter.

◆ ◆ ◆

Putting Dawkins aside for a moment and to gain insight into where we are, I need to point out that this old Pilgrim is very much aware of the demons who would prohibit his progress. The atheist philosophers of the 19th century, notably Marx, Engels, and Nietzsche, have to be front-runners. Antonio Gramsci and the Frankfurters, Theodor Adorno, Erich Fromm, Max Horkheimer, Herbert Marcuse, and others turned *doublespeak* into an art form. They all hated Western virtue and institutions, particularly Christianity. Marcuse had a massive impact on university campuses across the US, undermining family, traditional sexual morality, and patriotism. And I must say, on this point, I found Christopher F Rufo's *America's Cultural Revolution: How the Radical Left Conquered Everything* more than a little enlightening. One could also look to the Russians Dostoevsky and Solzhenitsyn for more insight and comfort, but I'm not sure about Tolstoy. Despite being enthralled by the book, I've never been entirely convinced by the first sentence in *Anna Karenina: "All happy families are alike. But each unhappy family is unhappy in its own way."* I have always believed that loneliness in all its forms is the ultimate cause of unhappiness. Maybe that is because someone said to me when I was young that in Hell, everyone is alone, having spent an entire life going their own way, God was giving them what they wanted.

Heaven is populated by those who have admitted their frailty and dependence on their Creator, that they are sinners. For a long time, I have believed that the peace of forgiveness is central to human fulfilment. God gives penitents what they need. Unhappy families are alike, overwhelmed by the loneliness of estrangement. On the other hand, happy families delight in the differences in each other's needs. Thankfulness is their default position, and in that sense, perhaps they are alike. It seemed to me that Tolstoy more closely resembled Friedrich Nietzsche and Herbert Marcuse than a believing Christian. Tolstoy went his own lonely way, and his death was desperately tragic. Paul Johnson, echoing T.S. Eliot, says it well.

> *"What makes the last months of his life so heartbreaking, especially to those who admire his fiction, is that they were marked, not by any enabling debate over the great issues the quarrel in theory embodied, but by jealousy, spite, revenge, furtiveness, treachery, bad temper, hysteria, and petty meanness. It was a family dispute of the most degrading kind envenomed by an interfering and self-interested outsider and ending in total disaster. Tolstoy's admirers later tried to make a scene of biblical tragedy from the death bed at Astapova Station, but the truth is, his long and stormy life ended not with a bang, but a whine."* [8]

When I first read this, I was overwhelmed by the unexpected horror of Tolstoy's death; it seemed unnecessarily tragic.

Enlightenment Daze

To make more sense of things, I'll delve deeper into my own 'enlightenment' and continue to support why I believe that subjectivism, the unrestrained sovereignty of instinct and feeling, is maturing into a bitter and deadly spiritual and cultural poison. Distilled to its toxic 'purity', the poison would convince us that the human imagination is the sole authority that can discern the difference between good and evil. It would have us believe that secularism, the fantastical domain of rational neutrality, is the only way to understand the world.

The explanation and most rigorous development of secularism as the foundation of a nation's vigour and vision can be readily discovered in the French notion of *Laïcité*. I have already mentioned that with my wife Mary, I spent considerable time in France every summer from 2008 until 2019. During that time, a friend's establishment of an independent Christian school proved enlightening. Even many of her fellow believers were so steeped in Laïcité that they had difficulty understanding the value of what she was doing. They were convinced that Laïcité was indeed a neutral philosophy. It seduced the French conscience; the rational Goddess of Wisdom had come down from the heaven that wasn't there.

Laïcité, because it appears to carry a certain inexplicable mystique, is not easy to translate precisely. Still, it can reasonably be interpreted to mean secular idealism, allegedly based on respect for freedom of thought and religion and the separation of church and state, with no state religion. Laïcité and the famous *"liberté, égalité, fraternité,"* have the same source. Indeed, the cry of the French Revolution, first announced by Maximilien Robespierre in 1790, encapsulates the notion of secular idealism. The secular trinitarian motto rolls off the tongue easily.

At the risk of sounding somewhat dogmatic and even self-important, Laïcité is fundamentally mistaken about the nature of freedom. I would argue that freedom of religious belief and practice is foundational to any idea of freedom. Without that foundation, freedom of speech is without convincing authority, and that authority can only be given substance if there is a transcendent Court of Appeal. Nevertheless, French theorists would argue that freedom of speech is based on Laïcité, which declares that freedom of thought and speech is the fundamental freedom. However, that concept of freedom suggests that the rational mind can independently discover a foundation for moral truth. Rational thought gives rise to self-authenticating rational thought. That appears to be a tautology to me. It fails to consider the psychologically and spiritually coherent biblical story of the Temptation in the Garden and its consequences. It does not explain human duplicity. Without the belief that human dignity is a consequence of being created in God's image, there is no Court of Appeal to determine the limits of freedom of thought or speech. Freedom will always be conditioned by what the state decides it should be. Most of us, I believe, would not think that the best state of affairs. The presumed authority of the secular mind is a consequence of a rebellion against the Genesis creation story. The hubris of that fallen mind would claim the power of the disinterested judge. That astonishing arrogance looks like the besetting sin of the contemporary progressive mind.

Drawing on *The Declaration of the Rights of Man and of the Citizen (DRMC)*, Robespierre turns to Article 4, which says:

> *"Liberty consists of being able to do anything that does not harm others: thus, the exercise of the natural rights of every man or woman has no bounds other than those*

that guarantee other members of society the enjoyment
of these same rights."

The nonsense of such a statement should have been evident to Robespierre. A foundation for rights based on harm minimisation is bound to end in conflict. Maybe the maturing of that conviction helped take him to the guillotine. The accusation that he was harming others was enough. Unfortunately, the assertion that *"Liberty consists of being able to do anything that does not harm others"* influences contemporary moral sensitivities. For example, it underpins the thinking of those who would legalise recreational drugs and our changing attitude to sexual behaviour. The doctrine of harm reduction or minimisation, designed to lessen negative social behaviour, originates from the DRMC, which is not a good foundation for anything. Any attachment to the message about a genuine shared community described by John Donne's *No Man is an Island* is likely to have sentimental value only. The biblical declaration that inspires a responsible community no longer influences our morality. Transitioning from the biblical *"do good for others"* to the utilitarian *"do not harm others"* is not a step forward.

For the definition of equality, Robespierre echoes Article 6 of the Declaration, which held that the law *"must be the same for all, whether it protects or punishes. All citizens, being equal in its eyes, shall be equally eligible to all high offices, public positions and employments, according to their ability, and without other distinction than that of their virtues and talents."* It's worthwhile pointing out that although the DRMC is utilitarian, the value of a thing, and by default, a person, is determined by usefulness. However, even that error could not have existed had it not been drawn clandestinely from the Declaration of Human Dignity.

Laïcité presumes dignity. It offers no foundation for it. Of course, *égalité* and *fraternité* were challenging to define because they had roots in the religion that the revolution rejected. The idea of brotherhood that transcends family and tribe is essentially a biblical concept. Despite that, *fraternité* nurtured the revolutionary imagination and triggered widespread self-righteous enthusiasm.

◆ ◆ ◆

In a society ruled by the authority of the secular, the human image bearer must wear the stamp of bureaucratic approval. The state must become God, and the sacred is absorbed into the profane. *The DRMC* has authority only to the extent that it is utilitarian. To repeat something I've said in another context, it makes the same mistake that J.S. Mill and George Eliot made when Friedrich Nietzsche accused them of being "English flatheads" because they assumed they could keep Christian morality without God. The revolutionaries' hatred of Christianity was so intense that they could not discern that the foundation for the *DRMC* could only be universal if the rights had transcendent authority, which, of course, they denied. But the revolutionaries did have a case. The church had become moribund, if not corrupt. When Napoleon restored the French monarchy after the death of Robespierre, the trinitarian motto, *"Liberté, égalité, fraternité,"* was awkwardly replaced by *"Liberty and public order."* The monarchy banned it altogether after Napoleon's defeat, but the Second Republic officially adopted it after the 1848 Revolution, only to ban it again during the Empire of Napoleon III. Restored by the Third Republic, *Liberté, Égalité, Fraternité* remains something of a French war cry that has spread throughout the West despite its chequered history.

The trinitarian motto influential in the modern West illustrates much about the nature of subjectivism and its affinity with utilitarianism. The motto makes only limited sense in a world that believes, or instead once believed, in the sovereignty of the God it rejects. Without that foundation, subjectivism's passion can only sustain itself for a limited time. We should not be surprised that its history has been patchy. Subjective sovereignty has to nourish the rebel's presumptive mind and impassioned heart. It's the forbidden fruit first picked in the Garden of Eden. The original sin of disobedience, the refusal to trust God, laid the foundation of subjectivism's imagined authority. The hubris of human sovereignty must know good and evil without God. Milton's *Satan,* that grand architect of subjectivism, preferred to rule in Hell rather than serve in Heaven; of course, what he wanted to do was reign on Earth, and that created Hell for the rest of us. In Christopher Marlowe's *Tragical History of Doctor Faustus, Faust* asks *Mephistopheles, "Where is Hell?"* He reveals, *"Why, this is hell, nor am I out of it."* Rejection of God must collapse into a narcissistic subjectivism, a terrible preoccupation with the self. In Hell, narcissism is the eternal torment. Everyone, at last, becomes his or her *"own true self."* Polonius' advice to Laertes in Shakespeare's *Hamlet* was wishful thinking. Loyalty to self has replaced the Decalogue in the twenty-first century.

Poetry often reveals and illustrates truths that are otherwise difficult to articulate. So, the overarching authority of subjectivism is Satan's Revenge, the Grand Seduction. The seduced conscience would claim to serve humanity by declaring the human imagination supreme. And that is the difference between education in the 1950s and the 2020s. The difference between self-respect and self-esteem is the slippage from the authority of the moral to the authority of the psychological. That should bring to our attention the difference between identity discovered in the bonds of the intergenerational family and the bondage of the politics of identity—the difference between the substance and permanence of virtue and the transient thinness of values.

My abhorrence of cultural pluralism is not only because it fails to be coherent; it also cannot tolerate those who still believe in the permanent authority of Transcendent Truth, certainly not in the God of the Bible. Why is it so difficult for so many to accept what the psalmist has to say?

> *"The heavens declare the glory of God, and the sky above*
> *proclaims his handiwork.*
> *Day to day pours out speech and night to night reveals*
> *knowledge . . .*
> *The law of the Lord is perfect, reviving the soul;*
> *the testimony of the Lord is sure, making wise the simple."*
>
> Psalm 19

It is more than a little disconcerting to be surrounded by the hostility aimed at Christianity enflamed by slippery notions like intersectionality—the ideology that would claim that any number of factors such as sex, race, ethnicity, sexuality, class, religion, weight, disability, plus, can all come together in one strange notion of self-selected identity determined by victimhood. I have come to believe that since the 1970s, I have lived in a deepening spiritual, intellectual, and cultural maelstrom that pilgrims must fight against. It has never been easy, but it has become vexatious for a young person to discern and assert the difference between good and evil with the confidence of an informed faith. Again, I should have recognised that canary in the mine. Whatever the case, it was initially intuitive, a consequence of my Christian upbringing, but eventually, I became more confident in my suspicion that something was amiss. Gradually, I realised that my ability to discern good from evil was fading. Moral judgements vacillated between the bland "appropriate" or "inappropriate." A new code of what one should approve or condemn was gathering its authoritative head of steam. Although the acolytes of identity politics frequently use the word "evil" to condemn unbelievers, few seem to comprehend that the practice of evil has real and eternal consequences, that it distorts any concept we might have of permanent and transcendent good. As time has passed, fewer 'educated' people seem to understand the significance of such a loss. They refuse to believe that the wilful refusal to trust God has worldly and eternal consequences.

If we call something evil, there must be a divine standard because the weight of the word suggests, at the very least, the authority of a higher power. 'Evil' can only be a matter of opinion in a Godless world defying coherent definition. Milton's Lucifer, of course, will permit no discussion about it, but he was a liar from the beginning, the manipulating patron saint of cancel culture. He cannot allow open debate because his annexation of supremacy would be exposed. Going back to Rousseau, his atheism was not so much a disbelief in a higher power but rather a conviction that he was that higher power. Evil to him, insofar as he understood its meaning, was anything that frustrated the exercise of his higher power. And in that, he is the archetypal father of cultural relativism, the product of envy.

The temptation for me to comment on envy here is too strong. In Christopher Marlowe's *The Tragical History of Doctor Faustus*, the errant Doctor is educated by a parade of the Seven Deadly Sins; Envy presents herself thus:

> *"I am Envy, begotten of a chimney-sweeper and an oyster-wife. I cannot read and therefore wish all books burned. I am lean with seeing others eat. O, that there would come a famine over all the world, that all might die and I live alone."*

One cannot think of a better insight into the nature of cultural relativism. Like *Envy,* it is undoubtedly illiterate and would have all books burned. Contrary to its claims of inclusion, the spirit of Procrustes controls it, that mythical innkeeper whose beds were all of one length. Guests with short legs were stretched on the rack, while those with long legs had their legs amputated to fit. The great levelling continued until the hero, Theseus, came along to stop it. Alas, one cannot see a hero descending from the clouds of Mt. Olympus to overwhelm the tyranny of the twenty-first century's great leveller. Well, not yet.

◆ ◆ ◆

One of my graduate papers from the 1960s, 'Absurd British Drama,' was a catalyst for me, although I didn't realise it then. I had no problems with the notion of 'the absurd.' Indeed, it seemed to shed some light on my pilgrimage, but I didn't realise that the absurd was posited as a 'rational' response to the loss of confidence and the encroaching submission to meaninglessness. The barbarians inside the gate were winning. Perhaps there was a clue in the bleakness of Absurdist humour. It encouraged the laughter of derisive nihilism rather than a benign chuckle of comedic incongruity. Nietzsche was reaching out with very long arms. In the 1970s and 1980s, it was unclear where the belief in absurdity would ultimately lead us. Again, in my most imaginative dreams, I had no idea it would lead to the dominion of the self-creating human being. Neither the leopard nor Lucifer would change their spots, but it didn't sink in. Subjectivism, taking refuge in the rational, will always prove a tyrant.

I read and absorbed the poignant message of Albert Camus' *The Myth of Sisyphus*: the universe remains silent on the problem of meaning. I struggled through his *L'Étranger (The Outsider)*. The indifference of the main character, Meursault, is hard to bear or believe. There was much more. Samuel Beckett's *Waiting for Godot* and Harold Pinter's *The Birthday Party* were there to enlighten us. Pinter's brief, secular private funeral in early 2009 seemed particularly poignant in the real world, offering nothing to comfort the mourners. Pinter had selected eight readings in advance of his death. They included seven extracts from his writing and a passage from *The Dead* by James Joyce. Antonia Fraser's quote from Antonio in Hamlet, "*Goodnight, sweet Prince, and flights of angels sing thee to thy rest,*" was an incongruous metaphor in Pinter's absurd world, tragic even, because Antonia was Pinter's wife.

With some reservation, I dare to claim that I am not without some experience in attempting to comfort a dying loved one. What could one do? I held his hand and prayed. I prayed because I believed God heard me and that he would take note of what I asked for. Without warning, I wept. Both of us were enriched. I still don't understand it, but the tears were a comfort. My friend's gratitude and my confidence in God made me thankful. He was heartened because he heard the prayer. He believed that God was his friend. More recently, I visited a dear cousin several times before she died. Her condition made it almost impossible for her to talk, but again, holding her hand and praying turned the grieving tears into *a 'sweet sorrow'* well beyond that experienced by Romeo or Juliet. Believing that one will never be separated from his or her Redeemer with those who share the same faith is strong medicine. Like nearly everyone else old enough, I have experienced the death of a mother and a father and many close and dear friends. And perhaps the most heart-rending of all, the death of a grandchild. Of course, the mystery of death remains, but its intimidatingly ugly claim of victory does not.

It is impossible to explain the source of evil convincingly in natural terms. It's a terminal disease infecting the body and deforming the soul of every human being, a spiritual force spreading its cold darkness, a bloodthirsty beast ready to pounce in that darkness. Neither Becket nor Camus had much to offer youth or maturity. They failed to come to grips with death or suffering. The best they could do was to say that we were all nuts and that there was no hope, which is not what a Pilgrim wants to hear along the way. A Pilgrim would much rather listen to what Saint Paul says towards the end of his first letter to the Corinthians about the resurrection of the believer's body:

> *"Death is swallowed up in victory. 'Oh death, where is your victory? Oh, death, where is your sting?' . . . Thanks be to God, who gives us the victory through our Lord Jesus Christ."* (vv. 54-57)

◆ ◆ ◆

Hoping to become a better-educated teacher, I returned to C.S. Lewis' *The Abolition of Man: Reflections on education with special reference to teaching English in the upper forms of schools.* After nearly twenty years of teaching in New Zealand, Canada, the United Kingdom, and Australia and postgraduate study, I was a somewhat unfulfilled Head of English at a large New Zealand secondary school. I started to read more widely than I had hitherto. I revisited some of my favourite Greek dramatists, especially Sophocles, with his examination of the power of sin and human impotence.

I suppose Aristophanes represented some relief. I remembered Frances Bacon's "*Reading maketh the man; conference a ready man; and writing an exact man.*" That made me feel better; I believed it. With increasing interest and intensity, I re-read most of Shakespeare's plays and those of his contemporaries, Marlowe and Webster. Middleton and Jonson. I looked more closely at sixteenth- and seventeenth-century poetry and the Romantics; the Metaphysical poets are still my favourites, especially Donne and Herbert. I rediscovered Dostoevsky, Dickens, Thackeray, and, of course, Austen and George Eliot. I loved Fielding's *Tom Jones* and the biting satire of *The Life and Death of Jonathan Wilding the Great.* How refreshing his satire would be today. I looked more closely at Søren Kierkegaard, trendy in the eighties. I re-read T.S. Eliot's *Four Quartets* and *The Wasteland* with what I can only describe as poignant delight. I tried to come to terms with Nietzsche. I even tried to read Michel Foucault's first two volumes on sexuality, to little profit, for goodness' sake!

Until the late 1970s, English literature was at the heart of the secondary school curriculum. It remained compulsory through to the seventh form (year 13). We believed, well, I did, that literature informs and arouses a young person's imagination. I was always sympathetic to the idea that it had the power to stimulate the moral sensitivities dormant in the human heart. Reading good books strengthens intergenerational continuity and affection. However, in the 1970s, the so-called "New English", given status and popularised by various academic conferences around the English-speaking world, appeared. Several academics enthusiastic about New English could be mentioned, but I'll examine two meetings to illustrate the issue.[9]

In September 1966, approximately fifty educationalists from the United Kingdom, Canada, and the United States convened at Dartmouth College in New Hampshire, USA. John Dixon of Breton Hall College of Education in Yorkshire wrote the official report on the conference, *The Anglo-American Conference on the Teaching of English,*" published in 1967 as *Growth through English*. The unintended irony implicit in the title eluded me at the time. I had no idea just how important the teaching of the *New English* would be.

Dixon identified three traditions influencing the teaching of English. He considered each one outdated. He thought the teaching of literature that stressed heritage ignored "*culture as a pupil knows it*." Contemporary knowledge was just as meaningful as historical understanding, indeed, even more so. Teaching English that emphasised the importance of spelling, a wide vocabulary, comprehension of complex sentences, and precision in syntax and grammar got in the way of a pupil's creativity. It is significant that the 'pupil' became a 'student.' The new nomenclature conveyed that the learner is not under the teacher's authority. One can't help but wonder how the intrinsic power of the uneducated young person's mind would learn to distinguish between fact and fiction, and how much faith in subjectivity has contributed to a young person's anxiety, overwhelmed by social media.

Slowly, the term 'culture' has taken on a new meaning. It replaced 'civilisation' as the doctrine of cultural relativism took hold.[10] It abolished any distinction that might have remained between what we once knew as high and low culture; high culture was associated with 'bourgeois values.' The 'culture' pupils experience must be emphasised because it is 'more real.' In the classroom, group discussions, such as discussing popular films and television programmes, or writing a diary, sometimes called a journal, became essential to awaken a pupil's creativity. Assimilation into the prevailing society was replaced first by sympathy for immigrants (particularly relevant to the UK and Australia) and their prevailing values. The sympathy was eventually to be replaced by multicultural doctrine. In New Zealand, this was obliquely reinforced by concerns about the apparent failure of Māori education and, to a lesser extent, Polynesian education.

Although teaching New English was 'reformative,' the result undermined the subject's historical and literary value in the classroom. Insofar as it remained focused, character development became more about the pupils' experience rather than presenting the content and honouring the purpose of literature. A literary canon was a damp squib sent to the back of the bus along with the already estranged syntax and grammar. That literature could transmit all that was best in thought and feeling became passé if not a subject for ridicule. Cultural confidence was undermined. Indeed, "traditional" was to become a pejorative term.

One more name must be inserted into this melee: James Britton, Professor of Education, University of London, Director of the School's Council Writing Research Project (1965-71) in the UK, and influential at Dartmouth and York conferences. Britton developed a theory around two different uses of English, 'participant' and 'spectator.' Enamoured by the doctrine of multiculturalism and his other learning theories, Britton reinforced a philosophy of culture that would interpret the past using superior contemporary knowledge.

By 1971, neo-Marxist social and political revision guided American, Canadian, Australian, British, and at least two New Zealand participants at another conference in York. The intention of the conference was to *"discuss, write, listen and read about their roles and responsibilities as disseminators of cultural values and attitudes associated with the most urgent social and political conflicts."* [11] In schools, the emphasis began moving away from the teaching of literature informing the pupils' moral and aesthetic sensitivities to examining its presumed political bias. The so-called urgent social and political conflicts were conditioned by the anti-Vietnam and anti-nuclear protests and the increasing profile of the women's and human rights movements.

In short, teaching English was increasingly filtered through the lens of a theory that would eventually reinforce identity politics in the classroom. Teaching literature to enlighten and strengthen character was defeated by neo-Marxist and critical theory ideologues. Child-centred theorists who emphasised 'pupil-centred' learning were given a boost. They were obsessed with creativity and topics relevant to the pupils' needs and interests. Multiculturalists, increasingly influential, emphasised the need to consider the needs of women, indigenous tribes, and ethnic minorities.

It was becoming difficult to find a place where I could comfortably teach. I was superfluous to the growing loss of confidence in the permanence of traditional virtue and the selection of literature to inform students' responses to social issues. The old idea that it had something to do with enriching character was left behind at the last bus stop. By the late 1990s, literature was being examined in the context of selected extracts that frequently pointed the reader in an approved political direction. Questions in school textbooks on selected literary passages were expected to discover what the selections had to say about women, war, violence, inequality, or another pervasive issue, social justice. Being told by a visiting "advisor in English" that a poem had as many meanings as it had readers got me going. It is now possible for a student in English to get to year 13 without having read a complete book.

Nevertheless, despite the inroads made by *New English* doctrine, pockets of enlightenment remain in some schools. Some teachers cling to the idea of a literary canon, and teaching continues as it once did. However, that is a rear-guard action, although the writer, with a small group of experienced teachers, did visit a sympathetic Minister of Education, Lockwood Smith, in 1993 to protest the dilution of the senior curriculum. The teachers were confronted by some of the Ministry's curriculum revisionists, but they undoubtedly made a convincing case not to dilute the curriculum. Indeed, all the guns seemed to be on their side. Alas, any success was only temporary; the erosion returned.

Into the gathering storm of politicised literary subjectivism, I became increasingly aware of its insidiousness. The virus had been seeking to overcome my traditionally informed cultural immune system. I became aware that I was in danger of being overwhelmed by the contagion that C.S. Lewis had warned about in his 1943 lectures, *The Poison of Subjectivism,* published as *The Abolition of Man* nearly forty years before 'the poison' began to taint the bloodstream of New Zealand's Ministry of Education. Lewis was responding to a popular school textbook he called *The Green Book.* He claimed that the book was unwittingly seducing pupils to accept a flawed philosophy that would ensure submission to the authority of subjectivism, the control of their language. Lewis was emphatic. *"The practical result of education in the spirit of The Green Book must be the destruction of the society that accepts it."* By the mid-1980s, I had grasped the significance of Lewis' warning. He develops his argument from a story told by Samuel Taylor Coleridge about two tourists visiting a waterfall. One tourist calls a waterfall 'sublime,' while the other thinks it 'pretty'. Coleridge is unimpressed by the second tourist's observation.

The authors of *The Green Book* attend to Coleridge's disapproval by claiming neither tourist was describing the waterfall; instead, they were expressing their feelings. The first tourist was saying, declared the writers of *The Green Book,* *"I have feelings associated in my mind with the word sublime; I have sublime feelings."* In response, Lewis quotes a revealing paragraph from the *Green Book.*

> *"When the tourist said, this is sublime; he appeared to be making a remark about the waterfall. Actually . . . he was not making a remark about the waterfall, but a remark about his own feelings. What he was saying was, really, I have feelings associated in my mind with the word 'sublime,' or shortly, I have sublime feelings . . . This*

*confusion is continually present in language as we use it.
We appear to be saying something very important about
something and actually we are **only** saying something
about our own feelings."*

Lewis points out, *"The immediate problem is with the word 'only'.
A pupil will have no idea that ethics, theology, and politics are all at
stake."* That hidden controversy is now poisoning the hallways and
classrooms of our education system: a duplicitous and aggressive
ideology that would deny the reality of any permanent objective truth,
that the Sublime is an eternal reality. The consequence undermines
the young person's understanding of virtue, cultural confidence, and
faith. Even scientific method is threatened by the loss of belief in
permanent truth. But that is not all. By using *"only,"* any confidence
the young person might have in his or her feelings is also compromised.
Any intimation of awe the pupil might have is nipped in the bud, even
demeaned. Lewis claims that the writers of *The Green Book* teach
students that all statements of value, such as calling the waterfall
'sublime,' are merely statements about the speaker's feelings.

The attempt to debunk all sentiments is like trying to amputate
the heart, which gives rise to *"men without chests."* Lewis followed the
classical philosophers Plato, Aristotle, and Augustine, the Christian
philosopher/theologian who believed that education was an exercise
that trained children in *"ordinate affections."* Children's emotions had
to be trained to respond to the permanent reality of objective truth.
I suspect, but I don't have the hard data, that the recorded decline in
mathematics and English in every English-speaking country is, if not

caused by, it's undoubtedly made worse by the failure to understand the authority of objective truth and its beauty.

Specifically, Lewis draws our attention to *veneration* and *humility,* two virtues necessary for maturing the human spirit. Like all other virtues, they are undermined, and much else besides, by the abolition of the authority of objective truth. If Coleridge's waterfall was merely 'pretty' and not objectively 'sublime,' if beauty's authority to arouse lies only in the feelings of the perceiver, then on what basis can anyone ever enjoy the uplifting pleasures of veneration and the rich and ultimate reward of humility? If feelings are to be ultimately authoritative, vanity is readily encouraged. One has begun a goosestep march through the institutions to narcissism. It becomes impossible for the pupil to consider anything concerning the cause and source of beauty. Indeed, insofar as it is even recognisable, appreciating beauty becomes an exercise to inflate one's ego rather than educate it.

The parade of traditional virtue and vice, any insight into the problem of sin and suffering, or any enjoyment of a redemptive vision that might suggest the healing power of forgiveness is wiped from the cultural memory. The poison of subjectivism pollutes the Lethe as it flows through the child's deconstructed mind to the faux Elysium. And that's the problem with *New English* and everything it touched. Rather than developing the imagination to engage with the best ideas, it inflates the student's impressions of his or her skills. The ability to criticise intelligently is undermined.

The Frankfurters' Fantasy

I hope I'm not a fool rushing where angels fear to tread. I can only report what I saw happening around me during what I have chosen to call my pilgrimage. I sensed the changes, saw, smelled, and tasted them. I'm aware that any attempt to discuss the so-called Frankfurt School is fraught with its range of snags and hurdles.

The Frankfurters were not alone in shaping the post-modern world, but were influential in revising traditional Marxism. And in the interests of fairness, I guess it must be said that, unlike either Gramsci or Nietzsche, they did have the motivation of the impending Holocaust. And for that, one tries to be as understanding as possible; Nietzsche is always there, hovering in the background. If the Frankfurters were in danger of being executed by the Nazis, and it seems that many of them were, it is easy to allow the softness of one's heart to overcome the hardness of one's head, to paraphrase C.S. Lewis. They were not always in agreement by any means. Gyorgy Lukacs accused other school members of luxuriating in the Grand Hotel Abyss. According to Stuart Jeffries in his book *The Grand Hotel Abyss,* he accused Schopenhauer of "musing on the suffering of the world from a safe distance." However, as their ideas developed, with more irony than one can imagine, they contributed to a tyranny replacing their attempt to eliminate the tyranny they despised.

When we went to the 'pictures' in the late 1940s and 1950s, 'movies' came later, we would watch news items and short documentaries. Quite frequently, we would hear the phrase. *"Man's Conquest of Nature."* We had taken it for granted that progress was divinely ordained. But of course, as I discovered, it wasn't, although I was to eventually believe that the conquest of man over nature is the conquest of some men over others. To make that claim, one hardly needs to be a professional philosopher: some truths seem self-evident. When we reject or ignore the authority of the Divine, any attempt to dispose of what we assume to be a tyranny is to replace it with another. If there is no standard set of rules to be applied unexceptionally to what we think and how we think, then there is no single standard for judging truth.

C.S. Lewis quotes from Bunyan's *Pilgrim's Progress* in discussing the issue. *"It came burning hot into my mind, whatever he said, and however he flattered, when he got me home to his house, he would sell me for a slave."* So, the inevitable became just that, the inevitable. The 'New English' became one of the primary weapons to reinforce post-modern 'freedom' in schools, assisted by its biggest gun, critical theory, and its derivative, critical race theory, which would sell us all for slaves. So, it seems to me as I look back. The most significant change in the classroom was that teaching English moved away from precision in writing and speaking, and an educated response to literature. The focus shifted towards the speaking and recording of personal experience. Teachers and students were encouraged to believe that social problems are problems of structure, not an essential flaw in the human heart. Rousseau et al. and Marx might well have passed on to their utopian never-never land, but their ideologies were being radically transformed as they shaped the contemporary imagination. The working class had not risen against its 'exploiters.' Neither did it look like doing so. The entire ideology needed a shake-up, and it got it.

I'm not suggesting that some shaking was not required; there always is. Nevertheless, we must confront the surging progressivism, which is the rejection of Christianity, dominating university campuses in the West. The point that I'm labouring here is that progressivism offers no new insight into the human condition or the world's nature. It has been my conviction for some time now that so much academic chatter and the popular journalism that depends on it can readily be described as loose. How else can one explain the incoherent ideology defending the increasing number of tribes' most recently discovered human rights? It is an outrage if any member of one of these groups is offended by any critical assessment of their fuzzy ideology. Social justice, with its demand for equal outcomes and the wickedness of emotional harm, incubates cancel culture, and that subjective fuzziness has contributed significantly to the transformation of society. However, for clarity and to illustrate its impact and defend my gathering animus towards the poison of subjectivism, I'll draw attention to four protagonists. I'm not suggesting this quartet is definitive in any way. It's just that much they have to say reveals how we got to where we are.

◆ ◆ ◆

On the periphery of the Frankfurt School, I'll start with the Italian Marxist Antonio Gramsci (1891-1937), the founding member and sometime leader of the Italian Communist Party. He was imprisoned by Benito Mussolini in 1926 and stayed there until he died in 1937. A tragic figure, he was one of the most original Marxists, and any examination of his life must encourage sympathetic admiration. His astonishing intellectual vigour, despite ill health, gave rise to a refreshed doctrine of power. How he managed to stay alive in prison for so long defies my imagination. Gramsci developed the concept of "hegemony" from an idea posited by a student. Essentially, it is about how power operates in any society. According to Gramsci, social elites, "the ruling class," impose their moral, intellectual, and political values on those around them. They make use of shared social values to retain control. So-called *bourgeois* values got in the way, but Gramsci believed all these could be brought down without violence. Civil society had to be reordered from the ground up to bring about the materialist social order originally sought by Marx regarding capitalism; property ownership, buying, and selling had to be brought down. However, for fundamental change to occur, activists had to reshape the consciences of a new elite who would reorder the foundational beliefs of the entire civilisation. A new and aggressive consensus (critical theory) had to be established, first in civil society and then in politics, not vice versa. Universities were the target. One could imagine them as the 20th-century evangelists of the Gospel of Woke. But I couldn't possibly say that.

I tried to come to grips with Max Horkheimer (1895-1973), a German philosopher, sociologist, and member of the Frankfurt School. I have been informed by those wiser than I am that he was an important figure to consider in any analysis examining society, mainly Western civilisation, that would challenge the "power structures." From what I could tell, Horkheimer developed what he called 'Critical Theory' and became the director of the Frankfurt School in 1930. A radical rethinking of history was necessary, with capitalism remaining the villain. The liberation of human beings from their unconscious enslavement would eventually come about. He seems to have been influenced by an attempt to combine the ideas of Marx and Freud, a conflation of Marxist economics with Freudian psychology. It looked like a marriage between what has become a student version of capitalism and far too much faith in therapy. For centuries, Western men and women were slaves to the limitations of Christian dogma. Nietzsche had already made this claim in the introduction of his *The Anti-Christ. A Curse on Christianity. Para 5:*

"Christianity has taken the side of everything weak, base, failed; it has made an ideal out of whatever contradicts the preservation instincts of a strong life; it has corrupted the reason of even the most spiritual natures by teaching people to see the highest spiritual values as sinful, as deceptive, as temptations. The most pitiful example is Pascal's corruption, who believed that his reason was corrupted by original sin when the only thing corrupting it was Christianity itself!"

I don't know if many of the students who shouted outside the gates of Stanford University had read Nietzsche. Still, they were nevertheless echoing their ignorance and perhaps their hatred of Christianity. And it is a complete failure to understand the redemptive power of Christianity that underpinned Marxism, Gramsci's neo-Marxism and Horkheimer's critical theory. Nietzsche's hatred was directed mainly at Jesus Christ, who would turn men and women into weaklings. Well, perhaps not entirely. He hated Jesus Christ, who died on the cross as a substitute for man's sin. Nietzsche was quite happy with Jesus the man, who failed in his struggle against a religious and hypocritical bureaucracy, dying on the cross because he was weak. I'm not entirely sure what Nietzsche would have accepted as evidence. I can certainly offer my testimony and the testimony of many of my friends as evidence of the Resurrection. Not to mention the millions of believers since the thief on the cross and their common admission of pardoned indebtedness.

Then, there is Theodore Adorno to consider; the value of his esoteric criticism of capitalism and his exchange principle left me out in the cold. My distaste was aroused in the context of his criticism of mass culture and Nazi propaganda. Adorno claimed that the radio broadcasts of Californian Christian preachers were *"would-be Hitlers."* Both were in the business of establishing a specious authority over their listeners. A small thing, you might say, but not for me. Now, I'm sure some preachers had feet of clay, Californian feet, I was to discover, had plenty of it. Nevertheless, most were preaching what they believed to be the Christian gospel: the revealed story of salvation. Adorno's failure to appreciate the difference between the preachers and Hitler exposed his inability to understand Christianity or his tradition of Judaism. Whatever his perception of dignity might have been, it was not based on the Genesis story. Like Marx, he was seduced by the secular claim of neutrality. Whatever the case, he was a poor guide for this Pilgrim. And just a reminder, I'm not trying to critique Frankfurter's exhaustively. I'm sure that's obvious already, and anyway, it's beyond the aim of this book and perhaps beyond me. I just want to observe how they influenced me and many of my contemporaries. Or perhaps more accurately, why they failed to influence me.

The Berlin-born German Herbert Marcuse (1898-1979) is one of the most significant players mainly because of his impact in the United States on the university campus. From 1943 until 1950, he worked for the Office of Strategic Services, which became the Central Intelligence Agency. In 1955, he wrote one of his most significant works, *Eros and Civilisation. "Today, the fight for life, the fight for Eros, is the political fight."* Marcuse says in the preface that modern science had the resources to shape *"man's world in accordance with the Life Instincts, in the concerted struggle against the purveyors of death."* It took me a while to recover when I first read that. The purveyors of death were, of course, traditional Christians. I searched unsuccessfully for a clear definition of '*Life Instincts*.' Slowly, too slowly perhaps, I began to realise that in *Eros and Civilisation*, I was reading a plea for the sexualisation of society that would take us back to the license of Roman times. It's just about where we are in this first quarter of the twenty-first century.

Marcuse's *"repressive tolerance"* spin on tolerance, it still seems to me, is influential beyond what it deserves. In his 1965 *A Critique of Pure Tolerance,* he declared that the cultural objective of his interpretation of tolerance would extend intolerance towards prevailing beliefs, political theory, and opinions while extending tolerance to beliefs, attitudes, and views that were illegal or suppressed. It was the intellectual's duty to open up the mental faculties so that '*utopian possibilities*' were not excluded. Traditional beliefs about the family and repressive sexual behaviour hindered the realisation of Utopia, whatever it might prove to be. The centrality of the family to civil society and the concept of Christian restraint on sexual behaviour had to be overcome. It must be evident to many of us now that the contemporary ideology that emphasises the struggle between the oppressor and the oppressed is simply a relabelling of the old Marxist division of bourgeoisie and proletariat.

> "*The bourgeoisie, wherever it has got the upper hand, has put an end to all feudal, patriarchal, idyllic relations. It has pitilessly torn asunder the motley feudal ties that bound man to his natural superiors, and has left remaining no other nexus between man and man than naked self-interest, than callous cash payment. It has drowned the most heavenly ecstasies of religious fervour,*

of chivalrous enthusiasm, of philistine sentimentalism, in the icy water of egotistical calculation. It has resolved personal worth into exchange value, and in place of the numberless indefeasible chartered freedoms, has set up that single, unconscionable freedom—Free Trade. In one word, for exploitation, veiled by religious and political illusions, it has substituted naked, shameless, direct, brutal exploitation." [12]

I quote this from the Manifesto because it illustrates Marxism's passionate intensity and religious nature. It's characteristic of the entire Manifesto, a creedal statement with insufficient evidence, a rejection of any traditional morality that might have restrained fallen human nature or regulated free trade. The Manifesto's simplistic rejection of Christianity, claiming it to be a tyranny, replaces it with an absolute tyranny. Adam Smith's '*Sentiments,*' which were Christian, are denied and declared villainous, replaced by an ideology that is thoroughly subjective despite being declared scientific by Marx.

Roger Scruton's remarks on the Communist Manifesto are revealing and encouraging. They echo my suspicions of cultural relativism's envy when confronted with differences.

"Behind the impassioned rhetoric of the Communist Manifesto, behind the pseudoscience of Marx's labour theory of value, and behind the class analysis of human history, lies a single emotional source—resentment of those who control things." [13]

Our idea of family has changed dramatically from the 1950s to the present. And I'm just not talking about the somewhat romanticised version of the nuclear family that Hollywood briefly promulgated in the 1950s. The comments below from T.S. Eliot, more penetrating than Hollywood's brief encounter, would have made considerable sense in the 1950s, although I doubt if they would make much impact today. Anti-Christian dogma, from Marx to Marcuse, has done its best to undermine the family and the sentiments of civil society it engendered.

> *"When I speak of family, I have in mind a bond which embraces a longer period of time than this: a piety towards the dead, however obscure, and a solicitude for the unborn, however remote. Unless this reverence for past and future is cultivated in the home, it can never be more than a verbal convention in the community. Such an interest in the past is different from the vanities in pretensions of genealogy; Such a responsibility for the future is different from that of the builder of social programmes."* [14]

Chesterton, Scruton, and Eliot understood that the post-modern cultural manipulator would be unlikely to appreciate any concept that even got close to enjoying a *"piety towards the dead"* or *"a solicitude for the remote unborn."* I know that Eliot and Chesterton were not the best of friends, at least not until Eliot's conversion to Christianity in 1929. Both became Christian believers as adults, Chesterton to Catholicism and Eliot to Anglo-Catholicism. Both understood the impact of Christendom on Western civilisation. Indeed, that is why they valued tradition. There were timeless truths that had to be passed on from generation to generation. They knew the rising *"poison of subjectivism"* would likely be Western civilisation's greatest threat.

I'm Not Surprised

I'm not surprised at what is happening in Western universities. To this seasoned observer, English, sociology, psychology, even history, and, God forbid, many law departments have become so doctrinaire. Indeed, there is considerable, if not overwhelming, evidence to support the claim that promotion depends on submission to the cult of diversity. Most academics are real or imaginary members of the political left influenced by the Marxist definition of capitalism, critical theory, and critical race theory. In New Zealand, it would be challenging for an applicant, even with the best qualifications, to get a job in a university if s/he was openly an unbeliever in the diversity cult and failed to make the right noises about the Treaty of Waitangi. University staff, supported by the taxpayer, are among the world's most privileged people.

It would be more than a little helpful if university academics, administration, and contemporary protestors were to consider just what gives protest lawful authority. It would come as a surprise to many of them, I'm sure, that Samuel Rutherford had already considered this in the seventeenth century. However, after the Israeli reprisals in Gaza following the Hamas terrorist attacks on October 7, 2023, the pro-Palestinian protesters seem to think that the authority for their protest lay in their own limited and emotionally derived definition of violence. That they could be the apex of subjectivism's annexation of authority is probably not in their minds. Seduced by the politics of identity, they cannot have any concept of the 'Just War' or its variations.

Their understanding of justice has limited historical context, and they fail to appreciate that a just government is founded on the rule of law. They want to demolish the principles that permit them to protest.

The pro-Palestinian protesters could benefit from reading or viewing Robert Bolt's play about Thomas More, *A Man for All Seasons*, first performed in 1960 and made into a successful movie in 1966. In his passionate excess, William Roper, Thomas More's future son-in-law, would cut down all laws to achieve his ends. But as More points out, where would he go when the *"Devil turned on him, the laws all being flat?"* Like William Roper, but without his integrity, the contemporary protesters would cut down all laws except the one that they imagine would protect their passion. Again, it would seem beyond their comprehension to understand the principles laid down by Samuel Rutherford in *Lex Rex* or *The Law and the Prince*, to give the book its full title. The protesting students cannot possibly appreciate that their rejection of transcendent law will turn law from a gift to a curse. Arbitrary power will demand passive obedience. Despite their protest, the antinomian servile protesters would willingly yield to the imposition of multiculturalism. They would resist any suggestion that their protest could rapidly eat up the truth. There is no way they could ever comprehend Gertrude in Shakespeare's *Hamlet*: "*The lady doth protest too much, methinks.*" The protesters act out their little play in an unbelieving world with astonishing confidence.

As my pilgrimage gets closer to its end, I become even more convinced that the prevailing anti-colonial invective has its roots in a rejection of transcendent law and a conviction that the past must be interpreted through the uninformed passion of the present. For example, in condemning the empire, noisy student protesters have failed to grasp its perennial nature and role. Nigel Biggar points out the obvious in the introduction of his excellent *Colonialism, A Moral Reckoning*, that empires have been with us for a very long time. The Assyrians were around, 4000 years ago. Then came the Egyptians, the Babylonians, the Persians, and the Romans, not to forget Alexander. Biggar points out that *"Empire first appeared in China in the 3rd century BC, and, despite periodic collapses, still survives today."* The Americas and Africa had their empires. The British Empire gave way to the Empire of the United States, and now we might be looking down the barrel of the revived Chinese Empire.

One of the most damning things that can be said about cultural relativism's creation of identity politics is that it tends to halt progress and obscure the truism; we are all in the business of learning to behave morally. Just as certain moral principles might be straightforward to an eighty-six-year-old but not to an eighteen-year-old, some ethical realities that might be obvious to us were not evident to our ancestors. One clear example is how attitudes to slavery have changed, although contemporary protesters don't seem to be aware of why that might be. They insist that racism, slavery, and white supremacy make up the evil trinity of Western civilisation. They either ignore or refuse to believe that slavery has been with us for millennia, and in some parts of the world, it is still going on. That slavery was first abolished within the British Empire seems to have gone unnoticed. Even more telling is that the impetus for that abolition came from politicians the Evangelicals had deeply influenced.

To take one newsworthy event discussed by Nigel Biggar. Echoing much student protest in 2021, an Oxford University professor, Robert Gildea, said of the Cecil Rhodes statue above an Oriel College entrance:

"Rhodes looks patronisingly down upon us . . . he blocks our treatment of history and therefore he should be taken down . . . the idol needs to be pulled down so that the racist spell can be broken." [15]

He went on to claim that Rhodes, sympathetic to slavery, represented the colonialist mentality of white supremacy.

The irony of Gildea's claim that Rhodes is blocking his treatment of history and that his statue needs to be pulled down should be obvious. Any interpretation of history that depends on contemporary ideology rather than the application of historical method for its analysis will be little more than propaganda. Gildea would rewrite history with the authority of his latter-day neo-Marxism. Now, if that sounds too severe, where does he get his animus other than from a simplistic and, therefore, unjustified rejection of tradition? After much debate, Oriel College decided not to take the statue down because of "regulatory and financial challenges." Nevertheless, they would make provision for students and academic and non-academic staff to be tutored in *"equality, diversity, and inclusion,"* along with training in race awareness. So, we had a make-believe solution to an imagined problem. Until recently, everyone knew that Rhodes' statue was there because he had been a significant college benefactor. He could only be condemned and accused of white supremacy by judging the past through the lens of contemporary prejudice, which is what submission to cultural relativism always engenders.

During the writing of this chapter, the hierarchy at the University of Liverpool gave staff instructions on how to diversify and decolonise the history curriculum. Of course, they are not alone. Similar universities in other Western countries are doing the same. They were precise at Liverpool in the request to *"problematise whiteness and heterosexuality in their seminars."* [16] Meanwhile, back in New Zealand, the statues of Captain Cook and Queen Victoria have been damaged or defaced in a frenzy of uneducated anti-colonial wrath. That Cook had nothing to do with colonising New Zealand or that Queen Victoria was at the benign end of colonial malfeasance was of no consequence.

There is no doubt that New Zealand universities are vexed about free speech. In August 2018, Don Brash, one-time leader of the National Party, was initially stopped from speaking at Massey University. More recently, a panel discussion about free speech at Victoria University in Wellington was postponed because of a backlash about the panel's *"lack of diversity and right-wing leanings."* [17] After listening to staff and students, the university reformatted the panel to cover diverse views, which means we will do nothing. The consequences of judging the past through the eyes of the immediate are immense. Not only do we get an inadequate understanding of our history, but our understanding of authority is invested in the self, oblivious to the need for self-examination.

Auckland University has introduced a compulsory Treaty of Waitangi/Matauranga Māori (Māori knowledge) course for all students beginning in the 2025 academic year. It would appear to take for granted that its limited understanding of colonialism should be taught to all students while they pay for the privilege. One commentator, Graham Adams, tells us that Eru Kapa-Kingi, a vice-president of Te Pāti Māori who develops and teaches courses for Law School, presumably echoing something approaching a consensus, said in an Auckland University newsletter (March 2025):

"We need to start realising that universities were one of the primary tools of colonisation in Aotearoa, replacing Māori philosophy, Māori ways of thinking, speaking and acting. That places an obligation on academics today to really contribute to the deeper, longer-term decolonisation project."

Subjectivism and Its Values

Teaching children how they should live has become very difficult. Every attempt to restore confidence results too quickly in an accusation of racism or some other 'ism.' Subjectivism acts like an anaesthetic. Tradition, in whatever form it is imagined, must become the enemy. Men and women will fail to believe that thankfulness is a duty to the source of the virtues that protect and prevent them; instead, they will repress any knowledge of the source and even grow to despise it. Lewis points out that, like the *Green Book's* pupils, they will not be aware that they have turned subjectivism into an absolute and insist on the permanence of their subjective values, the consequence of what 'I value.' Although they might still use words like 'justice' and 'courage,' they will not describe the old virtues but project their self-authenticating values instead.

Values have no recognisable and definitive concrete form, like the virtues of courage or moderation, for example. Diversity must be the primary de facto value in a society where values have replaced virtues. Not only must we accept that, but we must affirm its overreaching abstractions or be excommunicated. Virtues are observable characteristics of the individual that depend upon a recognised and permanent universal truth underpinning and sustaining the human condition. They are universal but not uniformly recognised and enforced. However, the universal presumption of values must have uniform recognition and a society that enforces that recognition. The value of diversity is a universal abstraction that must be obeyed. Inclusion is not only a value; it presumes the status of a modern virtue. The same might be said for equity (equality of outcome), the anaesthetic that would ease us into the sleepwalker's embrace of tyranny.

I recall reading somewhere, perhaps I heard it decades ago in Sunday School, that the Ten Commandments are not just something invented by a vindictive God to stop us from having a good time; they speak to our true nature. They describe reality. They don't undermine self-respect, although they certainly question self-esteem. The Genesis description of human dignity, the *Decalogue,* and the *Beatitudes* are enduring and universal. They are a permanent guide to life; if we deny them, we deny 'the ground of our being'. The apostle Paul, addressing all of humanity, tells us in his letter to the Romans, "*the law is written on their hearts, while their conscience also bears witness, and their conflicting thoughts accuse or even excuse them*" (2:15). Traditionally, we have understood that 'accusing' and 'excusing' require divine guidance. We knew the propensity for the human heart to go astray. A grandfather knows that only too well his heart and his children's and grandchildren's.

We get an entirely different kind of human being when we ignore the reality of human duplicity, traditionally called sin. Perhaps I might be forgiven if I introduce a little biblical psychology here, and quote something from Saint Paul's second book to the Corinthians. "*For godly grief produces a repentance that leads to salvation without regret, whereas worldly grief produces death*" (vv. 7-10). The point is that there is a definitive reality in recognising our sinfulness and guilt before the just and loving God. Such repentance gives us hope and destroys regret. It is the liberation that Christ promised his followers.

Notes:

1. Chesterton, G. K. *Orthodoxy.* Chapter 4

2. The background for this comment comes from Jonathan Haidt, *The Anxious Generation.* 2024

3. Paul Johnson. *Intellectuals.* Harper Perennial. 1988, page 2.

4. Walsh, Michael. *The Devil's Pleasure Palace.* Encounter Books. 2015. Page 139.

5. Voltaire. From *Les Delices.* 1775

6. Nietzsche's accusation was something of an exaggeration. It's unclear how much he had read on Eliot or Mill. However, his claim that Christian morality could not be continued without believing in God was proven correct.

7. Grant, Madeline, *The Telegraph* UK. April 3, 2024. Christianity's decline has unleashed terrible new gods. Richard Dawkins was the star of New Atheism, but now he tells us he is a cultural Christian. For some reason, which Dawkins does not explain, Christianity has utilitarian value that others do not.

8. Johnson, Paul. *Intellectuals.* Harper Perennial. 1988. p. 137.

9. A detailed description of these conferences can be found in *The Wayward Curriculum*, ed. Dennis O'Keefe, Social Affairs Unit 1986, an essay by G.H. Bantock: *The Attack on the Culture of Quality,* and Alan Barcan: *English: Two Decades of Attrition.* I draw much of my detail on the conferences from these two essays.

10. Nietzsche, Friedrich. *The Anti-Christ.* Para 41. See also "*Christianity remains to this day the greatest misfortune of humanity." Para 51.*

11. Editorial. *English in Education.* Vol.16. No.2 Summer 1982. Quoted by Alan Barcan. *The Wayward Curriculum.* p. 32

12. *The Communist Manifesto.* Marxist Internet Archive.

13. Scruton, Roger. *Fools, Frauds, and Firebrands.* Bloomsbury. 2015.

14. T.S. Elliot, *Notes Towards the Definition of Culture.* Faber. 1962. Page 4

15.   Biggar, Nigel. *Colonialism: A Moral Reckoning.* HarperCollins, 2023. p. 302 note 11.

16.   *The Telegraph* (UK) June 15, 2024

17.   *NZ Herald.* April 27, 2025.

IV

The Tricky Trinity: Identity, Politics and Therapy

The contemporary climate is therapeutic, not religious. People today hunger, not for personal salvation, let alone the restoration of an earlier golden age, but for the feeling, the momentary illusion of personal wellbeing, health and psychic security.

Philip Reiff, *The Triumph of the Therapeutic.*

Therapy is the necessary medicalisation of 'virtue' employed by multiculturalism and identity politics. By that, I mean the ideology replaces virtue with the values of cultural relativism, undermining the vocabulary of traditional morality. Good and evil must become a matter of tribal opinion controlled by the ideology's framework of oppressor versus oppressed. The tricky trinity is above rational criticism. Sustained by the authority of subjectivism and a destabilising refusal of self-examination, it can never supply what it promises. It cannot give peace of mind or cultural confidence. It impoverishes the human imagination while having no power to heal it. Although the patient (we're all patients now) will experience tragedy, s/he will have no satisfactory way to discern it. Comedy, especially satire, is consciously and subconsciously forbidden because satire might reveal the reality of the ideology's folly. Folly is a mere mistake, and any consequent anxiety about it is healed by therapy rather than absolved by admission of guilt. Virtue can no longer have victory over vice. People who conscientiously practice virtue are likely to be offered counselling. For example, humility may be treated as a loss of self-esteem, and chastity as sexual dysfunction. Virtue is not so much its own reward as a condition requiring therapeutic intervention because there is no cosmic struggle between good and evil. The only 'evil', if one can ever use that word, is to deny the validity of identity politics. Every desire and event must be assessed within the moral parameters set by the state. The human adventure ends in anticlimax. Indeed, there is no way for a story to reach a climax, for the hero to find rest and reward, without that cosmic battle between good and evil. The Marxist-inspired oppressor/oppressed paradigm sustained by cultural relativism undermines any awareness of the cosmic struggle. The ideology that gives the Tricky Trinity life is the way of no resolution; the overarching political dogma guarantees permanent frustration. Any version of heaven it promises to provide will always be out of reach.

The Tricky Trinity is forced to work within the context of a grand irony. Having rejected the traditional notion of sin, it still finds itself in the invidious position of dealing with the 'sin' of unbelief. It either convinces unbelievers of the error of their ways or condemns them to its version of purgatory. The unbeliever cannot be allowed to continue in his or her unbelief because it is infectious. Hate speech legislation and re-education are necessary. Always in a state of becoming, the patient must find comfort in the priestly counsellor's therapeutic bosom. I remember the debate around introducing school counsellors to secondary schools in New Zealand in the 1970s. Some claimed that we didn't need them, but if we did introduce them, we would need more and more. Well, for whatever reason, we're now told ad nauseam that we certainly need more. It seems likely that the public education system will become increasingly concerned with ameliorating psychological dysfunction instead of concentrating on what we used to call the three Rs. Well, it might appear to alleviate psychological dysfunction. Still, it will be about self-esteem and everyone reaching his or her 'full potential', that odd state of being that receives almost universal approval without anyone knowing what it might be. Because therapy is expected to resolve the angst of moral uncertainties, counselling replaces confession, and personality replaces character. Young people become less resistant to propaganda because treatment emphasising the subjective tends to undermine the status of moral certainty and prevents students from even considering it.

◆ ◆ ◆

It has already been suggested that C.S. Lewis warned us in *The Abolition of Man* that the student confused about the nature of the Sublime would not be aware that many profound ethical dilemmas are being glossed over. So often, in counselling, students accept the validity and function of identity politics without accurately understanding what they are doing. They will believe that tribal membership is the consolation of identity politics. The student is not encouraged to consider past wisdom because it wasn't wisdom. Discovering the supposed value of their righteousness, they are seduced into the worship of Narcissus. It will not occur to the student that therapeutic multiculturalism is a parody of the courageous Pilgrim's journey. Victory over the temptation to surrender is ignored because it is not recognised for what it is, and psychological safety becomes a condition that the state must supply. There is no place for virtue meaningful to the humble pilgrim and intrinsic to any rational comprehension of Western civilisation. Neither Homer's Odysseus nor Christian of *The Pilgrim's Progress* has a place in the multicultural assault on drama. Indeed, the concept of the overcoming pilgrim is not so much denied as it is not even considered. Life is not a journey in which difficulty is to be overcome. Instead, it is a journey of continuous victimhood as one struggles for recognition and vindication of tribal identity, which makes any transcendent declaration supporting human dignity impossible. The Genesis story becomes a mere fairy tale, not even rising to the level of metaphor.

Because the politics of identity are always underpinned by cultural relativism, the literary imagination is not allowed to explore and certainly not explain the psychology of godless and banal victimhood. There can be no journey to the Promised Land other than the receding Utopia, where social justice is promised but never finally realised. Neither Odysseus nor Aeneas can struggle against overwhelming odds on their journey home. Marlow's and Goethe's *Faust* are incomprehensible, Dante's *Divine Comedy* is a foreign language from another planet. Ironically, identity politics would make T.S. Eliot its unsuspecting prophet; "*This is the way the world ends, /Not with a bang, but a whimper.*" No wonder humanities departments in universities are beginning to fade from the scene.

In the 1960s, the English department was at the university's cultural centre. We still believed that we should study the best that had been written. Eliot's existential observations were a big deal. We talked and argued about them ad nauseam. We were up with the play; no one questioned it. But now that moral sensitivities have been politicised, the victory of utilitarianism has weakened the traditional reasons for studying literature and even history. Sociology, influenced by multicultural theory and identity politics, has given rise to ill-disciplined intruders like women's studies, anti-racist education, peace studies, indigenous studies, and so on. The point about these is that they have no controlling methodology other than their political bias.

Because of its levelling syncretism, the cult of subjectivism would have everyone see the world through its 'inclusive' eyes, and to do otherwise is morally wrong. Ideological fanaticism must increase, and if satire does manage to sneak in through a crack in the wall, it will increasingly offend. Perhaps we need not be too afraid. Fanaticism, in the context of Western civilisation's present devolutionary ennui, will probably fail to rise to the level of vicious revengefulness displayed by the Islamist terrorists who attacked the Charlie Hebdo office on the 7th of January 2015 in Paris, killing seventeen people. But the roots are the same: implacable self-righteousness that will not tolerate dissent.

Despite Promethean aspiration, there is no way that the inhabitants of a multicultural society could ever evolve into Nietzsche's Übermensch (Overman). We are much more likely to get 'underlings.' His concept of the hero is misplaced. The death of God does not allow us to create a new kind of hero. Instead, it is the death of heroism. What is there to be heroic about? We cannot kill the reason for heroism and expect new life from the decaying body. In the mature multicultural world, rising above it is impossible. Indeed, any attempt to do so would be an act of foolishness. Heroes can only act in a world where there is vice and virtue, where there is a heaven to gain and a hell to shun. Living under the Tricky Trinity's dogma, it becomes impossible to understand the reality of human suffering and the compassion of suffering for others. Suffering becomes an abstraction to be healed by therapy when it only has the power to suffocate it. Submission to the faux Trinitarian demands will not stop 'patients' from falling hopelessly back onto the couch of deconstructed virtue.

Like Huxley's Soma in *Brave New World*, subjectivism ensures the sleep of reason. There is no foundation for the hope that would make suffering bearable. The sacrifice of compassion hardly makes sense. It is difficult, if not impossible, to be compassionate without sacrificial love. Indeed, severe suffering is impossible to bear without compassion's support. Despite its claim to be universal, the ideology that would drive the politics of identity does not have and cannot have any coherent theology or philosophy of suffering. The biblical story of Job, which teaches the human creature humility as he pleads with the Creator for justice, is beyond comprehension. That Jacinda Ardern told New Zealanders to be kind when she was Prime Minister is entirely consistent with multicultural theory; it turns kindness into a cult, the new tolerance in action.

The Prime Minister could hardly have said *"be of good courage,"* a necessary component of humility, because that involves a much deeper understanding of the virtue of compassion than she could offer. Telling somebody to be kind costs nothing. It has no more moral content than the advice to 'take care.' The 'death with dignity' mantra that underpins New Zealand's assisted suicide law further illustrates the superficiality of Jacinda Ardern's subjectivism. Compassion is only meaningful when the needs of the other overwhelm the need to be safe and the desires of the self. Pity is not about sharing in the suffering of the loved one. Instead, it is about feeling sorry for the victim and getting rid of the suffering as soon as possible. Pity that does not mature into compassion short-circuits it. The sentimentality of the self-creating identarian is easily moved to pity because, in the material world s/he inhabits, preventing pain is the highest aim, or indeed the prevention of offence. In the real world, the union between the comforter and the suffering one is a poignant human mystery that arouses and gives insight into the power of compassion. And that insight comes at the cost of participating in the pain of another's life. Ultimately, it means giving oneself up for the other, modelled and made possible for us through the crucifixion and resurrection of Christ, the event the self-creating identarian would deny but can find no satisfying replacement.

Loving another will always demand sacrifice sooner or later. I remember a story about life around the 19th-century coal mines in Wales, sentimental perhaps, but illustrative. The miner, we will call him William, what else, was married to Myfanwy; their son was Dylan— every payday, William would give Myfanwy his complete pay packet. She would give him back a coin, maybe sixpence, to spend at the pub on Saturday night, where he would proceed to get blotto. Myfanwy and her son would take a wheelbarrow to the pub door when the pub closed. Dylan would go into the pub to get his father and bring him out. The pub was a place for men only, and anyway, Myfanwy chose not to go in. Dylan would bring out his inebriated father and put him in the wheelbarrow. Neither Dylan nor Myfanwy condemned Williams' drunkenness, although they probably looked forward to a day when the rescue missions would cease. Life was hard; love was real, and sacrifice was necessary. Truth reveals itself even if sentimentalised. In such a world, judgment was still possible; human weakness, even sinfulness, was intimately understood. The Tricky Trinity offers no insight. To give William's and Myfanwy's story a little context, by 1913, the South Wales coalfields, driving British industry, were among the largest in the world. That humility could exist in such a grand landscape must be a lesson. Despite the story's sentimentality, belief in compassion motivated by love's eternal reality overcomes the sentimental. A story is never satisfying while the love of innocence or maturity looks like it might just be defeated by evil. None of us can bear to live in a world where injustice prevails.

◆ ◆ ◆

Understanding compassion and participating in it gives us insight into the two contemporary and competing views of human nature. On the one hand, we all share a common flaw, which helps us understand our need for mercy and forgiveness. Being genuinely compassionate towards those who suffer suggests, at the very least, that one is beginning to enter the mystery of human suffering, to believe what Saint Paul wrote in his first letter to the Corinthians, *"And now these three remain: faith, hope, and love. But the greatest of these is love"* (v. 13 NIV) *Agape* is the word Paul uses here, the grace of sacrificial love. This is the love that leads the pilgrim forward.

The Tricky Trinity could never understand the power of faith, hope, or love; it does not recognise the essential crack running through every human heart that just might let the light in, as Leonard Cohen suggests. We are alone in the universe and must make our way in it. We are evolving creatures who are quite able to shape our nature. Consequently, virtue is a changing and sliding scale. We have the power to be what we want, with *power* being the operative word. Having rejected the source of beauty, a beautiful mind in a beautiful body remains the name of the game. Utility is all, and that must create a life less meaningful and bearable than that shared by William, Myfanwy, and Dylan.

The failure to recognise that we are all flawed creatures dramatically changes how we think about each other. For example, it changes the way we view the morality of assisted suicide. Bringing about the death of another whose suffering is just too hard to bear is fraught with understandable human anguish for all of us. When a relative or friend is called upon to hasten the death of a loved one, suffering great pain likely to end in death, few of us will condemn him or her. It's one of those situations where one is tempted to say, but for the grace of God, that could have been me. However, when a society writes laws to facilitate assisted suicide, it assumes the role of God. In doing so, it says it understands the mystery of life and knows who should die and who should live. That's why once an assisted suicide law is passed, it is subject to increased liberalisation because society has lost its anchor. At the same time, very few will admit that in an increasingly utilitarian society, the state will always come to value an individual based on his or her usefulness.

To return to Nietzsche, good is the will to power; anything reinforcing the feeling of control (self-realisation) is to be valued, the release of desire, for example. The claim that assisted suicide can be labelled 'Death with Dignity' suggests that the 'will to power' has already seduced the society that preaches it. Humility, too easily mistaken for obsequiousness, weakness, and dependency on the biblical God, is a catalyst for evil. Compassion for the one who suffers is wrongheaded. Practical sympathy for the weak is one thing. Power over one's life and body is what matters. It's about defining the self. In this context of self-creating identity, one can be as caring as one wishes, but that cannot provide insight into the searing impotence of human frailty and dependency.

Nevertheless, is there something welcome on the horizon? Are we beginning to see a kickback against identity politics? Over the last decade, some academics and politicians have been increasingly willing to explore the roots of Western civilisation. Tom Holland has this to say in the introduction of his seminal work *Dominion: The Making of the Western Mind (xxv)*:

> *"To live in a Western country is to live in a society still utterly saturated by Christian concepts and assumptions … Two thousand years from the birth of Christ, it does not require a belief that he rose from the dead to be stamped by the formidable—indeed the inescapable—influence of Christianity. Whether it be the conviction that the workings of conscience are the surest determinants of good law, or that church and state exist as distinct entities, or that polygamy is unacceptable, its trace elements are to be found everywhere in the West. Even to write about it in a Western language is to use words shot through with*

Christian connotations. "Religion", "secular", "atheist":
none of these are neutral ... They derive from the classical
past ... freighted with the legacy of Christendom. Fail to
appreciate this, and the risk is always of anachronism."

It must be encouraging to many Christian believers that a historian as erudite as Holland understands that Western civilisation owes its existence to the Christian understanding of order and its ethos of "love thy neighbour." Its *"trace elements"* are everywhere. Friedrich Nietzsche might well have thought that he could stand outside God's creation order and act as a judge upon it, that his unaided reason would guide him to the truth. While something might have been poignantly and absurdly heroic about Nietzsche, his contemporary self-creating disciples warrant our sympathy more than our admiration. Held in thrall by the original sin of pride, he could never have understood that the sovereignty of subjectivism is the consequence of historical forgetfulness and the exalting of cultural amnesia over the traditional religion that gave rise to Western civilisation. In this first quarter of the twenty-first century, it must be evident to many people, one would hope, that submission to the authority of secularism has not been a great idea. As a replacement for Christianity, it's a bit of a fizzer.

We used to understand that loving one's neighbour always has a severe sacrificial aspect of giving oneself to help another. We all knew the story of the *Good Samaritan*. The sacrifice of compassion demanded that he give time, effort, and money to heal the injured traveller. And if we go a little deeper, it must be evident that sacrifice and humility walk alongside each other. Unlike the hypocrites who crossed the road to avoid the injured man, the Samaritan crossed the road to help. Where will the cultic affirmation of identity politics get its rationale for sacrifice, or learn to comprehend the poignant beauty of compassion? We all know if we care to think about it for a bit. The subjectivism of cultural relativism with its children will play the parasite it is, and feed off its despised host until it dies without the powers of regeneration intrinsic to its host.

The parasite preaching tolerance cannot understand that humility and sacrifice are the only things that give meaning and a foundation to tolerance when confronted by moral differences. More irony, the dogma of inclusion demands we ignore fundamental differences and affirm competing values. That might appear tolerant, but it would seduce us into servility. If the subjectivism of cultural relativism were to reorder the legal framework, it would make hypocrisy compulsory and forgiveness impossible. Shifting the focus away from tolerance, which can discriminate, to tolerance that replaces discernment with affirmation, a society is created where forgiveness is meaningless. It stops people from saying what they believe. Justice is severely compromised by making it serve an ever-changing concept of human rights. Justice is not enriched; it is undermined.

It's not difficult to imagine what direction social order will take in New Zealand if we continue to lose the pervasive and salutary influence of Christianity, to comprehend the stories and images the Bible gives us as we attempt to describe and understand ourselves and the world around us. What will give our spiritual imagination indwelling and transcendent content, substance to the longing of our hearts, insight into the mystery of love, significance, honour, the delight of intimate friendships, understanding parents, respectful children, and cause posterity to admire us? The replacement religion cannot do any of those. Subjectivism is the poison in the little bottle that says, "Drink me." It swells the head and anaesthetises the spiritual imagination by turning it into superstition.

No matter what we call it, the new cultural narrative could never give rise to a poem of such theological and sexual subtlety as John Donne's *A Valediction: Forbidding Mourning*,[1] to offer one of hundreds of examples from the period. The poem's power lies in how its images (conceits) bring the *Sacred and Profane* together in one harmonious whole. Donne's poem is profoundly Christian insofar as it marries the poet's love for his wife with the transcendent without collapsing into sentimentality. Any attempt to write such a poem under the umbrella of the new religion would do just that: collapse into a deceitful sentimentality. It would prove to be an aggressive ideology that impoverishes everything sacred and human about us.

Culture War

There's a revealing story about four Jewish teenagers from the Old Testament book of Daniel: Daniel, Hananiah, Mishael, and Azariah. Their names are important. Taken from Jerusalem by the forces of Nebuchadnezzar to Babylon, they were young men *"Without any physical defect, handsome, showing aptitude for every kind of learning, well informed, quick to understand, and qualified to serve in the King's palace"* (Daniel 1:4 NIV). They were to be trained for three years and placed in the king's service afterward. They would have a Babylonian Bachelor of Artifice (B.B.A.). Significantly, their names were changed: Daniel (God is my Judge) to Belteshazzar (Lady, wife of the god Bel, protects the king); Hananiah (Yahweh is gracious) to Shadrach (companion of Aku); Mishael (Who is like God?) to

Meshach (invoking Aku again); and Azariah (Yahweh is my help) to Abednego (servant of Nebo). These four men struggled against the forces that would undermine their faith in the God of Israel for the rest of their lives. They were in the midst of a 'culture war,' a war to be won by radically changing the religious loyalty of the young men.

The plight of our young people in 2025 is not much different from that of the young Jews in Babylon. Two competing religions compete for their loyalty. Of course, it might be that not many people understand that, or believe it, but that's not the issue. It's what's happening, even if most don't understand it. Indeed, I suspect that the plight of our young people in 2025 is worse than that of the four young Jews in Babylon. The Babylonian exiles could draw on a deep commitment to their faith. The young people protesting on the streets today hardly have a slight suspicion about what they don't know. At best, they are the rebels' shadow searching for a cause.

So, what's the point? Well, it's a question of identity again. About whom one believes oneself to be. That is as much a religious question in the twenty-first century as it was during the reign of Nebuchadnezzar, 605 BC–563 BC. The story of the young Jews in the Book of Daniel is one of confident identity, and it was that confidence that not only preserved them but enabled them to prosper. The contemporary struggle that people have over identity within the overarching narrative of multiculturalism is vexatious by its nature. It undermines confidence, making it very difficult to understand what it means to be a human being, who is my God, or even the immediacy of the issue. The politics of identity, essential to the outworking of multicultural theory while denying divine pretensions, acts like a religion, insofar as it demands complete obeisance. The human heart shrivels without a grasp of or hope in the sublime. There may be no Babylonian fiery furnace or lions' den, but the threat of cultural exile has a similar purpose and effect.

So, to recap, subjectivism, blind to the sublime, always results in spiritual, moral, aesthetic, imaginative, and intellectual impoverishment. And it does that because, having no conviction of the Sublime, it has a diminished view of what it means to be human. It does not have the power within itself to catch and preserve the proper balance between the material and the spiritual. Worship of the material in cahoots with vague notions of spirituality becomes essential and reasonable. Such an overarching narrative has neither the ability nor the desire to examine one's reason for being; where does one start? It is quite without allegorical power, turning life into one long creep into the darkness of narcissism.

Nevertheless, as I write this, two interesting things are happening that we couldn't have written about even a year ago. The political right is no longer in reaction mode. DIE's folly in its flirtation with cultural relativism is becoming more evident. The cultural relativists are licking their wounds, opposition to the cult of transgenderism is gathering strength, and the entire social justice framework is under threat. But for how long, one wonders? The President of the United States, Donald Trump, tells us he is getting rid of the cult of diversity. Well, *bonne chance* to him. I hope he understands what he's up against. It's taken nearly one hundred years for the 'diversophiles' to get to the point where they rule over us. They are not going away anytime soon. The popularity of Trumpism may have disoriented them, but I fear it will prove temporary. I am eager to discover how our government will attend to what might be the beginning of a watershed in Western civilisation. The struggle between the White House and Harvard

University in the United States about the incompatibility of diversity and merit highlights the nature of the battle. There is a great deal of sound and fury, which may not signify much.

The White House claims that university diversity programmes inhibit free speech, encourage racism, jeopardise scientific progress, disorient public order, and undermine aesthetic sensibilities. Harvard, the oldest American University, has led in pleading for academic freedom; free speech is being threatened. This is a remarkable defence because diversity programmes, by their very nature, inhibit free speech. Speaking out against DIE in any university in the United States—and in New Zealand, for that matter—is likely to incur a severe penalty. It would inhibit promotion and could even result in the offender's resignation.

But even more interesting, for this writer at least, is the rise of what we've come to call cultural Christianity. Many writers and academics are now realising that Christianity has utilitarian value. That it has been and continues to be the cultural glue for Western civilisation has become self-evident. As I have already mentioned, even the poster boy of atheism, Richard Dawkins, is content to be called a cultural Christian. He's happy to accept biblical morality and culture, but faith, there's the rub. Faith is critical to civilisation, and biblical faith gives us our roots, the foundation for an understanding of restraint and the power of renewal. It should be evident to us now that unrestrained democracy is a failure. It must be said that it's a failure because its essential quality—the foundation of a shared religion that would teach us who we are—has been lost. If we accept that the Bible offers us the best cultural glue, then we should ask why. Why is it that, despite Christianity's utilitarian value, things are falling apart? The answer should be obvious. I'll start with a cliché: We want our cake and we want to eat it too. We accept the ordered freedom that Christianity can give us, but we deny the giver. That's why an institution as august as Harvard University speaks with a forked tongue. It fails to recognise its denial of free speech for others while demanding it for itself. The irony shouts out very loudly. Founded on believing in the universal Truth of the biblical God, it creates its version of truth. Where, for goodness' sake, does it think it gets the title 'University' from?

The institution designed to protect Truth now undermines the belief in a universal truth and the importance of the experience that gives rise to it. The 'constrained vision', emphasising experience, has been replaced by the 'unconstrained vision',[2] emphasising the power of reason. I take the critical difference to be two conflicting versions of human nature. The constrained vision accepts that human nature is flawed. It depends on learned, historically evolved social processes; tradition is significant but not absolute as a guide. It is open to adaptation, but within the boundaries of its experienced understanding of human nature. The constrained vision is suspicious of any ideology failing to accept human limitations. The unrestrained vision is utopian in its goal setting and frequently revolutionary. Human nature is malleable and in need of improvement.

Notes:

1. *A Valediction: Forbidding Mourning.* Donne, John. *Complete Verse and Selected Prose.* Ed. John Hayward. The Nonesuch Press. 1962. Page 36.

2. Any understanding I have of these visions comes to me from a reading of Thomas Sowell, *A Conflict of Visions: Ideological Origins of Political Struggles.* William Morrow and Company. 1987.

V

DIE, The Enemy of Character

The righteous lead blameless lives;
blessed are their children after them.

Proverbs 20:7 NIV

When I was in secondary school in the 1950s, the value of good character was taken for granted and built into the school curriculum. Courage, loyalty, and truthfulness took the front seat. It might have been sentimentalised in colloquialisms like 'playing the game'. I suspect compassion and temperance were there, too, but they didn't have the immediacy of courage for a boy. Reading good books made us better. We were convinced of that. It was the *l'esprit de époque*. Although we may not have understood it clearly, we believed that good books enriched one's character and imagination, and we read a lot. Books were the ammunition that fired our imagination. They didn't have to compete with the World Wide Web. So, courage was given considerable mileage at my boys' school for reasons that seemed obvious at the time.

The first Dickens novel I read was *A Tale of Two Cities* when I was fourteen. I still love the opening paragraph; it is just so timeless:

> *"It was the best of times, it was the worst of times, it was the age of wisdom, it was the age of foolishness, it was the epoch of belief, it was the epoch of incredulity, it was the season of Light, it was the season of Darkness, it was the spring of hope, it was the winter of despair."*

Our English teacher discussed Sydney Carton's moral courage despite his drunkenness. Carton's, that is, not our English teacher's. I don't think I understood it then, but now I believe courage has considerable redemptive power. Most of us had gone to Sunday School when we were younger, so we knew the biblical story of Joshua and the underlying context of what it meant to *"be of good courage."* Intuitively, we understood the spiritual significance, although I doubt that we could have talked about it with conviction. At primary school, extracts of the *Iliad* and the *Odyssey* were read to us. Before my secondary education, the Trojan Horse, Odysseus, and the one-eyed giant, Polyphemus, overflowed my imagination. The X-Men fighting for peace and freedom in Hollywood's fantasy world don't make the grade with my grandchildren, despite one of the heroes having my surname.

When one looks at movies, from *Superman* to *Star Wars* and *Dune*, they are much more revealing when understood in a traditional context. The old concept of the hero is lost in the belief of man's power to conquer nature, which is the conquest of some men by others. There is no ultimate Court of Appeal in the modern version of heroism. Faith in the beauty of truth is overwhelmed by the pursuit of power. The anti-hero, filling in for the hero, conquers in the name of power rather than truth. The search for the Messiah remains in the religious subconscious, but most seem to lack the insight to recognise his beauty. The politics of moral abstraction undermine the joy and aspiration of youthful imagination.

I loved the story of *Black Beauty*, and ever since, it has conditioned how I think animals should be treated. The emotional power when we learn the difference between right and wrong as children never disappears. The tears I shed for *Black Beauty* when she was treated badly and my anger towards the perpetrators helped to shape my idea of justice, enriching me as an adult. *Gulliver's Travels* taught me the elements of satire and human nature without even being told it was satire. It was more revealing than any explanation I heard at university. Fairy tales, before Disney bowdlerised them and turned pathos into bathos, were the warm milk of my imagination.

It seems self-evident to me now that what we read as children reinforces and deepens our adult response to metaphor. So, a young man was courageous, but only insofar as he was good. The faint vestige of nineteenth-century Muscular Christianity that remained, not to be confused with toxic masculinity, probably reinforced my perception. *Onward Christian Soldiers* had not yet been cancelled by the progressive definers of violence. The ethic of *Tom Brown's Schooldays (1857)* cast a shadow long enough to reach New Zealand. Although Rugby School was far from the classless school I attended, its ethos still shaped much of our imagination. Even boys who hadn't heard of Tom Brown, Flashman, Thomas Hughes, or Matthew Arnold tended to act like they had. Such was the belief in the power of courage to overcome injustice. Victoria might have been dead for over fifty years, but confidence in the Empire hadn't quite. But as we now know, the 1956 Suez Crisis ended that confidence.

I now understand something else—all the comic book heroes, except the more recent ones, lived in a world where good and evil were still present to shape our characters. Superman, Batman, Wonder Woman, Iron Man, and Captain America only made sense in a world confident about the nature of goodness. The prevailing loss of confidence, and we have lost it, would make cowards of us all. It's not a coincidence that the more recent incarnations of Batman have become darker. Superman, that symbol of hope, defends the American Way no longer.

This is not a lament for the passing of post-Victorian virtue. However, I am saying that the contemporary failure to appreciate the importance of teaching boys the importance of good character is a profound loss. We took the idea of character seriously. We frequently fell short, but in falling short, we seldom made excuses for our behaviour. We were realistic, especially when we applied that realism to others. And despite what is often said about the post-war period, bullying was not acceptable. In the playground, bullies were despised. When he was discovered, the bully could expect to be punished. Manliness was a big deal. To be manly and masculine was to be responsible and courageous. Perhaps a little muscularity was a matter of some satisfaction and gratitude. In our wildest rocking dreams, we had no idea that "manliness" would be misunderstood and pronounced toxic one day. We were taught to respect girls, even honour them, and dare I say, protect them. Of course, that ethic did not always prevail, but it was always there as the expected standard. We might not have always played the game, but we knew the rules. The contemporary notion of equality and certainly equity had not yet been applied with any rigour to the relationship between the sexes.

I can now see a vast gap in attitude to the past between the classroom I sat in and the one my grandchildren sit in. We were taught and retained a reverence for the past. We took it for granted that knowledge of the past helped us better understand the present and future. Now it seems my grandchildren have absorbed the idea that the past is a roadblock to progress. Taught by teachers seduced by multicultural dogma, the best thing they can do with the past is to rewrite it based on their superior knowledge. And that rewriting is necessary for progress, it couldn't possibly be an exercise in self-deception.

One warm sunny day, a well-educated English teacher, who had been a prisoner of war during World War II, read extracts from Baldassare Castiglione's *The Book of the Courtier* to us. Of course, we had never heard of Castiglione or the Book of the Courtier. Perhaps it was the teacher's way of coping with the sleepy period after lunch. Maybe it was the sunny day that encouraged the teacher to read to us, or maybe because Castiglione was Italian, I imagined the romance of the time. And I have not forgotten the name of the author. It still rolls off my tongue as easily as the day I first learned it.

Of course, our teacher didn't expect us to behave like Renaissance gentlemen. Not that we would have known what one was anyway. Still, he wanted us to understand that while the finer points of what went on between the sexes changed over time, they should always be marked by courtesy and mutual respect. We were respectful enough not to mock the notions of old-fashioned courtesy; we were civilised enough to know they had their value, well, some of us were. We knew the mythology surrounding King Arthur, although we might have been somewhat vague about Guinevere's imagined or real unfaithfulness; we were unsure. Even if we couldn't speak on the topic with clarity, we understood the power of myth to educate the imagination. And that imagination was still far from the spirit of protest shared by the 1980s Stanford students. If we could have been transported to the 1980s, we would have thought the protesters silly.

Looking back, I can see how my character was shaped by what I read. Although I don't think I understood it then, I became obsessed with the sacrificial hero. Alexander Dumas' *The Corsican Brothers* reverberated in my mind for weeks. The idea that conjoined twins, Louis and Lucien, separated at birth, could feel each other's pain was a mystery that still gives me pleasure as I remember the story. Then there was Dumas' *The Count of Monte Cristo* and the raging injustice suffered by Edmond Dantès. The book was long, but my fascination with the hero kept me going. I'm unsure why I retained interest in the 19th-century French novel. Maybe my young man needed to see that justice was done. If I remember correctly, *The Three Musketeers* was an easier read than the other two novels. Alas, Victor Hugo's *Les Misérables* proved to be beyond me. Hardly surprising, Hugo digresses so much, and I don't think I knew what a digression was when I was sixteen.

In spite of being sixteen, the school motto, in Latin, of course, *Non-Scholae Sed Vitae Discimus*, "not for school but for the life we are learning," was clear, meaningful, and practical. It seems caught up in all the multicultural chatter decades later, 'character' has no content. In the first quarter of the twenty-first century, anybody may be called a 'personality,' without embarrassment, as though that describes moral worth. I've already said that self-respect has been exchanged for self-esteem. So, what can an octogenarian do but recall Plato and Aristotle and what they had to say about virtue and character? I remember the *Golden Mean,* the balance between two extremes. The Delphic Oracle recommended nothing to excess. It seemed common sense.

Plato has Socrates, Protarchus, and Philebus discuss character in *Philebus*, and Aristotle describes the virtues in *Nicomachean Ethics Book II.* Courage, for example, was the mean between the deficit of cowardice and the excess of rashness. Believe it or not, I had been taught that at school in the context of the conveniently numbered seven virtues and seven vices.[1] And would you believe it? We read *The Parade of* the *Vices* from Marlow's Faust. I can remember how we all loved its raw imagery. We were fascinated when the teacher read us selected portions of Marlow's play. Discovering that Helen of Troy had the face that launched a thousand ships, and just where Ilium (Troy) was, made me think I was incredibly enlightened. And, I suspect, extremely fortunate that we had an educated and cultured English teacher for our last two years at secondary school. I could be tempted to say they are now thin on the ground, but I dare not.

I now have a large poster on a wall in my study, nearly two metres wide and over one metre high, with 'COURAGE' written over a graffiti background. It reminds me of what I would like to have more of. The graffiti background reminds me of the crazy, contrived ugliness of the world I now live in. It's not just the unwarranted suspicion of an old man; courage doesn't have the provenance or prominence it once had. The poster helps me remember the difference between the *Golden Mean* and the Genesis story, including the Decalogue given to Moses 1000 years before Aristotle. I now understand that Hebrew virtue was not in the balance between excess and deficiency because the Hebrews were monotheists. Instead, virtue found its power in faithful obedience to the revealed will of the Lord. The difference is critical. No matter how you spin it, the *Golden Mean* remains an abstraction. Well, it has become an abstraction without the old gods to support it. Helpful, no doubt, but an abstraction, nevertheless. The obedience of faith in a living God arouses the desire to love and serve. It's the difference between the secular god in the abstraction of reason and the passionate biblical God who completes personhood. *"The law of the Lord is perfect, reviving the soul"* is heartwarming. The rest of Psalm 19 is well worth reading.

◆ ◆ ◆

Although few of us in this first quarter of the twenty-first century might be able to identify the classical or biblical virtues readily, most of us still recognise them as having something to do with good character. Until the nineteen-sixties and seventies, the Bible generally, the Decalogue, and perhaps the Beatitudes still informed our moral imagination. With only the usual uninformed youthful suspicion of tradition, perhaps unconsciously, we accepted the value and significance of the four cardinal or hinge virtues and the Christian virtues of humility, faith, hope, and charity. They were there in the oxygen we breathed, informing us about the difference between right and wrong.

It was obvious that a blending, awkward as it might have been, of the Christian and Classical narratives, gave a foundation to the educated mind and its vision; we took it for granted, not sure that we understood the difference between myth and legend, but it didn't matter. I doubt the relationship between character and virtue would even be considered a possible topic of discussion in the contemporary secondary school senior classroom, and for obvious reasons. The language that would permit such a discussion is not there anymore. Of course, we might not have understood that the cross has been central to Western civilisation for nearly two millennia. There was no way we could have adequately comprehended how the story of the Crucifixion and Resurrection influenced our understanding of gratitude. We weren't old enough, and our grasp on the sweep of history was not up to it.

Alas, the contemporary senior secondary school pupil is unlikely to know about Jesus Christ and the meaning He gives to Western civilisation. Claiming that a literary canon might inform virtue and its effect on character development through the centuries has become controversial. At the risk of stating the obvious and going over everything lightly, there remains, if we were only to use it, the poetry and prose in Old English and Middle English from *Beowulf* to the *Canterbury Tales*. And then there's the drama of the Renaissance with Shakespeare, Marlowe, Jonson, et al. There is, too, the metaphysical poetry of Donne, Herbert, Shakespeare again, and Edmund Spenser's *The Faerie Queene*. The Christian vision remained influential. For example, John Donne's Sonnet X, *Death, Be Not Proud,* echoes what many believed: Christ had defeated the power of sin and death on the Cross.

Toward the end of my last year at high school, our teacher read Donne's sonnet to us. We were only kids, but we did have the nous to realise that the teacher was enjoying himself. With some help from the teacher, we slowly unravelled the imagery. Of course, it's doubtful that a teacher would even read such a poem to his or her class in 2025; it's too tricky, too 'religious', although it's undoubtedly inclusive. It proved to anticipate a double delight for me. My first English lecture at university included a professor reading us three or four of Donne's sonnets, including *Death, Be Not Proud,* in a rich Canadian voice. I knew nothing of the professor, but more than sixty years later, I remember him with affection. Such was the power of the poem.

During the upheaval of the English Civil War, the rise of Protestantism, and the Restoration in England, Christianity continued to shape behaviour, art, and music. Two of our most enduring works came from this period: Milton's *Paradise Lost* and Bunyan's *Pilgrim's Progress.* I don't think it's revolutionary to suggest that it's not until we get to what we now call the Romantic period that we see serious and extensive questioning and even rejection of the Christian story. The Christian Gospel of sin, repentance, and redemption is initially romanticised. For example, in Goethe's *Faust, Part 1,* the redemptive power of romantic love saves Gretchen. And even in Part 2, in the last act, we have *"He who strives on and lives to strive, can earn redemption still."* So redemption is not the consequence of repentance; it's the reward for striving. We find writers like George Eliot and Thomas Hardy rejecting the Christian story, but they would find a substitute for redemption in the duty of striving. In the works of both these writers, the loss of faith makes tragedy even more poignant. Looking back, it seems that the Sublime has been overwhelmed by pathos. The message of justification by faith has always been hard to absorb into one's being.

It was probably the early seventies when I began to sense a drift from understanding the arts based on the search for the Sublime to one grounded in psychologically conditioned values. I remember attending an exhibition in Toronto in 1969, *The Sacred and Profane* in *Symbolist Art*.[2] It was later that I realised it was a watershed for me. The individual exhibits collected worldwide remain the most revealing exhibition of paintings and drawings I have ever seen. It convinced me that the Sacred existed as a category of knowledge and that I could not correctly comprehend the Profane without knowledge of the Sacred. Indeed, without knowledge of the Sublime, one would have no means to assess or even recognise the Profane. Although a Christian believer, it was the first time I had come to an intelligent engagement with the Sublime and its exploration by an artist. I also began to understand what its rejection might mean.

Indeed, the Sublime became meaningful at this exhibition, and an explanation of the grotesque and pathetic was needed to help me understand the human condition. I embraced the Sublime with a sense of wonder and awe and understood why for many, it leads to worship. On the other hand, the grotesque distorts the Sublime, making us feel uneasy, even fearful. The preoccupation that contemporary art has with the grotesque seems normal to me. So much modern music has become banal. And if that's not bad enough, it's pretentious as well. Pathos helps us understand what it means to lose something important; it brings tears for what might have been. Perhaps most importantly, one learns to believe that engagement with the Sublime leads to a forgetfulness of oneself. And yet, simultaneously, the enjoyment of one's humanity becomes much more exciting. On the other hand, continuous participation in the grotesque would diminish us, as the *Faust* story reminds us. Pathos can engulf us in helplessness that would reduce much of life to the sentimental. The Grotesque and the Pathetic appear to make us too conscious of ourselves. I can't help but recall a few lines from T.S. Eliot's *East Coker* in *Four Quartets: "Love is most nearly itself when here and now cease to matter. Old men ought to be explorers."* Indeed, he could well have said that old men ought to be pilgrims.

◆ ◆ ◆

The most important discovery in my contact with the Sublime was the realisation that this thing we have come to call religion, and that somehow it is extra to everyday life, is a category error. To be 'religious' is no more alien to the human condition than having red hair. I learned that what one believes about the nature of oneself and the world gives meaning to everything else we know. I am not, nor ever was, a blank slate. Faith is not an optional extra. Like Marx, we might wish to ignore and step outside its influence, but all we will do is establish an alternative religion that must be a parasite. When art gets disconnected from its search for the Sublime, it will likely become a substitute religion.

The exhibition prepared me to understand the subterranean cultural reset that was taking place, from the importance of Christian-informed self-respect to the new dogma of the psychology of self-creation and self-esteem. I thought I saw a foundation for self-respect in the Sublime and the notion of self-esteem in the profane. The Sublime did not encourage self-centeredness, while the profane seemed to do just that. In the meantime, the transformation of virtue into values had become so successful that I had to, for many years, remind myself just what a virtue might be. I was reminded that in the fourth century, the theologian Ambrose affirmed virtues, which Plato identified as the essential characteristics of a good man. The Church was to describe them as the "human virtues." They are also found in the *Jewish Book of Wisdom*. In short, they have traction.

This is more than can be said for their contemporary parasite: 'values.' Gertrude Himmelfarb (to whom I will return presently) tells us that values are not identifiable characteristics of any human being. They do not become characteristics of anyone who might try to sneak them in by changing the verb to a noun. I might passionately claim to value justice or courage, but that makes me neither just nor courageous. I might even say that justice is one of my values, and because it is, I think of myself as just. When 'value' is changed from a verb into a noun, it is in danger of becoming an enemy of virtue because the observable reality of the material and ordered world (the objective) becomes subject to personal interpretation with the limited authority of the individual's feelings. The necessary distinction between opinion and fact is blurred. In an argument or debate, because one has learned to accept the authority of the subjective, one is readily seduced by the intensity of feeling. In such a situation, the conviction of faith is a product of emotion rather than the consequence of revelation, tradition, rational thought, and certainly not scientific method. Indeed, there is no need for the individual to exercise rational thought to examine the conviction because of his or her confidence in the rightness of passion.

For example, the authority and power of subjectivism underpins the "reigning discourse" around gender and race. It's a language game. Judith Butler is revealing here.[3] The trick is to get people to use the language that reinforces their ideology. The emotional power of what Butler calls *"gender norms"* exists because they are repeated. Sexual identities are established by *"performativity"*. A dreadful word, but there you are. We construct our gender by performing it. Sexual identity, or to be doctrinally correct, 'gender identity,' is a result of 'performativity' and is not biologically determined.

So, the identity of a man or a woman is always in the state of becoming. Even if the demands of the transgender claims recede, as they seem to be doing, we have absorbed a way of thinking where we are constantly shaped and reshaped by the intensity of our desires. Even if we reject the demand that pronouns must be fluid, but yield to the use of neologisms like 'cisgender', 'non-binary', 'gender-affirming', 'transgender man or woman', 'gender minorities', 'heteronormativity', 'pansexual', and the phobias, we will not have rejected the authority of passion. Denying the authority of the objective, the authority of self-creation remains in control of common sense or rational syntax. And that incoherence finds a recent manifestation in the claim that homosexuality is a biological reality: *"I was born that way."* At the same time, the identity of the recently discovered transgender is a social construct: *"I wasn't born that way."*

So, we might have begun to accept the subjectivity underpinning education in the 1970s, but now schools are scaling dizzy heights at the command of the state. Maybe John Stuart Mill was right, that despotism over the mind leads to control of the body.

> *"A general state education is a mere contrivance for moulding people to be exactly like one another: and as the mould in which it casts them is that which pleases the predominant power in the government, whether this be a monarch, a priesthood, an aristocracy, or the majority of the existing generation, in proportion as it is efficient*

and successful, it establishes a despotism over the mind,
leading by the natural tendency to one over the body." [4]

The despotism over the mind that leads to control over the body worries me. For example, my primary objection to the demands of gender/queer theory, the most aggressive contemporary expression of the victory of values over virtue, is that it reduces any possibility of discovering and living a coherent philosophy of human meaning and purpose. By denying or ignoring the objective existence of human essence and dignity, queer theory must create an alternative reality to survive. It must, for example, reorder everyone's understanding of human identity and purpose. The skirmish over the grammar of simple pronouns is a symptom and technique of deception. In a discussion of prisoners in jail, in his usual esoteric way, Michel Foucault writes,

> *"It would be wrong to say that the soul is an illusion, or*
> *an ideological effect. On the contrary, it exists, it has a*
> *reality, it is produced permanently around, on, within*
> *the body of the functioning of a power that is exercised*
> *on those that are punished."* [5]

Even the soul is an existential and psychological product of the body's pilgrimage. It is cultivated and formed by what is apparent but not defined. Foucault's *'reality'*, the real me, is entirely the product of material and psychological power. The body conditions a new definition of the soul rather than the other way around, as I had been taught in the 'sexist and racist' single-sex schools of the 1950s.

From the late 1960s to the 21st century, Foucault was a big deal in universities. I remember that nearly every student thought we were on to something new. I didn't understand it then, but Foucault was the anti-God grandchild of Friedrich Nietzsche. Knowledge gave rise to power, and power would always pass on its particular kind of knowledge, as Nietzsche tells us, ad nauseam, in *Beyond Good and Evil* (par. 168), *"Christianity gave Eros poison to drink; he did not die of it, certainly, but degenerated to Vice."* Foucault and Nietzsche would turn their spin on vice, the Christian virtue of sexual sanctity, into their spin on virtue, which inevitably was to evolve into sexual licence called freedom.

I now understand that neither Foucault nor Nietzsche nor all the others have taken us forward. They mimic Adam and Eve's temptation in the Garden of Eden. Lost in the labyrinth of all their wishful philosophising, they wanted to create their vision of good and evil. The Christian story stood in the way; it had to be eradicated. In that, Foucault was superficially successful in helping to develop the 'new' sexuality despite being a paedophile who tragically died of AIDS. Nietzsche's explanation of God's death gave impetus to the eugenics cult, which seems to be giving birth to an even more deadly cult: transhumanism. I can't bring myself to provide either the dignity of a philosophy. I'll come back to transhumanism later.

So, I suppose it's not surprising that I have come to believe that the imaginary authority of personal experience is not only the enemy of virtue but also of Christian doctrine and tradition, replaced by an ideology telling us what we must learn and unlearn.[6] To clarify things, I'm using ideology following John Adams' description in an 1813 letter to Thomas Jefferson. Adams said "ideology" is a good descriptor of a particular kind of political thinking.[6] It might describe an enthusiastic and confident structure for reform about its imagined benefits, but it has no intellectual vision rooted in political reality. Convinced of its righteousness, it is intrinsically and compulsorily judgemental; such is its addictive nature. Hence, the cancellation of those who disagree. History must be recalibrated, exemplified in its rewriting, the knocking over of historical statues, and censorship of literature, validating C.S. Lewis' phrase 'chronological snobbery'. Because values disguised as virtue don't have the support of rational thought, they must have the support of an authoritarian state.

It has become popular over recent years to talk of 'Kiwi values' as though they are unique. But despite all the talk, these values are entirely derivative and lacking substance. It is impossible to identify them with any authority, although there is an assumption that New Zealanders share them. They are the identitarian usurper glue that would hold us together. Because the progressive mind finds virtue's intrinsic and permanent nature anathema, it must find a replacement. And that replacement must submit to the cult of identity politics because political sanction is the overarching authority of control. Kiwi values have become a grab bag of conflicting, ill-defined ideas such as democracy, peace, harmony, respect, inclusion, freedom of choice, safety, equity (social justice), kindness, sporting prowess, etc. None of these can be used to describe a person's character meaningfully.

I have mentioned how I found a timely salvation in C.S. Lewis' *The Abolition of Man*. I must mention another book that informed the previous paragraphs and how I now think about education: virtue and values. Gertrude Himmelfarb convincingly explains one significant causal factor in the tension between virtues and values in *The Demoralisation of Society: From Victorian Virtues to Modern Values*. (1995). Himmelfarb claims that morality has "*become so thoroughly radicalised and subjectified"* that most are unaware of what has happened. A closer examination of the difference between the older concept of self-respect and the more recent self-esteem is revealing. A traditional understanding of character has always informed self-respect:

> *"Suffering produces perseverance; perseverance, character;*
> *and character, hope, and hope does not put us to shame*
> *because God's love has been poured into our hearts through*
> *the Holy Spirit who has been given to us."* [7]

The biblical description had been thoroughly secularised by writers like George Eliot and J.S. Mill in the nineteenth century. Despite that, the idea retained its working credibility until the beginning of the twenty-first century, when scientism finally ruled out the authority of the scientific method by declaring that sex was not determined by biology.

Although self-respect might work for a while without an appeal to tradition, it is nevertheless given its power to encourage behaviour by a belief in the God of the Bible. One's dignity is a gift from God and not a consequence of our actions or, as Judith Butler would have us believe, 'performativity.' Actions that satisfy are the result of insight into our dignity, and such insight permanently nourishes and honours humility. Self-esteem depends entirely on how one feels about oneself and the authority those feelings have. Perception is all. It supplies no framework for self-criticism and the concept of restraint that flows from that balanced appreciation of virtue that makes goodness possible. It appears to encourage pride. Let me restate that a little differently. Self-respect grows out of a belief in and practice of virtue. Self-esteem is sustained by a belief in the viability and integrity of emotionally perceived values. Therefore, we should not be surprised that identity or race is more meaningful than virtue. Martin Luther King's "*Dream*" appears to have been just that—a dream.

Himmelfarb places considerable responsibility on Friedrich Nietzsche for transmuting virtues into values. He was aware of what he was doing when he began to speak of,

> "... *values not as a verb, meaning to value or esteem something; nor as a singular noun, meeting the measure of a thing,(the economic value of money, labour, or property); but in the plural, denoting the moral beliefs and attitudes of society . . . He used the word consciously, repeatedly, to signify what he took to be the most profound event in human history. His 'transvaluation of values' was to be the final ultimate revolution, a revolution against both the classical virtues and the Judaic Christian ones. The 'death of God' would mean the death of morality the death of truth—above all, the truth of any morality. There would be no good and evil, no virtue and vice. There would only be 'values.' And having degraded virtues and values, Nietzsche proceeded to devalue and transvalue them, to create a new set of values for his 'new man.'"* [8]

Himmelfarb goes on to point out that the sociologist Max Weber borrowed 'values' in such a matter-of-fact way that he helped them become part of the accepted vocabulary and reinforced the idea that all moral ideas are subject only to custom and convention, that they have a purely instrumental utilitarian purpose peculiar to specific individuals and societies. In his maturity, Weber is said to have told a student,

> *"Today, a scholar's honesty, especially that of a philosopher, can be measured by his attitude towards Nietzsche and Marx. Whoever does not admit that he could not have accomplished crucial parts of his work without the contributions of these two men deceives himself and others. Our intellectual universe has largely been formed by Marx and Nietzsche."* [9]

The 'revelation' that gained its impetus from Marx and Nietzsche reinforced the downgrading of the biblical story and ethics. Still, as I have already suggested, it did not abolish the need for morality of some kind. Even Darwin is alleged to have said that when asked about God and religion, the idea of God was beyond the scope of man's intellect, but that man still had an obligation to do his duty.[10] And then there is the penetrating declaration from George Eliot, who declared, *"God is inconceivable, immorality unbelievable, but duty nonetheless pre-emptive and absolute."* [11]

A swelling assumption developed when I was a young man that morality, having the power to do what one believed to be right, had nothing more than a rational basis. Any morality you care to think about is a human invention. I now understand that the English utilitarians like Eliot and Mill had an impossible problem. They didn't catch on to what Nietzsche understood only too well. Although Eliot and Mill et al. rejected God, they were nevertheless dependent on the ethical underpinning that Christianity had taught them. The problem in Eliot's obsession with duty is evident in her novels. Her greatest novel, *Middlemarch,* could not have been written without the Christian morality hidden on nearly every page. Slowly, we get to the first duty of man, which is not *"to know God and enjoy him forever."* Instead, man's first duty is to know and love oneself. I suspect that Eliot would be horrified if confronted with the accusation that she had participated in such hubris. It has taken two centuries for us to finally be convinced that therapeutic self-love is the way to salvation. In our heart of hearts, I don't think any of us would ever admit this, but in practice, duty has been replaced by licence; the conviction that freedom is found in the liberation of desire.

With its roof fixed in place, DIE is the enclosed arena where we must play all our games. Entrance is free, but exiting is expensive. It is the enemy of character because it would reduce human beings to mere political constructs. Identity is not formed, discovered, nurtured, or explained within the intergenerational family's diversity of relationships. Social capital is not valued, and its effects are misunderstood. The family, the most important civil society institution, Edmund Burke's little platoon, is devalued and finally dissolved. So, too, are the shared benefits between family and community. Identity is discoverable only within group membership, more accurately called tribal, and each tribe competes with the other for its share of human rights. The outcome cannot be the harmony promised by the esoteric trinity of diversity, inclusion, and equity. Uniformity will be enforced, and free speech and conscience will be denied, not to mention religious belief and practice. We will get exactly the opposite of what the theory of multiculturalism presumed. There will be no diversity of thought, culture, or race; inclusion will be uniformity and equity on the road to tyranny.

Notes:

1. The four classical virtues are Prudence, Justice, Temperance, Courage, and the theological virtues, Faith, Hope, and Charity. Lust, Gluttony, Greed, Sloth, Wrath, Envy, and Pride are vices.

2. Second-hand copies of the catalogue are still available from Mare Booksellers, Toronto, or eBay.

3. Judith Butler. *Who's Afraid of Gender?* Penguin Books, UK, 2024; *Undoing Gender.* Routledge. 2004; *Gender Trouble.* Routledge. 1990.

4. John Stuart Mill. *On Liberty, 1859.* Chapter 5, Para 13.

5. Michel Foucault. *Discipline and Punishment: The Birth of the Prison.* London, Penguin. 1991. p. 29

6. See *What is Ideology?* An event co-hosted by Public Discourse and the Lumen Christi Institute, Chicago, May 2, 2024.

7. Romans 5:3-5

8. Himmelfarb, G. (1996) *The de-moralization of society: from Victorian virtues to modern values.* New York: Vintage Books. p. 10

9. Bendix, Reinhard and Roth, Guenther, *Scholarship and Partisanship: Essays on Max Weber.* Berkeley. 1971, p.22

10. *Darwin Correspondence Project.* Letter 8873. Darwin, C.R. to Doades, G.H. Nov. 27. 1878.

11. Gordon S. Haight. *George Eliot: A Biography.* (Oxford, 1968) p. 64

VI

When Rights Are Wrong

For my people are foolish;
they know me not.

Jeremiah 4:22

The Universal Declaration of Human Rights, adopted in 1947, encouraged the assumption that human rights are discerned by reason, and are, therefore, universal. However, I have come to believe they are neither, and the claim that they are both leads to folly. My suspicions were reinforced when I heard the term 'animal rights' sometime in the mid-1990s. Similar to the first time I heard the word 'multiculturalism', it was at a dinner table, where a young academic who had just completed a PhD became excited about the idea. I was reasonably sure that it was an ideological development from the inroads made by cultural relativism and the necessary confusion around human nature that followed. Whatever the case, anything she said that resembled an argument failed to capture my mind or heart. I was no longer the soft touch I might have been in the 1960s or 1970s.

I was inclined to blame multicultural theory because I suspected its pervasive relativism was causing too many people to *feel* their way to truth rather than *think* their way. The simple phrase "I think" had been replaced by the vague ambiguity of "I feel." There seemed to be an unspoken assumption that to feel was more authoritative than to think—or, if not more authoritative, certainly kinder. Criticising what another felt was insensitive, the accusation of 'bullying' was just below the surface. Transgenderism hadn't quite arrived, but on looking back, I suspect the climate necessary for its acceptance had reached us.

Wendy, with her new PhD, I'll call her Wendy, would not be dislodged from her conviction. She was a child of her time, quite sure in her heart, and that was enough. She could have been one of the students taught by the teachers Lewis describes in *The Abolition of Man*. The purity of unexamined affection ruled in her heart and mind. She was kind to animals and believed everyone else should do the same. That the entire concept of rights has a necessary connection to duty seemed to have passed her by. Without that connection, rights floated freely in her mind, although they were nothing more than demands. Had she been prepared to confront it, her dog and mother shared a common dignity. Of course, she would have denied that, but it was still a reasonable conclusion based on what she was saying. Whatever the case, the claim that animals have rights is an assertion; it is not a fact. I'm unsure what the claim can be based on other than an extraordinary sensitivity to animal suffering. What I feel, must be true.

There are good reasons for treating animals with diligent care, but animals are hardly the possessors of rights of any kind. Taking my insight from the Genesis story, I had always assumed that duties and rights were interdependent. And for that, I must thank the English philosopher, Roger Scruton, who consistently pointed out that only human beings have duties, and therefore, only human beings have rights. That connection between duties and rights still monitors my thinking about human rights generally. I don't think anyone can argue sensibly that animals have duties. Australian philosopher Peter Singer,[1] for example, explains some of the equivalence of interests of animals, including humans, but does not solve the problem of duty. Whatever the case, I no longer worry about Wendy's claims. There are more critical things to think about.

So, back to the real stuff. After World War II, it became necessary to discover a justice system acceptable to the Allies, and indeed to the Germans as well, to prosecute the Nazi war criminals. Duty might have been a contentious issue, as many on trial claimed they were doing their duty. On the other hand, the observance of the rights of others was also within the province of one's duty. The Allies knew it was important that as many people as possible believed that justice was being done. Something convincing to everybody had to be found. The first of the Nuremberg trials took place during October/November 1946. Taking its cue from British and American law, it had numerous prosecutors and defence lawyers, although a panel of judges imposed the sentences. Of necessity, the actual trial was shaped by a range of legal traditions:

> *"The defendants were allowed to choose their own lawyers, and the most common defense strategy was that the crimes defined in the London Charter were examples of ex post facto law; that is, they were laws that criminalized actions committed before the laws were drafted. Another defense*

was that the trial was a form of victor's justice–the Allies were applying a harsh standard to crimes committed by Germans and leniency to crimes committed by their own soldiers." [2]

So, in the interests of justice, something better than 'victor's justice' needed to rule the proceedings.

◆ ◆ ◆

On my way to dizzy octogenarian heights, it's probably inevitable that I should wonder about the nature of justice and freedom, specifically in the context of expanding human rights. For a long time, I have been surrounded by human rights chatter without any definitive and workable definition. In 2001, when I was Director of the New Zealand Education Development Foundation, Professor Rex Ahdar (University of Otago) wrote *Adrift in a Sea of Rights* for the Foundation. It described the human rights scene well. I suspect that if it were to be written in 2024, *Awash in a Sea of Rights* might be a more accurate title.

It might be an exaggeration, but not much, to accuse the Human Rights Commission of making up rights as it goes along. For example, the Commission has this to say in the foreword to its *Conversion Practices in Aotearoa, New Zealand:*

> *"Imagine a future where Rainbow people can live authentically and with pride. A future where Rainbow people are affirmed within their religious and faith communities, their ethnic communities, their schools and youth groups. This is the future most of us want for*

ourselves and our loved ones, and many people have worked and continue to work to remove the barriers that prevent Rainbow people from experiencing this."

One is surprised that the writers of this foreword did not notice the internal contradiction of this passage. On the one hand, they commend religious freedom, but only if the religion conforms to their notion of inclusion. On what grounds does the Human Rights Commission have the right to determine religious doctrine? Is the irony not obvious? Despite contemporary attempts to be progressive, most traditional religions do not approve of homosexuality. Indeed, they are frequently pressured to conform, making their disapproval sound like a denial of human rights.

Christians, maybe because Christ told them to love their enemies, are more susceptible to pressure here than Muslims. Whatever the case, we have a conflict over the nature of freedom and what it means to be human. The Human Rights Commission would have us believe homosexuality is a human right but freedom of religious belief and expression is not. It would have the Christian who believes God has created men and women in His image affirm what s/he considers wrong. The language of bureaucratic obsequiousness will not do. Taking the language of the Human Rights Commission seriously, religious communities must have the right to affirm their fellow believers according to *their* theology of the Divine and human nature. It should be evident to the most casual observer that the Human Rights Commission, true to its identity politics, is establishing itself as a surrogate deity; taking its cue from Marcuse's *repressive tolerance,*

tolerance is affirmation. The Human Rights Commission is not protecting human rights. It's inventing them.

◆ ◆ ◆

The penchant for invention brings me, I believe, to one of the significant problems of our time concerning human rights. For all my life, I have believed that human rights are about protecting the individual by the law and from overreaching laws. The Universal Declaration of Human Rights says as much. However, multiculturalism and its progeny, identity politics, have moved the focus away from the protection of the individual to the preservation of the rights of the group. Because identity is now a matter of political determination, new groups presuming oppression constantly press for legal recognition. That is particularly evident in the number of letters added to, and sometimes taken away from, the LGBT+ label. The obvious question is: How can we agree on the nature of freedom if we have to make it up as we go along? How can we confidently contemplate any notion of "justice as fairness" without an explicit insight into what freedom is and a clear understanding of what human rights are based on?

Allow me to offer an illustration of the problem. The *Declaration of the Rights of Man and of the Citizen* inspired the French Revolution. Its seventeen articles, adopted between August 20 and August 26, 1789 by France's National Assembly, served as the preamble to the Constitution of 1791. The declaration says, *"Men are born equal and remain equal in rights."*

And here, I would claim, is the beginning of our problem. On what ground does the French National Assembly decide that all men are born equal and remain equal in rights when simple observation would deny it? Although they rejected the authority of Scripture, their concept of dignity still came from the story of Genesis. They confused aspiration with reality. It is this ambiguity around the foundation of human rights that continues to plague our understanding of human rights to this day. The American Declaration of Independence (1776) says,

> *"All men are created equal, and they are endowed by their creator with certain inalienable rights . . . these include Life, Liberty, and the pursuit of Happiness."*

These two declarations might look similar, but they are radically different. "Born equal" is not the same as "created equal" because the American Declaration, although political rather than overtly religious, refers obliquely to the Genesis story. However, the claim to *"life, liberty and the pursuit of happiness"* echoes more of Rousseau than the Genesis story, although *"All men are created equal, and they are endowed by their creator with certain inalienable rights"* suggests a recognition of a power beyond the state.

The French Declaration does not suggest an authority higher than the State. However, the *Concordat of 1801* between Napoleon and Pope Pius VII restored, in part, the status of the Church. Nevertheless, any explicit connection the Church might have had with human rights is overruled by the concept of *Laïcité,* the victory of reason over revelation. This victory shaped the French understanding of the individual and seeped into the English-speaking nations. The American Declaration of Independence (1776) still credited God for its sense of freedom. However, the American Declaration of the Rights and Duties of Man, known as *The Bogota Declaration (1948),* assumes that *nature,* apparently discoverable by reason, becomes a more significant player in creating human dignity than God:

> *"All men are born free and equal, in dignity and in rights,*
> *and being endowed by nature with reason, and conscience,*
> *they should conduct themselves as brothers one to another."*

The roots of the Declaration are still there in the language of brotherhood, but that brotherhood has been given to them by nature. The preamble in chapter two says:

> *"The fulfilment of duty by each individual is a prerequisite*
> *to the rights of all. Rights and duties are interrelated in*
> *every social and political activity of men. While rights*
> *exalt individual liberty, duties express the dignity of*
> *that liberty."*

The connection between rights and duties is not clear. It seems to be saying that rights gain their validity by fulfilling duty. However, how does one know what that duty might be? The Genesis story would suggest that duty is the consequence of a loving and thankful response to the God of creation. If we accept the Genesis story as true, even as a metaphor, we must say liberty is a consequence of the dignity God gave us, bringing with it its own set of responsibilities. We do our duty because we understand we owe it to God who gave us our dignity. Duties neither express nor describe our dignity. (The Bogata Declaration would take us back to George Eliot's view that duty is *"pre-emptive and absolute".*) Duty is a natural consequence of love, expressed in the pleasure of responsibility.

When the Genesis explanation of human dignity is removed, so is any foundation for universal human rights. Neither rights nor duties have a foundation other than the power of reason, which has no more authority than communal or personal opinion. Under the contemporary umbrella of cultural relativism, any theory of human rights must be influenced by the perceived demands of identity politics. The helpful distinction between negative (natural) and positive (political) rights tends to be lost because the concept of natural rights depends on the dignity given to men and women by God. When that is forgotten, the way is opened up for the state to ignore the differences between negative and positive rights. Negative rights require that no one, including the state, interfere with your ability to get on with the business of living, and you have these rights because of your God-given dignity. Freedom of religious belief and expression, speech, assembly, and property rights are prominent examples. Positive rights, sometimes called entitlements, require someone else to provide the means for their execution. As the foundation on which one can establish individual dignity crumbles, dignity becomes indistinguishable from identity sustained by group membership. When a group is identified because of its oppression, the perception of entitlement becomes increasingly vocal.[3]

◆ ◆ ◆

To maintain a workable vision of rights, a nation must also have a robust civil society. Without the moral vision nurtured by tradition and civil society's primary institution, the family, the French Revolution's version of human rights tends to take over. Instead of human identity grounded in the transcendent and expressed through generational continuity, it is determined by group membership, which tends to undermine traditional notions of nationhood. The dignity, sacred origin, and nature of individual identity are ignored. The kind of freedom implicit in negative rights is overwhelmed by untrammelled positive rights. And when that happens, rights are frequently found to be in conflict. So, without apology, I repeat: *By rejecting the biblical foundation of human dignity, the sovereignty of the subjective presumes the reasonable existence of that dignity and consequently can shape human dignity according to its imagination.* No wonder the Human Rights Commission thinks it's a source of revealed truth. It presumes human beings have dignity, but it doesn't know why. It might appeal to a form of natural law that might be described rationally without understanding its source. But even that doesn't help us. Having rejected the God of creation, justice—everyone getting what he or she deserves—is fused into a mutable concept of social justice, giving rise to an ever-increasing number of unsustainable human rights. Human rights will always prove promiscuous; there will be too many of them because they will have nothing to be faithful to. The idea of a rationally derived and universal human rights declaration by a government agency to ensure justice for all is *"vanity on stilts,"* to manipulate the famous Benthamite phrase.

◆ ◆ ◆

So then, the most valuable question to ask about human rights is: are they universal and intrinsically religious? I can't think of anything better at this point than to quote two opposing views. The first by R.H. Tawney:

"The essence of all morality is this: to believe that every human being is of infinite importance and, therefore, that no consideration of expediency can justify the oppression of one by another. But to believe this, it is necessary to believe in God." [4]

The second by Ronald Dworkin:

"We almost all accept . . . that human life in all its forms is sacred . . . for some of us, this is a matter of religious faith; for others, of secular but deep philosophical belief." [5]

I'm going with Tawney for several reasons, not least because of Dworkin's use of 'sacred.' His definition of sacred is weak because it is based entirely on an undeclared conviction that the subjective is intrinsically reasonable and sufficiently authoritative. He may say his idea is based on *"deep philosophical belief."* Still, no matter how deeply or rationally that is considered, it remains a secularised and, consequently, a reconstructed perception of the Sublime. The sacred and secular are mutually exclusive because the secular denies the authority of the Sublime. Perhaps Dworkin would like to consider why his secular belief in human rights is entirely Western or why all forms of human life are sacred. His claim of sacred resembles that of the claim made by the writers of *The Green Book* when they declare that the viewers of the waterfall do not see anything sublime; instead, they have sublime feelings. The Transcendent cannot tell them anything about the nature of truth. With its self-inflicted limitations on truth, the secular mind can find nothing in itself to suggest the sacred. It has cut itself off from the doctrine of objective value, the kind of thing the universe is, and who we are.

◆ ◆ ◆

Now that my mind is 'desecularised,' I am persuaded that the belief declaring every human being sacred is inescapable if we are to take meaning and purpose seriously. Suppose we are not created by God and given dignity by Him. In that case, any claim to dignity has to be residual, the fading consequence of a Judaeo/Christian civilisation, or simply a matter of opinion. As Hannah Arendt says,

> *"The conception of human rights, based upon the assumed existence of a human being as such, broke down at the very moment when those who professed to believe in it were for the first time confronted with people who had indeed lost all other qualities and specific relationships—except that they were still human. The world found nothing sacred in the abstract nakedness of being human."* [6]

And that is the point. Nothing in the abstract nakedness of being human would give rise to any notion of sacred dignity. The *"abstract nakedness of being human"* is an inadequate foundation for a theory of universal human rights. I repeat, any talk of *inherent dignity* cannot make sense in the presumed neutral context of secularism. The presumption of secular authority is similar to what I have already said about scientific method. Rational thought cannot be the foundation of rational thought. Claiming its overarching, disinterested neutrality is no more than a tautology.

◆ ◆ ◆

For a practical outworking of human rights criticism, I'll go to Mary Ann Glendon's survey of the Universal Declaration of Human Rights (UDHR) 1948 in her 2001 seminal text, *A World Made New*, and some of her lectures. I do so because the editing of the drafts of the UDHR is a gauge for what would go on in the succeeding decades: the gradual and deliberate de-Christianisation of Western civilisation. And just in case you have missed it, this book is about the de-Christianisation of Western civilisation and the total failure to find a replacement.

After an extensive survey of the history of establishing the UDHR, Glendon addresses the problem of universality in a multicultural, multinational world. While she does not explicitly say that universal rights only make sense in Western civilisation shaped by biblical thought, she is well aware of the problem. She points out that the stakes are high. Particularly in the post-war context, any suggestion to give up on the viability of human reason and choice was unthinkable. To do so is to accept that human affairs are shaped only by force or accident. And just in case I have not been clear enough, the UDHR is entirely Western with its source in the Genesis story, whether it says so or not. Suppose non-Western nations see some value in universal human rights. In that case, they do so because they accept they might have limited practical value, not because they have suddenly come to believe in the Genesis creation story and its explanation of human dignity.

So, Mary Ann Glendon tells us, an official but undeclared pretence had to be established to get the UDHR over the line. John Humphrey, the distinguished Canadian international lawyer who worked closely with the commission preparing the Declaration, suggested, *"What we need is something like Christian morality without the tommyrot."* Another significant figure, the French social philosopher Jacques Maritain, suggested, *"Yes, we agree about the rights, but on condition, no one asks us why."* In an outburst of multicultural enthusiasm in 1947, the American Anthropological Association (AAA) sent a letter to the Human Rights Commission warning *"that a statement of rights conceived only in terms of the values prevalent in the countries of Western Europe and America, would not do."* The AAA pointed out that any statement of human rights must consider the social group of which any individual is a member and *"whose sanctioned modes of life shape his behavior and with whose fate his own is thus inextricably bound."* The idea of universality was based on a necessary but unadmitted pragmatism.

Considering the moral anxiety of the postwar world, the AAA's reservations seem more than reasonable. Nevertheless, the UN philosophers, who had not yet developed the language of rights as we might understand them today, did accept that European, Confucian, Hindu, and Muslim thought shared some common values. The problem, later to surface, was that there was no agreement on what these values might rest upon other than a shared conviction about the evils committed during the Second World War. With time, even these convictions would slowly fade away.

◆ ◆ ◆

The *Universal Declaration of Human Rights* begins well enough, affirming negative rights and the sovereignty of the individual, which resembles English common law. However, by the time we reach Article 26, we find:

"Everyone has the right to education, which should be free at least in the elementary stages and compulsory. It emphasizes that education should promote the full development of the human personality and respect for human rights and fundamental freedoms."

From the perspective of the 21st century, this might seem more than reasonable. However, Article 29 widens the range, revealing the road we must travel down:

"Everyone has duties to the community in which alone the free and full development of his personality is possible. In the exercise of his rights and freedoms, everyone shall be subject only to such limitations as are determined by law solely for the purpose of securing due recognition and respect for the rights and freedoms of others and of meeting the just requirements of morality, public order and the general welfare in a democratic society."

These rights are no longer about letting the individual get on with his or her life. They are wide-ranging, imprecise claims, cast as human rights, demanding the use of the public purse. Eventually, this shift in our understanding of human rights brings about non-discrimination law, which devalues the sovereignty of the individual. In New Zealand, this development continues to give the Waitangi Tribunal its emotive and hegemonic power. Having accepted non-discrimination law as authoritative, government agencies and groups, sustained by identity politics, will inevitably conflict with the state, demanding that it yield to their will.

Glendon points out that the drafters of the UDHR aimed to provide *"A framework within which divergent philosophies, religious, and even economic, social and political theories might be entertained and developed."* [7] With ambition akin to that of Alice's Mad Hatter, the framework had to be sufficiently definite to be an inspiration and guide in practice, but sufficiently general and flexible to apply to all cultures. It had to be capable of modification and suit people at different social and political development stages. This was nothing like John Keats' philosophy of *negative capability,* which allowed the artist to hang onto a mystery when reason might suggest otherwise. One had to pretend that the mystery wasn't there. [8]

The framers of the Declaration insisted on making the impossible reasonable. The embrace of human dignity while denying its source had to be glossed. That such a denial would strengthen the authority of cultural relativism was yet to be realised. Like any good politician, those who signed the Charter claimed *"faith in freedom and democracy,"* which meant faith in the assumed dignity of men and women. However, as Glendon points out, *"faith based upon a faith was not much to go on."* Faith in freedom and democracy hardly makes sense unless a universal truth sustains them. But what universal truth? I don't think it's unreasonable to suggest that an implicit but unspoken ambiguity underwrites the UDHR.

> *"When the third committee took up the preamble as its final term, a last vain effort was made (by the Netherlands) to insert the mention of a deity. Charles Malik, who earlier*

in the drafting process had proposed a reference to the creator, seems to have come around to Chang's and Mrs Roosevelt's view. Arguments about the use of words like "God" and "created", he later wrote, "are often concluded silently by sheer sensing that the prevailing climate of opinion will never admit such terms." [9]

So, we should hardly be surprised when the Human Rights Commission, back here in New Zealand, continues to discuss obscure human rights issues, because it has not moved on from the ambiguous underwriting of the UDHR. Indeed, it has gone further by presuming that it is the authority on human rights. It has to continue the pretence of a foundation when it has none.

Perhaps such ambiguity over the two years of drafting the UDHR contributed to the confusion on what Glendon calls *"the traditional political and civil rights—the ones now most labelled Western."* There is considerable disagreement among philosophers and legal experts about the boundary between civil and political rights. I have already tried to explain them. With a little more content and context, I'll try to be specific. Civil rights are those rights, frequently called negative, sometimes natural rights, that stand to shield the individual against overreaching state action. Negative rights let people be left alone by the state to get on with their lives. At the very least, they include freedom of religious belief and expression, freedom of speech, freedom of assembly, and freedom of movement. Positive rights, sometimes called political rights, always require someone to deliver them, usually the state. Depending on the theories underpinning them or a nation's political posturing, they can include extensive claims such as the right to social and economic rights, cultural rights, and, most recently, the right to a range of sexual behaviours and identities.

Not too infrequently, political rights enter into conflict with negative rights and with each other. Perhaps the most controversial of these rights now is the struggle between those who believe that one's sex is biologically determined and those who think it is assigned at birth or any other time. That contradiction compromises the *Conversion Practices Prohibition Legislation* (CPPL) *Act 2022*. It presumes homosexuality is biologically determined, while the transgender lobby tells us that sexual identity is not biologically determined. Despite that apparent contradiction, the CPPL would inhibit counselling for those who are doubtful about their sexual identity. It would have the state lecture parents on what they should think about identity and, consequently, about human nature. I'll examine this issue in more detail under the topic of civil religion. However, one point is worth making. Such a contentious debate illustrates how far we have moved away from the UDHR belief, ambiguous as it might have been, in a shared conviction concerning human nature sustained by a universal foundation for human rights.

Confusion is increased when diversity is no longer an observation about human differences but a dogma that delineates the nature of those differences, determining the legitimacy of a particular right. This theory attempts to create a new value system by declaring human identity a political construct. I must say it took me a while to realise I was being seduced into accepting a new vision of the human creature. When we reject our God-given identity, all values are up for grabs. Diversity rules, and the primary moral driver must be the imagined virtue of 'inclusion.' DIE, a political construct torn from its traditional moral foundation, is swollen into the madness of self-righteousness beyond examination. The devotees think they have discovered a new ethic no one has ever known.

Western civilisation, shaped by the Genesis declaration of dignity, is no longer happy to believe in the authenticity of that dignity but continues to presume it nevertheless. Any alternative conviction about responsibility for others tends to lose any coherence it might have because human rights and duty informed by the Christian faith take for granted the needs (rights) of the other. Such an understanding accepts the need for personal restraint, a necessary component of social order, and for human rights to succeed. Remembering Scruton, rights are intimately tied to duties. However, when the idea of universal human rights is divorced from duty to the Transcendent and to each other, there is no defence against the power of human desire. Any residual notion of duty alone proves to be ineffectual in shaping moral behaviour. It can be replaced by servility too easily, and private and public morality are reordered and enforced by the state's civil religion of the Woke elite (No apology for using those words) and its priesthood of educators.

◆ ◆ ◆

A news item in the *Daily Telegraph (UK), 25/6/2024,* might help illustrate the fundamental problem. Kimi Badenoch (then Equalities Minister) was critical of the Scottish actor David Tennant, who said he wished that *"She did not exist anymore"* because of what he thought to be her views on women's rights. The then Equalities Minister responded by identifying Tennant as a *"rich, lefty white male celebrity."* He had just been given an accolade by the British LGBT+ Awards, where he said:

> *"Everyone has the right to be what they want to be and live their life how they want to live it, as long as they're not hurting anyone else . . . It's common sense, isn't it? It is human decency. We shouldn't live in a world where that is worth remarking on."*

A question arises. On what is Tennant basing his concept of human rights? Is he unaided, always able to evaluate the nature of harm? Is 'common sense' whatever he might think it to be, really enough? Does he have unique insight into the consequences of all human actions? He may well be making a plea for human rights. Still, he has destroyed their foundation, declaring that his perception of harm must be permitted to determine right from wrong. If we were to take Tennant seriously, he would undoubtedly undermine and exclude freedom of religious belief and expression, not to mention free speech. He would have the Equalities Minister silenced because he finds what she says offensive. A peripheral issue, but a significant one, Tennant ignores the importance of the struggle between the old-school feminists and the trans lobby. Why all the hostility in calling Germaine Greer and JK Rowling TERFS? We really are involved in the struggle over what it means to be human.

◆ ◆ ◆

When I was a young man, we assumed it was the business of those in positions of responsibility to restrain human passion and preserve our traditions. I didn't understand that as a child, but it was one of the reasons I trusted a policeman. Indeed, he was there to prevent crime and preserve peace, but to do that, he also had to safeguard our traditions. Now, I observe that the role of an elite, celebrity, or bureaucrat is to break down those traditions and encourage the release of human passion and the proliferation of human rights. The new tolerance is elastic, giving passion a destructive authority that would drive identity politics. That such a state of affairs exists, I'm pretty sure, is not the mere product of my octogenarian imagination. It's beyond the scope of this book, but it is worthwhile noting that it was during the Enlightenment that we learned to undervalue the restraint of passion.

◆ ◆ ◆

Allow me to defend my claim by returning to Marcuse and his pretentiously titled and co-written essay, *A Critique of Pure Tolerance*. Robert Paul Wolff and Barrington Moore Jr. were his co-writers. The allusion to Immanuel Kant's *Critique of Pure Reason* is obvious and deliberate. Michael Walsh quotes this extract from Marcuse in *The Devil's Pleasure Palace*. It's long, but it's just so revealing that I can't resist using it.

> *"The realisation of the objective of tolerance would call for intolerance toward prevailing policies, attitudes, opinions, and the extension of tolerance to politics, attitudes, and opinions which are outlawed or suppressed . . . Surely no government can be expected to foster its subversion, but in a democracy, such a right is vested in the people. (i.e. in the majority of the people). This means that the ways should*

not be blocked on which such a subversive majority could develop, and if they are blocked by organised repression and indoctrination, their reopening may require apparently undemocratic means. They would include the withdrawal of toleration of speech and assembly from groups and movements that promote aggressive policies, armament, chauvinism, discrimination on the grounds of race and religion, or that opposed the extension of public services, social security, medical care, etc . . . liberating tolerance, then, would mean intolerance against movements from the Right and toleration of movements from them." [10]

Walsh suggests we have *"tolerance for me, but not for thee."* That is precisely the issue. Marcuse's theory of 'repressive tolerance' underpins the contemporary diversity ideology, which is a temporary state of affairs. It creates the social conditions necessary for the replacement of traditional morality by liberal values. The transience and changeability of identity politics reign supreme.

We cannot overestimate the importance of the shift from moral behaviour based on traditionally informed personal conviction to moral behaviour determined by political allegiance. A morality shared by the community that depends on each citizen being convinced about the permanent nature of Truth is no longer meaningful. The new tolerance's version of truth must now be imposed to preserve public order. Antonio Gramsci shouts his secularised version of *"Hallelujah"* from the grave. Hence, there is a shift in schools from education to propaganda. Schools are places where children no longer learn how they got to where they are and how to cope in the world. Instead, they have usurped the parents' role by telling children who they should be and must become.

◆ ◆ ◆

In his 1993 essay, Daniel Patrick Moynihan, scholar, diplomat, and member of the Democratic Party, gave us the phrase *"defining deviancy down."* He claimed that society, notably American Society, was becoming morally confused and would eventually be ungovernable, although he wasn't given mainstream approval. His 1965 report *The Negro Family: The Case for National Action,* had blotted his copybook. Nevertheless, *"defining deviancy down"* proved to be prophetic. Moynihan claimed it happens when deviant behaviour increases beyond the level the community can afford to accept. Subconsciously, deviant behaviour becomes "normal." The new "normal" behaviours become the only acceptable behaviours because they determine public ethics. Class is not abolished; it is reordered to consider race and sexual identity. Those who support cultural relativism join the new elite, while dissenters are written off as morally and intellectually impoverished; 'deplorables' perhaps.

Same-sex marriage is an excellent example of 'defining deviancy down,' bringing with it profound political and sociological change. For centuries, we believed that marriage was the natural consequence of having been created male and female. Monogamy, that great rediscovery of the early Christians, stripped the Roman paterfamilias of his power and offered protection for both women and children. Marriage was neither an invention of the church nor the state. However, with the legalisation of same-sex marriage, the state became not the protector of marriage but its inventor and controller. Not only does the state now decide what marriage is, but also what a 'legitimate' family should be. Advocacy for one particular kind of family, the natural family, for example, is now discriminatory, as the charity *Family First* discovered when it lost its charitable status in 2022 for doing just that.

The legalisation of same-sex marriage in 2013 in New Zealand has created a tidal wave of consequential legislative change, especially insofar as it results in the continuous erosion of citizen freedom. It's not just that marriage is a human right, but that anything the state includes as its version of marriage is a human right. The dogma of inclusion that approves same-sex marriage is an exercise in exclusion. Those who disapprove cannot express their views without accusations of discrimination.

Perhaps it wasn't understood when the law changed; maybe it still isn't understood, that there is an explicit doctrine of what it means to be human within the ideology of same-sex marriage. Until recently, a human being's God-given identity has been reinforced within the generational continuity of the family. The state accepted that and wrote laws around it. However, now, after the grand march through civil society's institutions, the state can decide that being human has nothing to do with generational continuity or family identity. Although a homosexual union cannot, without artificial means, contribute children to the next generation, it is now declared to be the legal and cultural equivalent of the intergenerational family. That its continuing existence depends on the normality of the intergenerational family seems to have escaped the notice of the legislators. Indeed, one can no longer talk of the 'normal' family. A legitimate family structure is a reward the state can dispense at will.

We should not be surprised that in New Zealand and elsewhere in the West, we have witnessed a decline in marriage. For many young people, cohabitation has become a substitute for marriage. The negative data is overwhelming; cohabitation is detrimental to children. In the United States, the figures vary somewhat from state to state; 17% to 55% of children are born to single or cohabiting mothers, and only about half of these children are living with both of their biological parents by their mid-teens. On the other hand, over three-quarters of teenagers remain with their married parents. In the United Kingdom, approximately 40% of births are extramarital. In New Zealand, extramarital births rose from 10% in 1965 to nearly 50% by 2021, although a slow decline in the number of young single mothers has been observed over recent years. Alas, legislators continue to ignore the fact that children born to married parents, who continue to live with their mother and father, have better mental health, do better at school, and cost the taxpayer a great deal less money.

◆ ◆ ◆

For the new elite, the truth is what they say it is, and that truth determines their definition of freedom. The biblical description of truth is personal and eternal; like its Creator, it is unchanging. However, if the truth is fluid, its priesthood must always be in the business of finding ways to defend it, and one of the ways they do that is to inhibit freedom of speech. It is not a coincidence that as the number of human rights increases, the demands for hate speech legislation also increase, because political constructs are always open to revision. The elite always want to control what people can and cannot say, and everyone must use language that reinforces his or her ideology. One becomes a victim of what we might call an elitist lexicon, which starts to look ominously like Orwell's *newspeak*.

Consider the term 'social justice,' which on the surface seems harmless, but in reality signifies a significant shift in our perception of justice, indeed a redefinition. It moves us from a system where everyone receives their dues to one where equal outcomes for everyone are established for 'disadvantaged' groups. Justice and human rights cease to be about individual justice and become more about asserting group equality. The net result is a transfer of the power to interpret and evaluate justice from the general population to the state, which, in its wisdom, can determine how to redress group disparities.

Social justice assumes the authority of its contrived version of religious dogma while shielding itself from close examination. It is a deconstructed parasite feeding off divine justice. It turns God's revelation of his justice, explained in Romans 8, into an evolving, unanchored construct. It introduces a new, obfuscating language that runs parallel to the old, altering the essence of words and phrases we use to comprehend the world. It owes its parasitic existence to the biblical description of the good, true and beautiful. All the while, our understanding of what is sublime, grotesque, and pathetic stews itself in its own waste.

Social justice would seduce us into thinking that traditional morality and legal structures are oppressive and that power needs to be redistributed from that oppression to pursue equality of outcome. The whole deal has no objective foundation. Even determining the difference between the oppressor and the oppressed is a matter of opinion. Its underpinning relativism has no idea of how to distinguish good from evil. No society has ever flourished or will ever flourish based on a relative standard of truth and morality. I would also dare to add that no free society has ever been based on a secular foundation. One would hope that it's apparent to any wise observer that if we continue to submit to the overarching narrative of cultural relativism, the end will be either anarchy or totalitarianism, entrenched lawlessness, or capricious and arbitrary government. Such an outcome is inevitable in any society that rejects the concept of objective value described by C.S. Lewis in his criticism of *The Green Book*.[11]

◆ ◆ ◆

I have already claimed that diversity ideology deconstructs the biblical command to "love thy neighbour." On the surface, it appears to be about mutual respect, but it is really about the imposition of identity politics. It has to be; the cult can't survive otherwise. One must accept the notion of diversity as an absolute truth or be considered 'a hater of mankind.' Hater of mankind is not an exaggeration. The early Christians were sometimes called "haters of mankind" because they would not enter festivals associated with worshipping the ancient gods or the emperor.

The contemporary Christian finds himself or herself in a similar position. Although Roman culture, in many respects, could be tolerant, that tolerance tended to fade when an equally exclusive religion called it into question. The solution was to persecute followers of the new exclusive religion, although they did it somewhat unevenly, even erratically, depending on who the emperor was. I don't think it's drawing too long a bow to claim that critics of identity politics are the contemporary unbelieving haters of mankind who must be cancelled because they seriously doubt the doctrine of social justice. Inclusion, which is no more than a mutation of the virtue of tolerance into a value that constantly affirms, would turn identity politics into an absolute.

Because equity, that impenetrable term, exchanges equality under the law for equal outcomes, the individual citizen is forced to live out the fantasy of the gospel of diversity while equity is imposed. Such mindless, protective nonsense makes a country difficult to govern and, ironically, even more challenging for it to discover its folly. The role that human rights have traditionally been expected to play is exchanged for a version of rights affirming the passion that revitalises tribal identity. From within that bubble, language can impose the contemporary version of government-sponsored puritanism, and censorship is needed. It is impossible to accept anything that is not an endorsement. Allowing 'toxic' ideas to increase enables error to prevail. It is a moral duty to silence them.

◆ ◆ ◆

Alongside the imposed self-censorship that seems to have become part of our way of life, we must contend with a phenomenon known as *concept creep*. Words lose meaning through continued manipulation and misapplication, but not necessarily their potency to silence. The language of the Silencers is a primary example. Words like *sexist, fascist, Nazi, far-right* or *alt-right, extremist,* various words with *phobia* attached, and *white supremacy* are concept creepers protected from critical examination. In the contemporary scene, *racism* is the ubiquitous concept creeper, having the appearance of a morality that would take us where we want to go. One proves his or her case simply by using the word.

And there is another significant issue. The mainstream media (MSM) frequently fails to use the above terms accurately, which reinforces the impression that we have more fascists, racists, white supremacists, and so on than we do. Their hyperbole and overuse distort the truth. They reinforce the disingenuous trend by which human rights claims become accepted as rights. A new concept of discrimination based entirely on cultural relativism is locked into the legal system. And just what determines discrimination is decided by agencies like the Human Rights Commission, which asserts the 'rightness' of all the members of a self-identifying group. Any hope we might ever have had in coming to grips with the idea of universal human rights is lost because it is left up to the state to decide when claims can become human rights. Lex Rex has become Rex Lex. Divine law is no longer king; the king is law, or the state is absolute.

Finally, to use Mary Ann Glendon's phrase, *"A World Made New"* is what we got, but not in the way intended. The concept of universal human rights underpinning the United Nations' mission has helped maintain a certain level of world peace to the present day. The Universal Declaration of Human Rights was effective because people accepted it, especially those in the West, even if they didn't acknowledge its origins. Now, without any commitment to a belief in objective truth, subjectivism, as expressed in the cult of cultural relativism, has rendered it impossible to pretend that universal human rights have any authority. Rights have become disconnected from their duties, making it difficult to distinguish between rights and claims. The state, supported by institutions like the Human Rights Commission, is God. Human rights theory is no longer bound by either common or natural law. Human rights theory now determines what the law will be.

Notes:

1. I don't think I am biting off more than I can chew here. I understand the theory of equal consideration of interests for all animals. Singer's 1972 essay, *Famine, Affluence, and Morality* in *Philosophy and Public Affairs*, seems to be an example of a philosopher living off the biblical idea of the responsibility of the rich for the poor, which takes its authority from the Genesis story of human dignity. Because the Genesis claim is ignored or rejected, an alternative framework has to be found, hence the complex problem around the equivalence of interests. Mysteriously, the interests morph into rights. The question of why human beings should have rights anyway is not considered.

2. Taken from www.history.com/topics/world-war-ii/Nuremberg trials.

3. For an authoritative examination of positive and negative rights, see Isaiah Berlin's famous 1958 lecture 2, *Two Concepts of Liberty*.

4. Michael J Perry quotes Tawney in *The Idea of Human Rights: Four Enquiries*. OUP, 1998, p. 11

5. Perry p. 11

6. Perry p. 12

7. Glendon, Mary Ann. *A World Made New*. Random House N.Y. 2001. p. 78.

8. "Negative capability" permits writers to explore sublime mystery when it defies rational examination. First used by the Romantic poet John Keats in 1817 to comprehend 'truths' beyond the reach of what Keats called 'consecutive reasoning.'

9. Glendon. p. 112

10. Michael Walsh. *The Devil's Pleasure Palace*. Encounter Books. 2015. Page 45. (Quoted from *A Critique of Pure Tolerance*. Herbert Marcus)

11. See Kreeft, Peter. *C. S. Lewis for the Third Millennium. Six Essays on the Abolition of Man*. Ignatius Press, 1994. Page 44. Kreeft points out that the word 'value' might be misleading in this context. He thinks Lewis would have been much better by using 'law' that values sounds, too Nietzschean, too much like something posited by human will rather than objectively existing.

VII

Sex Is a Big Deal

Let my beloved come to his garden,
and eat its choicest fruits.

Song of Solomon 4:16

When I was a young man in the early 1960s, sex was a big deal indeed; well, the naughty bits. We were, if I remember rightly, pretty primitive about it all. I played rugby for several years, and after a match, a warm shower, and a few drinks, a young man was raring to go. And just in case I am misunderstood here, rugby is not the villain. We were young, randy, and fit. Alas, randy has now been replaced, like so many words we used to use, by the American 'horny,' although I don't think it means quite the same thing. Whatever the case, we knew our chances of being lucky were low. Lust was usually an unsatisfied vice; nearly always, the girl said "no" to overbearing sexual advances. She was probably still living with her mother and father or certainly in close contact with them; such knowledge tended to cool a young man's lust. Anyway, it was very likely that the young man had his parents somewhere in the background. A more significant percentage of young people today attend a tertiary institution away from their hometown.

Going back to the 1950s, sex did not thrust itself on us with such boldness. I was younger. Nevertheless, that did not stop me and two friends from taking advantage of the opportunities that came our way. One of the cinemas in the town where I lived hosted a French Film Festival, likely the first of its kind. Because the films were shown under the label 'Festival,' the usual censorship rules didn't apply. That's what we believed; whether it was true or not, I don't know. Maybe it was cultural cringe. We knew the cinema manager was lax in enforcing the rules. Trying to look as old as possible, and out of uniform, we wagged school and watched *The Wages of Fear*. The title alone was enough to get a fifteen-year-old boy excited. Such was the naivety and innocence of the 1950s. The movie was gloriously exciting. In a village somewhere in South America, four unemployed men were hired to transport a shipment of nitroglycerine without the necessary safety equipment. The road was hazardous, and the truck's suspension was unreliable. And, for a brief moment, near the beginning of the movie, one of the men's girlfriends gave us a glimpse of her breasts. In the 1950s, that was a big deal indeed for fifteen-year-old boys.

Unfortunately, somebody recognised us at the cinema and reported us to the headmaster. We were caned. We did the crime; as they say, we did the time. Now, I tell the story because, like our response to the movie, it reveals more about the mood and ethics of the time. We were punished, accepted the punishment, society supported the process, and the 'crime' was forgotten. The school did not inform our parents of our waywardness. Instinctively, we understood the dynamic of forgiveness, what the game was, and the position we were expected to play in that game.

It was ten years later when I saw *The Seven Deadly Sins*. It reminded me of when I had wagged school to watch *The Wages of Fear*. Both films introduced me to what I think the French excel at: creating an atmosphere of poignant sleaze. Maybe that's why I now find French cabaret music so hauntingly sad. Anyway, in *The Seven Deadly Sins*, presumably to illustrate the deadly sin of lust, a commercial traveller's car broke down on a cold, wet night, and he sought shelter in an isolated farmhouse owned by an inhospitable farmer with a much more hospitable and beautiful wife. Of course, the commercial traveller was young and handsome, and the wife young, attractive, and ill-matched. The dynamic between the traveller and the farmer's wife was evident. She prepared a meal for her husband and the commercial traveller, finishing with the most delicious cheese. After putting the cheese back in the locked cupboard, the farmer didn't take long to go to bed, snoring in the background; it had been a hard day. The farmer's wife, somewhat provocatively, got undressed, brushed her hair, and put on her nightgown behind a flimsy curtain. For some time, the naive or provocative wife, I wasn't quite sure which, and the commercial traveller chatted with the heated expectancy of hopeful lust.

"You know you can if you like," she said.

"Please," he said. *"May I?"*

"Yes."

"I'd love to."

After some more ambiguous exchanges of a similar nature, she went to the cupboard and, with a knowing smile, gave him some more cheese, to his apparent delight. So, as it turned out, there are eight deadly sins. The eighth is imagining sin when it isn't there. It proved to be a helpful lesson.

I didn't notice it much then, but now, looking back, I can see a definite change in our sexual sensitivities and behaviour by the late 1960s. It was, of course, brought about to some extent by the advent and use of the pill. *"Are you on the pill?"* became a common question by the mid-sixties. At the time, I had no idea just how revolutionary the widespread use of the pill would prove to be. It was there and accepted by a proportion of the population. It took several years for health issues to become an apparent problem, although I suspect for many women, not quite so long. Neither did I know anything of the coterie of academic influencers who had been working in the wings for a very long time to change our understanding of sex. Perhaps I had heard of Freud but not of Michel Foucault. I had heard of *The Kinsey Reports,* two allegedly scholarly books on human sexual behaviour, *Sexual Behavior in the Human Male (1948)* and *Sexual Behavior in the Human Female (1953)* by Alfred Kinsey, Ward Pomeroy, and Clyde Martin. They were kept under the counter in our local library. I have since discovered they were far from scholarly and later discovered to be fraudulent.

One grows older and hopefully wiser. Now, I believe that the sexual revolution brought about more deep-seated societal change than anything else in my lifetime—a recent rereading of Carle C. Zimmerman's seminal text, *Family and Civilization,* has confirmed my suspicion. I started to take it all more seriously when I discovered that there had already been a sexual revolution—nearly two millennia before the one I was living through. It wasn't a complete surprise to me, but the details uncovered by reading the works of several historians and others proved to be revealing.[1] Knowledge of the first sexual revolution helped me understand the second better.

By 100 AD, Christians were beginning to get noticed. However, by 400 AD, Christianity had become the majority religion in the Roman Empire. I suspect that no Roman citizen had any idea of the revolution that Christian sexual morality would eventually bring. Indeed, it was to bring about a groundbreaking change in the Roman sexual psyche, its philosophy of patriarchy, and a revolutionary theological awareness of the body, marriage, and children. Kyle Harper claims, *"Few periods of pre-modern history have witnessed such brisk and consequential ideological change. Sex was at the center of it all."* [2]

The power structures changed dramatically. The patriarch (*paterfamilias*) determined sexual morality in the Roman world. The restraining influence of the old Republican virtues weakened as the pride of empire became dominant. The male erotic impulse was in control; the patriarch had control over his wife, children, and slaves. Male sexual desire could be legitimately satisfied by slaves, prostitutes, and boys. The morality of shame controlling same-sex relationships was ambiguous. It was shameful for older men to pursue boys and to act in a passive role in same-sex relationships. It was not shameful for the boys to give themselves to older men. Pederasty was met with reserved approval, although there was no concept of legal same-sex marriage. The sometimes explicit and salacious satires of the Roman writer Juvenal (55–127 AD?) hardly suggest approval of sexual promiscuity or homosexuality. In passing, we have him to thank for some quotable and timely scepticism of his poetry, including *"Bread and circuses"* and *"Who will guard the guards?"*

Any suggestion of equality, as we understand the term today, between men and women, slaves and freemen, did not exist. Certainly, Stoic philosophy encouraged a particular kind of restraint without interfering with the patriarch's status. But it's not as easy to describe the status and role of women as precisely as we might like. Most Roman writers were men, and women's lives were, to a considerable extent, overlooked. We know that women had very little, if any, political power. Opportunities for negotiation came through their husbands. Nevertheless, there are some examples of influential women. Fulvia, the wife of Julius Caesar, enjoyed the title of Co-ruler of Rome for a short time. Valeria Messalina, the third wife of Emperor Claudius, was known for manipulating many of her lovers but was eventually executed for plotting to overthrow the emperor. And then there was Livia Drusilla, the wife of Augustus and mother of Tiberius. According to at least one ancient historian, she poisoned her husband by handing him figs smeared with poison, although she remained influential until she died in 29 AD. Revealingly, perhaps the most influential woman of all was Helena, the Christian mother of Constantine, who became emperor in 306 AD. In tune with the time in which she lived and bearing the title of Augusta Imperatrix, she was instrumental in helping establish the early church and many of its buildings.

We know that the *paterfamilias* had power over others, including their sex life. For women, undoubtedly wealthy women, it was *pudicitia*, a kind of modesty conditioned by shame. A reputation of modesty and chastity was expected. While this mainly applied to free women, it also applied to slaves insofar as a slave's honour depended on the discretion of her master. Harper tells us that the sexual life of a freewoman was controlled by rules around marriage, which could come in the early teens. (The minimum legal age for marriage was twelve years for girls and fourteen years for boys.) Virginity was the primary requirement for girls, and faithfulness within marriage was expected. That is hardly surprising, as girls were often married at a young age. Indeed, marriage was so universal for women that spinsters were almost non-existent. A girl's father was the leading player in deciding who she would marry; the marriage would facilitate an economic partnership between the father and the prospective husband whose family she would join. Adultery was only taken seriously because it was seen mainly as a crime against the husband. Anything that might suggest the modern concept of women's liberation, which would find its roots in Christianity, was yet to be born.[3]

The rules controlling, well, hardly controlling, the sex life of a young man were decidedly different from those around a young woman.

> *"Prostitution was a boom industry under Roman law. In the densely urbanized and highly monetized economy of the Roman Empire, sex was a most basic and readily available commodity. Girls stalked the streets. Taverns, inns, and baths were notorious dens of venal sex. Brothels were visible everywhere."* [4]

Without any safety net and few opportunities for employment available to women, they could be desperately vulnerable. It's hardly surprising that prostitution and slavery formed a common partnership. The familial patriarch had more control over the slave's body than she had over it herself. Indeed, there were different classes of slaves, and those with special skills were treated more humanely than those without. Nevertheless, a young girl, or a young boy for that matter, could be used to satisfy a patriarch and his friend's sexual proclivities. Sexual morality in the Roman world involved a rigorous regulation of women's sexual behaviour while giving men considerable freedom. Men married late, and women married early. Nevertheless, there were still some restrictions on men's behaviour according to their position in the hierarchy and the protocols surrounding that.

◆ ◆ ◆

Although most people living in the West no longer believe in the central doctrines of Christianity, they remain influenced by the biblical vision of dignity and sexual faithfulness. While they may reject the creation story of Genesis, they still tend to accept its declaration and description of human dignity subconsciously. And that residual recollection of human dignity makes it difficult for the modern mind to comprehend the Roman concept of power and the sexual psyche.[5] Because the modern mind assumes that our understanding of human dignity has been rationally discovered, most believe it to be self-evident. But it isn't. The Romans had no concept of dignity that resembled the one we still falteringly cling to in the West. It was entirely a Jewish concept until the early Christians began to appreciate its foundational value.

It took nearly three centuries, but Christian sexual morality gradually overwhelmed the sense of hierarchical entitlement enjoyed by influential and powerful men. Christianity brought the centrality of monogamy and the belief that marriage was for life. As the faith became increasingly influential, it taught that a man should love and respect his wife. Theologically, marriage was sacred because it symbolised the sacrificial love that Christ has for his Church. Adultery was no longer just a crime against the husband but a sin against God. Unsurprisingly, many early converts to the new faith were women because they discovered a convincing foundation for their freedom and dignity. The elevated Christian vision of marital sex completely swallowed up any idea that the Romans might have had about marriage. Included in the creation story was the commandment, *"Be fruitful and multiply."* The consequence of being created in the image of their maker, Man and Woman, is that they share in the Creator's creative power. The man could no longer sow his seed wherever he wanted. The nature and responsibility of marriage were explicit.

If the early Romans had a laissez-faire attitude to fornication, the early Christians certainly did not. And this difference probably reached its sharpest point in the Christian and Jewish condemnation of male-male, female-female sexual relations. The Apostle Paul, in Romans 1, describes homosexual relationships with deep disapproval:

> *"Women exchanged natural relations for unnatural and the men likewise gave up natural relations with women and were consumed with passion for one another, men committing shameless acts with men. And receiving in themselves the due penalty for their error."*[6]

God's created order reveals His character to Paul and, indeed, to the Church. The Creator's power and deity were displayed in the things that He had made. Homosexual relations were unnatural because they are a denial of God's order.

Something else foreign to the Roman world underpinned all that: the biblical concept of sin that was still culturally significant during my secondary education. Christianity has taught us that we are all sinners and have fallen short of God's glory. And it's this idea of falling short that describes what the Bible means by sin. The word used in the New Testament *(hamartia)* to describe sin was not unknown in the ancient world. From Aristotle to Shakespeare, falling short was the fatal flaw and the stuff of tragedy. However, as the implications of the Gospel of sin and redemption made headway, it became clear that everyone had fallen short.

As that idea filtered through the culture, it significantly impacted the authority and power of the *paterfamilias*. Sin is no more and no less than a failure to trust God and to believe what he says. As Milton tells us in *Paradise Lost*, disobedience in the Garden was the beginning of all our problems. The attempt to discover the source of good and evil without God had to become the cause of pride. And it was pride, the deadliest of all sins, that kept men and women away from God. Pride underpinned the notion of the ruling elite's 'natural superiority.' They maintained control by manipulating fear and shame, a feature that remains true of tribal cultures even today, including the new ones shaped by identity politics.

At the very least, the story of Genesis tells us that men and women have agency and sexual purpose. Obeying God in the context of that agency and purpose was the source of freedom. It was inevitable that Christians would develop a radically different understanding of freedom from what prevailed in the Roman world. Freedom for the believer meant having the power to do what he or she knew was a rightful duty. Knowing what was sexually permissible was the great chasm between the Christian and Roman worlds. And nowhere was that great chasm wider than in the Roman and Christian attitudes to marriage. The contemporary abhorrence of marital abuse, particularly of women, although not unknown to the Romans, had a low profile. For the Christian believer, marriage is God-ordained and, therefore, the natural consequence of a world populated by men and women. So, they enter permanent marriage as complementary partners. Indeed, the outworking of complementarity was influenced and modified by changing social sensitivities, but the concept remained significant.

◆ ◆ ◆

In the very early days of Christianity, it would have seemed impossible that Roman sexual morality would change so radically and that by the reign of Justinian (525-565 AD), the sexual revolution would be over. Of course, not everyone approved of the new sexual ethic or the new religion. That it improved the lives of women, children, slaves, and the impoverished, there can be no doubt. Because the Christian faith, with its theology of sex, is radically different from the Roman world, there could be no compromise. So it's hardly surprising that the Romans and the early Christians had very different ideas about the body, what it meant to be human, and how the sexual ethic reflected that humanity.

For Christians, marriage is a sacred union. Faithful marriage is an exercise of obedience to God. It is a symbol of Christ's union with the church and a mysterious manifestation of it. Within marriage and the care of children, one is confronted daily with the mystery and power of forgiveness. A mother or father forgives estranged children. A child might bring himself or herself to forgive an abusive parent. An abused wife can forgive her husband even if she can't live with him. Divorce is heartbreaking, but even here, faith in Christ's forgiveness can heal the pain and guilt of the breach. I don't think I comprehended the depth and cultural significance of marriage and divorce until I was nearly forty. Now, as cultural relativism has become the accepted controller of Western civilisation, we are witnessing not the continuing victory of Christianity over paganism but the victory of secularised paganism over Christianity, the state of affairs imagined by Nietzsche. And Marx's version of science, replacing Christianity, was no more than a return to natural religion. The eventual result is the revival of a sanitised pagan mythology of personhood, marriage, and family; a civil religion.

Instead of the comfort offered by the biblical declaration that men and women have been created in God's image, we have a politically constructed identity based on assigned function. Forgiveness and faith in a loving God cannot relieve the harrowing poignancy of lost love. Any insight into the holiness of the body cannot be considered. Judith Butler's ideology, described by the appalling word "performativity," comes to mind. By denying the declared naturalness and, indeed, sacred nature of male-female marriage, we return to the utilitarian domination by the powerful, who would judge all in terms of their usefulness. The ideal of complementarity between men and women, accompanying marriage and family as the central institution of civil society, must be denied. The rejection of the Genesis story and the undermining of our history must contribute to an all-encompassing but disconnected ideology that undermines traditional religion and its stories. Inevitably, detractors supporting the new paganism will concentrate on the periods and incidents when complementarity, cooperation between men and women, and family order appeared to break down.

◆ ◆ ◆

Contemporary sexual morality cannot accept the fallenness of human nature; it must reflect the promise of Utopia's moral and political order. Paganised secularism has no rationale for the family's privacy as the cradle of individual identity because it erodes civil society's power to protect individuals from state intrusion. The liberation of women that feminists have fought for over the last several decades has lost its foundation because they no longer have a convincing foundation for their identity. They are in danger of slipping back into second-class status, which will always happen when we deny the Genesis story. It's helpful to observe that secular means something quite different from its original use when it described a particular branch of Christian clergy. It now means non-religious and neutral, the product of rational thought. However, as I have said in a different context, it is not neutral; prevailing beliefs always condition it. Nietzsche's *Overman* was not the product of some new morality. His energy had no new source and depended entirely on his rejection of Christ's resurrection, the victory of the weak over the strong.

Alas, there is now an increasing animus against Christian sexual morality, although its influence remains. Feminists, indeed, women in general, are beginning to have difficulty with their own identity in a world that has become increasingly sexualised. We are experiencing a return to the patriarch's sexual appetite of Roman times, although the biblical claim of the sacredness of female dignity still lingers in the background. The hollowed-out post-modern progressive mind seems unable to admit that an encultured, enduring marriage protects children. There is a prevailing denial that a stable and committed sexual order is the consequence of men and women believing they have been created in God's image.

The beguiling problem with the contemporary sexual revolution is that it continues to assume a meaningful notion of identity can be found within the confines of progressive ideology. While busily preaching its notion of identity as its own, it has no idea it is cutting off the branch on which it sits. This self-imposed folly makes the contemporary sexual revolution similar to, but with very different results from, the revolution during the first 400 years of the Roman Empire. The Roman-Christian revolution enriched marriage and family life with mutual liberation and the disciplining of sexual relationships by humanising both men and women. The paterfamilias ruled over identity no longer because human value is God-given. The contemporary revolution would reverse the achievements of the first revolution if it hasn't already done so. For example, the refusal of transgender ideologists to accept the limits and demands of biology undermines the liberation of complementarity.

The sentimentalised concept of the person is initiating the old claim that sexual behaviour is a matter of choice and not of moral responsibility. The only thing preventing the State from becoming a post-Christian bureaucratic version of the paterfamilias is the residual but fading belief in the intergenerational family as the primary institution of civil society. As identity politics becomes central to our understanding of social order, the way is opened up for a tyranny like that of the paterfamilias to return. It is this creeping power of identity politics that is one of the main drivers of transgenderism eroding female identity. One of the significant differences between the Roman understanding of sex and the Christian understanding of sex, perhaps the main difference, was the status and role of women. A sensitive reading of the New Testament will discover Christ's teaching that men and women share a common civil and familial dignity. Just two examples are illustrative. We have the story of the Samaritan woman at the well, and the fact that women were the first to see the Risen Christ and tell others of their discovery. It would seem self-evident that Christ restored something of the Edenic harmony between men and women. Now, spiritual and cultural advances around the status of women are about to be undone. However, there are, particularly in the United States, encouraging signs that transgender ideology could well be losing its appeal.

It remains a struggle to preserve what our sometimes biblically educated civilisation has taught us about what it means to be human. But there is nothing new about this. We have been seduced into thinking that the Genesis Creation story, the Temptation in the Garden, and the Fall are fairy tales that have nothing to say about who we are. We don't consider Tolkien's and Lewis' claim that all myths point to the one true myth, and the one true myth reveals the richness of the others while also exposing their inadequacy. The story of the Garden tells us what happens when we try to know good and evil without God. We continue to be seduced by Satan's lie to Eve, dramatised for us in Milton's *Paradise Lost: "Queen of this universe! do not believe/Those rigid threats of Death. Ye shall not die."* Okay, you might insist and say it's just a story, a myth, a fairy tale. Well, find a better story to explain the mystery of good and evil. Why do all of us have trouble with temptation? Why is temptation something that we resist and embrace all at once? Why is the self-preserving power of rationality that Richard Dawkins tells us about defeated so frequently by temptation? Why are we divided against ourselves so often?

◆ ◆ ◆

So, who am I? That's the question. The sexual (Christian) revolution during the first five centuries of the Roman Empire delivered one explanation; the contemporary (neo-pagan) sexual revolution offers up quite another.[7] Michel Foucault's claim for self-creation is just too thin. He seemed to understand that. For example, he has this to say while rejecting the Christian theology of the self:

> *"I wonder if our problem nowadays is not, in a way, similar to this one, since most of us no longer believe that ethics is founded in religion, nor do we want a legal system to intervene in our moral, personal, private life. Recent liberation movements suffer from the fact they cannot find any principle on which to base the elaboration of a new ethics. They need an ethics, but they cannot find any other ethics than an ethics founded on so-called scientific knowledge of what the self is, what desire is, what the subconscious is, and so on."*[8]

Although Foucault talks generally of religion, the specific context is a Christianised civilisation; he finds himself between a rock and a hard place. Christianity may well have sustained the cultural ethic for nearly two millennia, but it has become unpalatable to the pseudo-scientific rationalist mind. The demands of the Transcendent for people everywhere to repent and trust God is embarrassing, if not foolish. However, neither science nor scientism can teach us a new ethic because there isn't one. The revolutionary task was much easier for the Christians in the first few centuries than for Nietzsche, Foucault, and the latter-day diminished 'wokerati'. The Christians pointed out to the Romans the intended potential of their humanity. They were not in the business of trying to conjure a new ethic out of the ether. Drawing attention to the flawed nature of the human heart, they gave their contemporaries a better understanding of themselves. They showed the Romans how to control their rebellious Promethean passions, but now Nietzsche, Foucault, et al. would set Prometheus loose amongst us again.

In our vain attempt to create a new ethic and that elusive new identity, we undermine everything from marriage, family order, and the welfare of children to the meaning of love. Alas, this is an issue that very few sociologists, members of parliament, or government bureaucrats will confront because finding a solution would undermine the entire progressive enterprise. It would demand an unpalatable return to the Christian explanation of human meaning and purpose. Unfortunately, the present imagined solution of inventing new human rights and throwing money at the problem will likely continue for some time, despite the contemporary sexual revolution having brought about social disorder of an unprecedented nature. Neither the paterfamilias (well, not yet) nor God is the boss. The morality of sexual life, marriage, and family is determined entirely by an elitist imposition of identity politics that would make freedom of choice primary, certainly above other moral considerations. There is no sign of any grassroots demand to replace biology with ideology or scientific methods, based on the needs of the individualising self-creating self.

◆ ◆ ◆

It is always gratifying to agree with those once considered the enemy. Recently, I discovered Jennifer Bilek and her *Transsexual Transgender Transhuman: Dispatches from the 11th Hour*. I sat up straight as I read what she had to say because she is a progressive and a self-described pro-choice atheist. She points out that deep pockets with a political agenda support the contemporary human rights movement. This is not top-of-the-head stuff; the evidence is overwhelming. Her research makes Judith Butler look like an amateur. In a biting criticism of transgenderism, Bilek claims that we are watching *"A glamorous ad campaign generated by elites, invested in tech and pharma, to normalize the changing of human biology."* That is a mighty big claim.

Of course, every society has its elite in hock to the super-rich. When I was a child at school, some wealthy people did have more power and influence than the rest of us. Nevertheless, we tended to think that integrity and professionalism went together. We still accepted the difference between high and low culture, although we might not have considered it in those terms. We knew some people were better educated, and some had more money than others. But we were not a divided society in the way we have become. Despite the great levelling promised by the multicultural theorists, we have a small number of extraordinarily rich people and too many ill-educated and influential celebrities telling us how we should live, simply because they can. Hypocrisy always values wealth and status above integrity. It shouldn't come as a surprise that most of us now find ourselves caught up in the so-called battle between the oppressed and the oppressors while an elite rewrites the blueprints. No civil society social contract is at the heart of the sexual revolution; the new elite is in control. Unlike the Roman sexual revolution, initiated from the bottom up, the contemporary revolution is imposed from the top down. The self-appointed priesthood would create men and women in their image.

Malignant Euphemism

'Malignant euphemism' is, of course, a contradiction, just like the language of transgenderism. The condition we used to call gender dysphoria, a denial of one's biological sex, is not so much a medical or even a psychological issue as it is one of propaganda reinforced by an aggressive ideology and an unreflecting media. There are plenty of red lights to caution us. For example, why is the battle fiercer around the claims of transgender women than transgender men? We all know that a man who claims to be a woman is a more significant threat to social order than a woman who claims to be a man. A transgender woman in a woman's space is a threat, and not just because of the immediate discomfort felt by women in that space. The social acceptance of transgender women in women's spaces erodes any hope for complementarity while reordering the power dynamic between men and women. And in that reordering, women are the losers.

Implicit in the belief that one can be born in the wrong body is the claim that one's sex is not the consequence of biology. An old grammatical term, 'gender,' is given an entirely new meaning to fudge the issue. A new category of human beings is created out of thin air. One can be described as 'trans' rather than male or female. Both maleness and femaleness are fluid. This is an astonishing outcome with even more astonishing consequences. Again, the Genesis story, which gives dignity to both male and female, is undermined, denying a fundamental assumption of Western civilisation: that men and women are equal in dignity and that dignity is displayed in their differences. The consequence is a complete loss of belief in the dignity of the human individual. The fantasy of transhumanism is beginning to look less like a fantasy and more like a threat hovering on the horizon.

On June 9, 2014, the edition of *Time* magazine had Laverne Cox professing womanhood on the cover. According to the magazine, it was a "transgender tipping point." *Vanity Fair* picked up the baton and had Bruce Jenner, *"I've always been a woman,"* on the cover as Caitlyn. Perhaps in the interests of balancing the books, *Vogue* magazine followed in Paris with Andrej Pejic, a refugee from the Bosnian War; she fled to a refugee camp outside Belgrade with her mother, grandmother, and brother. In 1999, they emigrated to Melbourne. In 2015, she underwent gender reassignment surgery, now euphemistically called gender confirmation surgery. Her genes, however, did not change. In her adolescence, Andrej, with her mother's eventual support, took puberty-suppressing hormones. Obsequiously, *Vogue* says, *"She engages—and dismantles—all one's visceral perceptions of gender."*

The transgender lobby, by concentrating on highly publicised gender reassignment apparent successes, has managed to create a mystique around them. I feel that I am a woman; therefore, I am a woman. To deny that claim is to be transphobic. Another neologism that would describe an imagined state, Ruth Barrett tells us that the transgender woman will not permit discussion in her presence or groups about anything related to her female identity or anatomy because it hurts her feelings. She doesn't want to talk about childhood or adolescence because she didn't experience what the young female body experiences. She goes on to say:

> "... if you speak about this, I am then reminded that I am not female, and therefore not really a woman. **My experience of feeling like a woman must not be invalidated by your experiences of being a woman,** therefore I will shame you for being female, teach you in university to estrange your body from your mind, make your distinct physicality and oppression that is specific to your sex irrelevant in the laws of the land or anything that names our differences until there is only the mind. Now only how I think about your body is real. Mind over body. Mind over matter. Spirit over matter/mater/mother. A woman is anyone who says they are a woman. My word is now more real than your mitochondrial DNA. Accept that by my word, you really don't exist.[9]

Barrett's sentence in bold is the point. Feeling like a woman or a man must not be punctured by reality. It is the estrangement of the body from a mind that underpins the entire transgender (transhuman) ideology. The transgender lobbyists claim that the biology of the body is malleable, entirely under the control of the mind. Old words must be given new meanings to label the imagined state of self, creating fluid bodily autonomy: 'gender' or 'cisgender.' What the mind feels about the body controls reality. Ironically, surgery becomes a tool not to heal but to manipulate reality. A latter-day and secularised gnosticism has seduced the transgender lobbyists into believing that transgender men or women have insight into a higher kind of knowledge.

Wall-to-wall propaganda is essential. For example, we have the ubiquitous case of Jazz Jennings, a young man who claimed to be female. A documentary on Jazz's life has been played breathlessly on New Zealand television at least twice. According to Jennifer Bilek:

> *"He began being exploited by his family and the media and promoted as a 'transgender child' when he was just two years old. Jazz liked sparkles and mermaids, and soon became the poster child for promoting dissociation from sex reality as a progressive new lifestyle for young people."* [10]

If the story around Jazz did not initiate the right to deny one's biological sex, it certainly reinforced it. In New Zealand, rational criticism of the programme was not permitted on MSM. Quite suddenly, it seemed, we began to hear of children born in the wrong body. They became heroic figures in their attempt to change their sex. They were to join the ever-burgeoning group of the oppressed. In November 2024, the leading television channel in New Zealand (NZTV) enthusiastically advertised and provided the unbelievable story of a transgender man giving birth. Although the story came from Christchurch in New Zealand, the *Daily Mail* (4/11/24) in the United Kingdom published a lengthy article. The NZTV programme lingered on the emotional state of the man giving birth and his partner. Of course it did. There could be no examination of the underlying and critical issues; they were glossed.

◆ ◆ ◆

Ten years ago, few people understood that gender ideology would attempt to reorder society from the ground up. Nevertheless, I'm hopeful we are beginning to see an existential crisis bubbling away underneath. After all, is changing one's sex a human right? The bodies of women and children are being violated, and that matters. The new legal language that would allow the assimilation of one sex into the other is malignancy disguised by euphemism. And all this without any convincing evidence. A 2024 Post-Primary Teachers Association (PPTA) position paper, *Amending Gender Pronouns*, continues the deception. Of course, they must eliminate regular pronouns; that is just the beginning. The old constitution *"did not recognise male identifying teachers who were adopting, nor those male teachers who were pregnant."* The paper goes on to say that the old provisions were not inclusive; they did not align with their values. This is an astonishing example of the victory of propaganda. Is the PPTA a priestly caste that can give absolution to those parents with a conflicting theology of human identity?

Just a little reminder about values here. The PPTA did not admit they were introducing a new morality, which is what they are doing. Instead, they claimed that the old constitution did not align with their values. However, these values could have no inherent substance. They are ideological reconstructions of 'inclusion' contrived from the old virtues, such as compassion. The PPTA has not only accepted transgender theory; it is acting as a propagandist for it. '*Amending Gender Pronouns'* presumes too much. Teachers paid by the taxpayer should not tell parents how they should live. If such a dramatic moral shift is required within our schools, then the demand should come from parents, not from a coterie of ideologically driven teachers. *Amending Gender Pronouns* is a jerry-built Trojan horse, bringing its corrosive ideology within the city's gates. If we are going to accept that one's sex is not biologically based, then the rule of law is likely to become ideologically determined.

It might be that the PPTA does not understand what it's doing or what's going on amid its self-righteous exhibition of values. Preoccupation with the self tends to lead to spiritual and moral myopia. Having rejected the past, the PPTA is condemned to misunderstand the future. It does not comprehend what Jennifer Bilek does, that transsexualism and transgenderism morph into transhumanism, a belief that human beings should use all the technological power they have at their disposal to rise above the limitations of body and mind. It's doubtful that the PPTA understands that 'transgender' is a softer and deceitful term for transsexualism, and it hides what is going on to make it more likely to appeal to an uncomprehending market. Transsexualism refutes the permanence of male and female, while transgenderism affirms the right to change one's sex. Once that is done, transhumanism is not far away, and the foundation of our humanity is destroyed.

Many of us must wonder why so many politicians and academics find it so difficult to define a woman but do not have the same difficulty with 'man.' Something odd is going on here. It's already been pointed out, but it must be evident to most of us now that the entire transgender movement has had a more significant impact on women than on men. We should not be surprised. If each person's sex, call it gender if you must, is merely assigned at birth, men who 'change' their sex will not become female. In nearly every species, the male is more sexually aggressive than the female. A transgender woman with or without a penis is unlikely to be less aggressive. However, the ideology cannot bear that, so it must ignore the obvious in women's private spaces and impose the rights of transgender women on the sports field. A woman's identity, critical to family life and civil society, is compromised at best and threatened. In a civilised world, a humane social order revolves around the demands of her biology.

◆ ◆ ◆

This octogenarian has no difficulty believing the claim that transhumanism, highlighted by the eugenics philosopher Julian Huxley in the 1950s, underpins the transgender movement. The eugenics movement, particularly in its early days, was optimistic that a new kind of human being could be manufactured. Genetic codes could be manipulated to improve future generations. Although Francis Galton was the first to use the term in 1883, it had already been introduced into public consciousness through Darwin's theory of natural selection. Galton posited that "the more suitable races or strains of blood have a *better chance of prevailing speedily over the less suitable.*"[11] Although eugenics has been discredited because of its unscientific bias and association with the Nazis, the spirit of eugenic theory now operates under the shroud of transhumanism. Even if the issue of 'transgender' fades away as it is likely to do, the problem of transhumanism will remain. We will think that we can live out a diminished version of the Nietzschean dream.

Although transgender advocates might argue that puberty blockers for children and adolescents are not experimental, they are. Fastidiously documented by Jennifer Bilek, a great deal of money is going to those surgeons, particularly in the United States, who practice such procedures as feminising facial features, phalloplasty, vaginoplasty, and urethral redirection. Overwhelming evidence suggests that wealthy and influential individuals are key promoters of the transhuman movement. According to Bilik[12] they include George Soros, Jennifer Pritzker, a transgender woman, Warren Buffett, Martine Rothblatt, another transgender woman, and numerous wealthy gay men, all of who are outspoken advocates of identity politics.

The most important thing about these supporters of transhumanism is that they believe their ideas about human meaning and purpose are the right ideas. Seduced by the eugenic spirit, they are largely unaware of any debt they owe their Creator, as there is none. They are free to deconstruct the human body for profit. Any awareness that the ideology of gender identity ravages the uniqueness of male and female lies outside their powers of comprehension. We have the medicalisation of what is essentially a spiritual problem of identity. Ultimately, transhumanism would try to prevent all human beings from experiencing what it means to be an embodied spirit. The kind of 'rest' explored by George Herbert (1593-1633) in his poem *The Pulley* is worse than a fairy tale. To the transhumanist, it's threatening.

> *The Pulley*
> *When God at first made man*
> *Having a glass of blessing standing by,*
> *"Let us," said he, "pour on him all we can.*
> *Let the world's riches which dispersèd lie.*
> *Contract into a span."*
>
> *So strength first made a way;*
> *Then beauty flowed, then wisdom, honour, pleasure.*
> *When almost all was out, God made a stay,*
> *Perceiving that, alone of all his treasure,*

Rest in the bottom lay.

"For if I should,' said he.
"Bestow this jewel also on my creature,
He would adore my gifts instead of me,
And rest in nature, not the God of nature;
So both should losers be."

"Yet let him keep the rest,
But keep them with repining restlessness;
Let him be rich and weary, that at least,
If goodness, lead him not, yet weariness.
May toss him to my breast."

Maybe the 'transhumanists' will become weary when scientism and hubris run out of puff. Their inevitable and devastating exhaustion may finally toss them to the divine breast. Perhaps they will realise that the sexual revolution they lust after will end in agony rather than ecstasy.

Notes:

1   Melanie Phillips, *The Sex-Change Society; Feminised Britain and the Neutered Male.* The Social Market Foundation. 1999; Mary Eberstadt, et al. *Primal Screams: How the Sexual Revolution Created Identity Politics.* Templeton Press. 2019.

2   Kyle Harper, *From Shame to Sin; The Christian Transformation of Sexual Morality in Late Antiquity.* Harvard University Press. 2013.

3   Leon J. Podles, *The Church Impotent: The Feminization of Christianity.* Spence Publishing. 1999

4   Harper. p. 47

5   Of course, there have been exceptions. Friedrich Nietzsche, for example. He despised the biblical expression of dignity, wanting it replaced with the old notion of power of the strong over the weak.

6   Romans 1:26-27.

7   Harper, pp 94ff.

8   From an interview conducted by Paul Rabinow and Herbert Dreyfus at Berkeley, April 1983. See *The Foucault Reader,* Paul Rabinow. Penguin Books, 1991. Page 351.

9   *Female Erasure: What You Need to Know About Gender Politics, the War on Women, Female Sex and Human Rights.* Ed. Ruth Barrett. Tidal Time Publishing. 2016. Sentence in bold indicates the author's emphasis.

10   Jennifer Bilek. *Transsexual, Transgender, Transhuman.* Spinifex. 2024. Page 11.

11.   Francis Galton. *Inquiries into Human Faculty and Its Development.* 1883. MacMillan. Page 25.

12.   Bilek. Page 19.

VIII

Civil Religion

The power of Man to make himself what he pleases
means the power of some men to make other men what
they please.

C.S. Lewis. *The Abolition of Man.*

A civilisation's religion and ethical behaviour are determined by who people believe God or the gods to be and what they think about human nature, and to reiterate, religion precedes culture and politics. In the Christian West (or, the Christianised West, if you prefer), we cannot avoid the problem of God's existence and nature. The difference between a Christian West and an increasingly distant Christianised West is significant in this context. The Christian West, sometimes called Christendom, fizzled out in the context of the Enlightenment's passionate faith in the power of reason, giving rise to the authority of secularism and a declining belief in the biblical God and the deity of Christ. Although it might have appeared otherwise, neither God nor Christianity died. The unavoidable question remained: where did we come from, and where are we going? The

Enlightenment enterprise from modernism to post-modernism has failed to answer either question, so we should hardly be surprised that residual Christian doctrine continues to shape our thinking subconsciously. As I have repeatedly said, the contemporary secular mind still depends on the biblical declaration of human dignity. It is a mind peculiar to the West, a heresy, living off the fruit of the tree it fails to cultivate.

◆ ◆ ◆

Politicians can only fumble out of the darkness if there is a light to guide them, so what will that light be? In its various incarnations, Marxism has unsatisfying explanations to guide us. The almost unrecognisable revolution is now so advanced in New Zealand that it has evolved into a civil religion; a replacement religion that must serve as the nation's religious, cultural, and legal foundation. I'm not claiming conspirators have been beavering away in the wings somewhere, although perhaps they were. Whether we are conscious of it or not, we follow their gods. The civil religion's legitimacy was symbolically and unconsciously confirmed in 2018 when Trevor Mallard, Speaker of the House (2017-2022), revised the 164-year-old parliamentary prayer to exclude reference to Jesus Christ. He defended his decision because New Zealand, a secular nation, had to be more inclusive. Why a secular nation should prove more inclusive than one founded on Christianity was not explained. God and the Queen remained in the prayer, but it was not the God of the Bible, the Father of Jesus Christ.

I suspect the Speaker had no idea he was helping to create a situation that made establishing a civil religion inevitable. He had accepted the great lie of his generation: the secular state is underpinned by philosophic and moral neutrality. He had no idea that the omnipotent secular state is an unsustainable by-product of the nation's rejection of Christianity. It was taken for granted that the secular state had sufficient authority within itself to be the foundation of New Zealand's culture. It must have slipped his attention entirely that the philosophy of the separation of church and state involved active belief in authority above the state if democracy was to continue. Following Marx, he collapsed the church and state into one. The point about the old prayer was that those who believed what the prayer meant understood that justice would ultimately depend on an authority above the state.

Of course, Mallard's prayer was not the only reason or the main reason for the inevitable establishment of a civil religion. He merely reinforced what was happening in society by giving it Parliament's blessing. Inevitably, with the rejection of belief in a Creator, the mystery of human sinfulness, and a Redeemer, the philosophy of human nature changes as its transcendent source is denied. People become valuable in proportion to their obedience to the state.

To some ears, that might seem an outrageous thing to say. Nevertheless, the unravelling of civil society institutions that have taken place over the last six or seven decades has created such an atmosphere of moral and legal uncertainty that the state has become the moral arbiter by default. Laws are now added to the statute books, affirming the state's power to decide who we are. They include new legislation on human rights without recognising their source, marriage, the family, and other legally recognised relationships are redefined. Assisted suicide, a range of laws defining discrimination, and an increasing trend toward speech censorship are introduced. Free speech censorship must be called hate speech legislation because dissent would prove intrinsically destructive. It cannot be called what it is, dissenting speech. That would give the game away. The legal concept of discrimination must overwhelm personal discernment and freedom of thought.

According to the Encyclopaedia Britannica, *"Civil religion is a public profession of faith that aims to inculcate political values and prescribes dogma, rites, and rituals for citizens of a particular country."* In New Zealand, such a *"profession of faith"* must find its authority in state power rather than God because civil religion reverses the historical relationship between Christianity and the democratic process, shaping politics from the bottom up. Civil religion is a religion imposed from the top down. It might appear to have the people's assent, but now that the authority above the state, which gave every individual his or her dignity, has been rejected, that assent is no longer necessary. I have already mentioned this, but just in case you missed it, democracy is only practical and possible when there is an agreed-upon authority above the state, a shared and enduring belief in what it means to be human. Something else that dawned on me slowly, but there you are.

Particularly in a decaying democratic nation, civil religion, shaped only by secularised political theory, will influence and eventually determine public moral consciousness. Conviction supporting and sustaining that consciousness will be fuzzy, but that doesn't matter. It's politics first and religion after. It's a state of affairs that the Queen of Hearts from *Alice in Wonderland* would approve: *"verdict first, evidence after."* Political theory becomes religious doctrine, and civil religion is the official enforcer of that doctrine.

◆ ◆ ◆

On the New Zealand Government website, one can find *Te ao Māori Strategy 2022-2025* signed by Rafael Gonzalez Montero, Executive, Parliamentary Services, and David Wilson. Clerk of the House of Representatives. Te ao Māori, we are told, *"is a way of perceiving, understanding, and interacting with the world that has been developed by successive generations over several centuries in Aotearoa."* Nothing revolutionary there, you might say. That's what cultures do. The issue is, however, how they do it. The claim that *"Te ao Māori . . . has been developed by successive generations over several centuries in Aotearoa,"* suggests a historical analysis that doesn't exist and a sense of order akin to scientific method; that Māori were a nation and not a loose connection of warring tribes, each with its pantheistic spin on the world.

Written in English and Māori, the English version is replete with Māori words that few of us understand. Perhaps it doesn't matter. The document tells us, *"the stars will guide us."*

> *"Together we are aboard our waka, and our guiding stars assist us in navigating our way through our mahi and the shared journey ahead. Along with He Waka Eke Noa, He Ao Takitaki acknowledges and commits to the work of both agencies' People Strategies and the shared Parliament Engagement Strategy."*

This is undoubtedly the language of civil religion. Replete with confusing and misleading heliographic language reminiscent of an idealised biography, we have,

MANAAKITANGA

We will express empathy, consideration and compassion, empowering others and enhancing the understanding of te ao Māori for all of our people. We will manaaki ourselves, manaaki our colleagues, manaaki others we work with, as we manaaki Parliament.

WHANAUNGATANGA

We respect differences and value diverse experiences. Central to te ao Māori is the concept of the whole self; by bringing and being acknowledged for our whole selves, we will support the growth of whanaungatanga.

Te ao Māori finishes with a karakia, which translates into a hotchpotch of sentimentalising secular prose written in the form of poetry, recalling John Lennon, astrology, and what looks like deliberate ambiguity.

> *We acknowledge the celestial entities*
> *We acknowledge our guiding stars*
> *The coursing of the stars is invoked*
> *Inspiring the path we follow through our world*
> *In this endeavour, heaven and earth come together*
> > *Let it be.*

Conscious or unconscious syncretism is the central issue. Te ao Māori would bring heaven and earth together! Attempting to combine two incompatible religions, Pantheism and Christianity, and expect that fusion will be a cultural foundation is wishful thinking in the extreme. A civil religion can be the only outcome.

Doubtless, some might argue that we've had a Christian civil religion for a long time. In the language of post-modern liberalism, the Christian ethic has shaped our narrative. However, such a comparison misunderstands how civil religion works. In New Zealand, Christianity, the people's faith, despite its warts, shaped the morality of civil society and its politics; it influenced Parliament's thought, not only because of Christian prayer at each sitting but also because beliefs that gave rise to the individual's dignity, the rule of law, and civil society were thoroughly Christian. And by the rule of law, I am not talking about judicial activism. I mean the law based on the biblical declaration of human dignity and the Decalogue. The contemporary manifestation of civil religion gains much of its motivating energy from a reaction against the Christian doctrine of sacred personhood. Consequently, its deconstructed perception of the holy cannot help but influence our understanding of human nature. The authority to determine what human nature might be and how it should be controlled must be decided by the secular state that takes its presumptuous neutrality for granted.

◆ ◆ ◆

It is important here to point out that the secular mind always underestimates the significance and power of prayer. For the Christian believer, being in communion with God is critical. The continuing erosion of parliamentary Christian prayer is the rational consequence of losing belief in Christian theology that underpinned civil society and made the Treaty of Waitangi possible. So, the rise of civil religion is a necessary consequence of the prevailing attempt to deny the influence of traditional (revealed) religion. Slowly, the ideology of cultural relativism has infiltrated Christianity to the point where it is overwhelming it and weakening its impact on public policy.

Perhaps that influence began to bite in New Zealand significantly with the *Family Proceedings Act 1980,* when no-fault divorce was introduced. There might have been good reasons for reforming the Act, but it moved away from the traditional and Christian view of marriage. Having lost faith in the marital union's sacredness and even practical value, monitoring and disciplining it became too difficult. Marriage's pivotal role in shaping the culture of civil society's institutions was either deliberately ignored or forgotten. We began to believe that hedonism is benign rather than malignant. It became inevitable that we should have a revision of human rights theory, the legalisation of prostitution, assisted suicide, liberal abortion laws, and same-sex marriage. All these were the inevitable consequences of a reductionist perception of freedom released from the restraints of Christianity. They could only come about by replacing the Christian theology of the body with a utilitarian concept of human nature.

This shift in our understanding of the theology of the body is evident in the legalisation of same sex marriage. We used to understand that the act of intercourse between a man and a woman consummated a marriage. Consummation reflected the belief in the sacredness of marriage; the man and the woman become one flesh. The biblical creation story tells us that marriage is written into the nature of the human creature. The question arises: How is marriage between two men or two women consummated? Acceptance of sexual complementarity gives rise to and reinforces the creation of the family; when it is ignored, radically different lifestyles become legitimate. The refusal to believe in the sacredness of the human body and the complementarity of the sexes must muddy the water when we think about marriage or come to consider what it means to be a man or a woman. That confusion cannot last, and it must be sold by civil religion, which will tell us what marriage and family are and what it means to be a man or a woman. And when that fixation passes, which it will, we are left with the question of what it means to be human.

◆ ◆ ◆

Something must be said about the nature of language in this context. We must know what we mean when we use a word. When words no longer describe reality, they encourage error, conscience is seared, and sin becomes normal. Loaded neologisms, frequently tautological, are used to silence conscience. They include 'love is love', 'marriage equality', 'my truth', 'consenting adults', 'gender identity', 'family is fluid', 'inclusivity', 'affirming tolerance', and 'hate speech'. They assume the self is the final arbiter of morality. For example, 'love is love' denies love's objective content, reducing it to mere sentiment. 'Marriage equality' hides a lie. It presumes different kinds of marriage, claiming they are equal. None of these terms has objective content. None of them has any concept of human dignity or moral clarity. They deny humanity's God-given purpose, generative power, and privilege. A civil religion might seem to liberate the 'enthroned self'; however, all the enthroned selves will find that the state has replaced God.

However, it has to be said that Christianity has always had the problem of being infiltrated and undermined by those hostile to it. Deciphering the changing and wavering influence of Christianity throughout its history is not easy. It is particularly challenging when those who hold and interpret the nation's story are hostile to Christianity. With the increasing influence of civil religion, young people are given an entirely different historical perspective. They don't understand that their moral intuition is rooted in the Christian faith, looking after the weak and loving your neighbour, for example, or that social justice distorts Christian justice, which is a revelation of God's character. They take it for granted that their hollowed-out ideas, specific to the Bible, are natural to the human condition. Therefore, they can't comprehend that rejecting Christian tradition means that the continuation of Enlightenment revolutionary fervour will consume itself as it did in eighteenth-century France and twentieth-century Russia. It becomes difficult to accept or even consider that the prevailing ideology is a parasite with nothing to replace what it would chew up and spit out. Young people don't have the historical knowledge to understand that civil society institutions are devalued and that social capital is lost. An ideological fog envelops the past, and young people, mainly, are left without a guide.

In the classroom of my last year at primary school, I can remember a chart hanging relatively high on two walls. It listed the events, stories, and people significant in shaping Western civilisation. It began with the Greek period (5th century BC) and went right up to the Second World War. The more important events and people were highlighted. We understood what BC meant and why the dates leading up to Christ's birth diminished and afterward increased. Most of us in the class found the stories around whatever was on the chart fascinating when they were explained. Had somebody in the 1950s tried to introduce BCE and CE, we would have known what they were up to. At the very least, we grew up to believe that history was intriguing and vital and that Jesus Christ was its climax. Doubtless, we got a few things wrong. We were influenced by the prejudices of our time, but nothing that couldn't be corrected. As I have grown older, understanding my errors has been enriching. It's unlikely that any such chart would be available in a primary school today. In the atmosphere of increasing ignorance, it would be viewed as Eurocentric and, therefore, not available for consideration. One thing the chart didn't do, because it wasn't an issue, was to tell us who we are and who determines who we are. It was the confidence we had in our identity that gave rise to the chart in the first place. Goodness me, I even thought the British Empire was a thing.

◆ ◆ ◆

One way to help understand what is happening is to return to Karl Marx. It's not that Marx is the leading player in the de-Christianisation of Western civilisation, although he must be close. For example, Marx's 1843 essay, *A Contribution to the Critique of Hegel's Philosophy of Right,* is revealing, even if Marx was speaking mainly about Germany:

> "... *criticism of religion has essentially been completed, and the criticism of religion is the prerequisite of all criticism. Religious suffering is at one and the same time the expression of real suffering and a protest against real suffering. Religion is the sigh of the oppressed creature, the heart of a heartless world, just as it is the spirit of a spiritless situation. It is the opium of the people.*"

He goes on to say,

"The abolition of religion as the illusory happiness of the people is the demand for their real happiness. To call upon them as to give up their illusions about their condition is to call upon them to give up a condition that requires illusions. The criticism of religion is, therefore, in embryo, the criticism of that veil of tears of which religion is the halo."

Now, I will leave it to the reader to decide whether these quotes *"are a claim to legitimacy by the facile turns of phrase,"* as Michael Walsh claims, or something else.[1] Whatever the case, the claim that *"Criticism of religion has essentially been completed,"* and *"the criticism of religion is the prerequisite of all criticism,"* are a dismissal of Christianity, leaving the way open for a new ideology to seduce the Stanford students in the 1970s and all the rest in the following decades. Marx thought he could stand outside the culture and assume a philosophic neutrality that would give him the tools to criticise the religion he despised. But as soon as he did, he had no foundation on which to stand other than bold assertion, which begs an obvious question. By what authority does Marx speak? He may have claimed his ideology to be scientific, but he had already rejected any sane understanding of science by rejecting the divine order on which the scientific method was posited. Any attempt to create a new ideology (religion) must become totalitarian to preserve itself. Like Satan, who enters the Garden telling Adam and Eve that God did not mean what He said, Marx would offer the same alternative vision based on the same lie. Adam and Eve disobeyed God's command and ate from the Tree of the Knowledge of Good and Evil, thinking they knew good and evil better than God.

It must be emphasised that the seizure of God's knowledge of good and evil would give subjectivism its authority. But God is not dead. He remains the judge of right and wrong. Marx is not getting rid of religion at all, merely the one he doesn't like for the one he would control. His pretentious term, *Scientific Socialism,* is not even his own; it came from the French socialist Pierre-Joseph Proudhon in 1840, who wrote the aptly titled *What is Property?* A brief examination of the quote from Proudhon below is rewarding.

> *"In a given society, the authority of man over man is inversely proportional to the stage of intellectual development which that society has reached; and the probable duration of that authority can be calculated from the more or less general desire for a true government,—that is, for a scientific government. And just as the right of force and the right of artifice retreat before the steady advance of justice, and must finally be extinguished in equality, so the sovereignty of the will yields to the sovereignty of the reason, and must at last be lost in scientific socialism."* [2]

One could spend the rest of the section on civil religion discussing this dense quote. However, the last sentence will do because it sheds considerable light on the origins of social justice, which is critical to the authority of civil religion: *"And just as the right of force and the right of artifice retreat before the steady advance of justice, and must finally be extinguished in equality, so the sovereignty of the will yields to the sovereignty of the reason, and must at last be lost in scientific socialism."*

This must be one of the first attempts to explain and defend social justice. The belief that the sovereignty of the will and human passion could be controlled by reason, scientific socialism alone was the dream. Still, it was to become the Achilles' heel of Western civilisation. The 'artifice' of Christian justice has not yet finally retreated before the untrammelled rationality and equity demanded by *scientific socialism*, now called social justice. Proudhon's quote sounds like something Nietzsche could have said, except that he said it four years before Nietzsche was born.

◆ ◆ ◆

Marx's so-called non-religion was the product of his faith in the supreme power of his reason. His heresy, because that's what his faith was, meant that the replacement of Christianity would not get rid of religion but replace it with another: a civil religion. Marx did not abolish religion at all. Instead, he helped to establish a climate for a civil religion to flourish. It's tempting to slip into metaphor and continue the comparison of Marx with Satan; both were rebels who denied God's authority (objective value if you prefer), and in doing so, both had to establish their alternative religions. Marx laid the foundation for the latest in totalitarian states, and in the Russian context, this led to the tyranny of Stalinism, which, by the way, gets too much of a free ride from its apologists.

With his failure to understand the significant power of natural religion, always lurking in the shadows, Marx, acting against his own Jewishness, would replace the revealed biblical faiths of Judaism and Christianity, thinking he had abolished religion. He might well have claimed that scientific evolution rationally and justifiably brought about the death of religion, but his condemnation of religion is all smoke and mirrors. In rejecting the society and religion that gave him birth and succour, Marx failed to consider the individual's critical importance intrinsic to the biblical revelation of human dignity. By casting history into an abstract struggle of opposing historical forces, he laid the foundation for the quote often attributed to Stalin: *"A single death is a tragedy; a million deaths is a statistic."*

Whether Stalin said this or not, it doesn't matter. But what matters is the context in which such a thought becomes possible. Time has abundantly displayed that brutal totalitarianism is the necessary consequence of Marxism. It might well be that critical theory, Marxism's grandchild, leads to soft totalitarianism, but it's still totalitarianism. Belief in the individual's dignity and the concept of freedom that flows from it is lost, whether totalitarianism is hard or soft. Perhaps one of the worst things about a civil religion is that it must always reduce human nature to an abstraction that conditions its necessary totalitarian impulse. The satisfying life for the individual is always secondary to the tribe's rights. That is one of the inevitable tragedies that overwhelms us when we reject Christianity as the guide to social order. Having rejected the sacred, which would give the individual dignity, there is no machinery to recover the individual's unique worth.

An Inevitable Discovery

One of the most revealing discoveries one can make is that somebody always wants to be in control. Compare the quote from C.S. Lewis at the beginning of the chapter with Rousseau's influential claim that *"all men are born free, but everywhere they are in chains."* Lewis was sure that human nature was deeply flawed and that the political process would not solve that problem. Although he never said so precisely, he could have said that all men are 'born in chains.' They are sinners and need to be liberated from the power of sin by God. So we have what Friedrich Nietzsche hated so much: Christ died on the cross and rose again, declaring victory over death, so that all men and women might be saved from the consequences of their sin, but not necessarily their folly.

Rousseau, anticipating Marx, thought that whatever the problem might be, he was confident that it could be solved politically. However, to leave it there would hardly be fair. Rousseau said a great deal more than his famous quote. Indeed, in the last chapter of his *Social Contract*, he tried to tell us how a civil religion should work. Rousseau didn't break away entirely from Christianity. Although he might have rejected the Bible as the primary religious authority, the idea that the weak should be protected and the oppressor punished remained strong. But even that creates a serious problem for Rousseau and his acolytes: how does one decide what is just? An ambiguous vision of an afterlife and a tolerant God seems to have remained part of his consciousness. Not quite an atheist, Rousseau was more of a wavering deist; God might be there, but divorced from the intimacy of day-to-day life. Anticipating Trevor Mallard, praying for one's country might revitalise politics. However, just who one should pray to was not clear. Not much help to a pilgrim, Rousseau's intuition and contribution to social justice theory were just the beginning.

Anticipating Marcuse, Rousseau believed a civil religion would tolerate all faiths. However, as a matter of dogma, a civil religion would not tolerate the intolerable. Those who did not yield to the civil religion would suffer a penalty. Although the state could not force someone to believe, it could banish or even execute an offender. Nevertheless, Rousseau, aware of control problems, thought they could be solved if the correct political process was followed. Unlike Lewis, his vision of humanity was utopian. That is another critical difference between civil religion and Christianity. For Christians, *"Thy kingdom come"* is about the need for personal salvation, the recognition of the individual's dignity, and God's sovereignty. It is not about attempts to create a counterfeit dignity designed by bureaucrats who have forgotten that natural law protects the dignity of the individual made in God's image. The state overreaches when it thinks it can create human beings in its image and write their rights because of that creation.

◆ ◆ ◆

Just a little observation I can't resist. Christians frequently suffer the accusation that their faith concentrates on the hereafter; pie in the sky, as they say. However, the progressive religionist looks forward to the forever receding pie in the sky, the Grand Socialist Utopia. Life is no more than a struggle to get there. The Utopian misunderstands and devalues Christianity, and in doing so, he or she is bound to the task of seeking something that will never be enjoyed because it must always be on the horizon. The value of the individual is lost in the utilitarian demand that everyone must struggle towards whatever utopia seems appropriate. And in the utopian muddle, many utopians become obsessed with their own particular Armageddon.

Civil religion in New Zealand will be entrenched because submission to cultural relativism cannot deliver justice unless the individual's identity is determined by group membership (tribe) authorised by the state. It is impossible to overstate the importance of this issue. The dignity and uniqueness of the individual are essential to the democratic process, a belief that has shaped New Zealand society since 1854, the first year of the New Zealand House of Representatives. When the gift of divine identity is rejected, civil religion finds its notion of identity in the political process. A new concept seeps into our consciousness that we have come to call the politics of identity, now intrinsic to New Zealand's civil religion, which focuses on balancing the groups' competing rights because identity is determined by group membership. In any society increasingly dominated by the oppressor/oppressed model, the tribe replaces the divinely ordained natural family as the protector of identity and civil society.

Such an outcome was dramatised for the Western world in February 2025. Preaching at his first church attendance after his inauguration, the Bishop, Right Reverend Mariann Edgar Buddle, asked President Trump to show mercy to LGBTQ+ people; she claimed, like many of her contemporaries in the United States and far away New Zealand, that his rhetoric and policies were making them afraid. She didn't seem to understand that her convictions about sexuality were crafting her concept of dignity. Politics was shaping her theology. Tribal membership determined identity, and for that reason, politics must reorder and control religious faith. She seemed to think that sexual orientation and identity were more fundamental to human meaning than the identity given to every human being by their Creator. The validity of tribal membership in determining one's identity could not be questioned. A diminished doctrine of human dignity infiltrates, its authority transferred to the State, and the control problem is on the way to being solved. Politics first, religion after.

Most of us are now living through a serious break in historical continuity. The consequential ignorance brought upon by such a break makes civil religion not only possible but necessary; it is essential to replace the forgotten national story. The new story must regard the old story as irrelevant and probably immoral, with its determination to produce heaven on earth. Slowly, it seems to happen slowly, everyone must be released from the restraints of the old order.

Perhaps one of the worst things a civil religion does is diminish the human spirit because, to be true to its nature, it must be authoritarian in making a great fuss about the efficacy of feeling, it must reorder what and how we should feel. Condemned to parody the lamenting chorus in a Greek tragedy, it has no machinery within itself to even begin to understand the nature of tragedy. Civil religion does not permit the catharsis of weeping; it fails to explain or explore the dreadful mystery of the tragic life. Indeed, it cannot because its utilitarian persona can never bring mercy and justice together. The only kind of citizen a civil religion will tolerate is the unfleshed and servile robot.

Democracy and Its Enemy

Just who will control one's life has always been an issue. In the de-Christianising West, most recently, we have tried to solve it by an increasingly inclusive democracy, a way of seeing the world through social justice doctrine, emphasising equality of outcome. However, democracy can only work well when citizens believe they are responsible for each other and that human dignity is not just the product of their imagination or government power. That democracy is presently under stress as we cease to believe we are embodied spirits should not be difficult to understand. Democracy, because we have become less confident about what it might be, cannot survive without a shared conviction about what it means to be human. A civil religion will always have an inadequate theology of the person.

It cannot admit that human beings are embodied spirits because that would be to undermine and eventually deny its authority. And that is the critical weakness of the neutral secular state. It cannot and will not examine the essential duplicity of its stolen foundation. Therapy becomes an exercise of control rather than healing the body by cutting out the tumour of hubris. The old sin problem must be resolved by therapy rather than by the recognition of error and forgiveness. Therapy is the theology of civil religion.

The following extract from John Adams' brief letter to the Massachusetts Militia remains as true today as it was in October 1798, even if we abandon Christianity's description of human nature:

> *"Because We have no Government armed with Power capable of contending with human Passions unbridled by morality and Religion. Avarice, Ambition, Revenge, or Gallantry would break the strongest Cords of our Constitution as a Whale goes through a Net. Our Constitution was made only for a moral and religious people. It is wholly inadequate to the government of any other."*

Without apology, I repeat: what a tribe, a nation, or even an empire believes about the human condition shapes its understanding of the past, present, and future. Anthropology and history teach us that religion informs culture, and religion teaches us how we might adapt to the reality around us. Contrary to the implicit claims of cultural relativism, not all religions have the same aim, means, and outcome. Muslims submit to Allah and all that that means. Its political framework demands that submission. Jews, to whom Christians are in debt for much of their theological understanding, learn to obey and honour the great I AM of revelation, who, for Christians, is the risen Jesus Christ. For Jews and Christians, faithful submission is voluntary and independent of any political system. The Romans sought good fortune by appeasing their gods and participating in festivals. A civil religion would, like Islam, demand submission and, like Roman religion, demand that we appease the gods of relativism and attend its festivals and practice its rituals.

While continuing to worship the great I AM, the trinitarian God of the Bible, the early Christians learned to thank God for His character, whose saving grace was revealed in Jesus Christ. Conforming to and obeying God's will is the Christian's privilege and duty. The great mystery of the Christian faith is that the Christian's joy is to honour God by obeying Him, not out of fear but out of love. The Bible tells us in the first commandment that God demands we believe, trust, and love Him. By failing to believe and trust in our first duty of love, we demean our humanity and start thinking we are our own self-creating deity. The second commandment tells us to love one another because God has declared each of us sacred. Contemporary civil religion short-circuits all that by attempting to accommodate reality to human desire, presuming it can control both. An elite, latter-day gnostic priesthood would initiate a religion out of its imagination in an attempt to give order to the cult of diversity, inclusion, and equity, which revises tolerance, undermines human purpose, and distorts meaning. Tolerance is no longer about holding your nose and getting on with it. Freedom is conditioned by a new kind of tolerance that affirms the politics of identity as the overarching story defining the human condition. The inclusive human being is progressive and committed to social justice, cultural relativism, and a race-based version of revised Marxism. The priesthood distributes freedom based on human rights doctrine, which may change as enlightenment proceeds. Civil society institutions are weakened by ideologically driven protests hostile to democracy.

◆ ◆ ◆

The writer of the Gospel of John tells us that *"God is Love"* and that is worth more than a passing thought in this context because it has been picked up by queer theorists and turned into *"Love is God."* Of course it has, because as soon as we strip away the idea of love from God-given dignity, we can inject the fallacy of passion's purity into it. Love loses its power to consider the other, so we have the theological reversal, *"Love is Love."* John's insight into God's character is turned into a tautology that supports an entire ideology.

We have known for a long time that democracy works if we all share a common dignity. It is this realisation of shared dignity that allows democracy to work. Without that, voting would be fraudulent. Civil religion does not need to be supported by the votes of individual citizens to impose its deconstructed and parasitic version of dignity on all of us. Because it snatches at the source of dignity, it will not permit any alternatives. The Jewish and Christian faiths are its greatest enemies because it has stolen its diminished and reconstructed understanding of human meaning and nature from the Bible. At heart, it's a fraud, and we cannot be allowed to see that.

When Christ told his disciples, *"My Kingdom is not of this world"* *(John 18:36),* He pointed out that his followers would always live in two kingdoms as long as they remained on Earth. He went on to say that there would always be tension between the two. The events of the last two thousand years have proved this to be true. The kingdom of this world has always tried to overcome Christ's Kingdom. Another way of saying this is that the government is always in the business of extending its power. Governments will always become autocratic unless there is some good reason for restraint. In New Zealand for nearly two hundred years, the Christian faith offered that restraint with its belief in human sinfulness, forgiveness, and salvation. Every man and woman, king and beggar, is subject to God's judgement. Neither a king nor a democratic state possessed the wisdom to determine what it meant to be human.

◆ ◆ ◆

Perhaps this is the right time to address social justice specifically. The first thing to note is that social justice is a redefinition of justice. Justice, under the influence of the Bible, used to mean that the law was based on the biblical explanation of human dignity. Justice was definite and permanent; sin has eternal consequences. Indeed, justice is frequently not completed on this earth, so a final judgement is necessary to ensure justice is done. However, it must also be acknowledged that the administration and dispensation of justice are not easy in life or literature. It lends itself very quickly to the folly that comedy can expose. I suspect that's why Shakespeare's *Measure for Measure* is one of my favourite plays. Lucio, the lecherous and ludicrous villain, is a hypocrite, and in the foolishness of his hypocrisy, he highlights the character of many of the others who are also hypocrites. The ducking and diving of every character make it clear that no one can stand outside the demands of justice, which God must consistently and finally deliver. The writer of Romans, quoting Deuteronomy tells us, *"'Vengeance is mine, I will repay', saith the Lord"* (12:19 KJV). Social justice is relative and lacks definition; it evades and dodges like Lucio without being amusing. For example, social justice declares that abortion is acceptable to maintain the mother's financial comfort and mental health, or that divorce may enable self-actualisation (we used to call it selfishness) of the separating partners. Social justice lets the irresponsible father off the hook because it fails to understand that duty is a loving action and not one of compulsion. Only the imagined specifics of each case determine whether something is just or not. Personal opinion and prevailing sensitivities are all one needs to consider. Social justice is happy with the destruction of public and private property, provided it's done under the protection of perceived racial injustices. It would convince us that it is caring (an inadequate word) and just to assist a loved one who wishes to kill himself or herself.

When social justice ideology controls our understanding of justice, we are left with the bias of an unstable subjectivity to bring about social order. The politics of identity becomes normative, and various groups claiming oppression rely on a mixed view of truth and morality that is totalitarian, naturalistic, post-modern, and Marxist. Social justice has no foundation other than that built by the politics of the time. Its application is secularism's attempt to replace Western civilisation's legal traditions. However, Western civilisation cannot flourish if its standards of morality and truth are not based on traditional justice, ultimately grounded in God's revelation of Himself. The necessary consequence of the encroaching civil religion is the evacuation of the democratic spirit, which, I repeat, depends on recognising God-given dignity. Freedom of religious belief and expression, which underpins free speech and conscience, and a rational response to faith in the biblical God, must be cancelled. Those freedoms validated by the Genesis creation story cannot be entertained, not because they've been discredited but because they're dangerous.

The Source

Western civilisation could not have happened without the Bible, both the Old and New Testaments.[3] For many people living in a de-Christianising, re-paganising culture, that will be another outrageous claim, although attempts have been made to justify it in previous chapters. However, it needs to be re-emphasised in the context of civil religion. The Genesis creation story uniquely introduces and declares in its explanation of human dignity what kind of creatures we are. The creation of male and female in God's image, along with the command to be fruitful, is the permanent foundation for marriage, family order, structure, discipline, and a civil society that functions effectively. As it has developed in Western civilisation, especially in the Anglophone countries, the rule of law is a rational consequence of belief in the individual's unique dignity. *"Innocent until proven guilty"* is a tremendous legal achievement inspired by the biblical concept of dignity.

The loss of the concept of dignity, or an unwillingness to accept it, was the problem confronting the Universal Declaration of Human Rights' framers, who presumed human rights to be universal without understanding why. In addition, and to be more specific, I have long believed that the Genesis creation story gives us the foundation for objective value. The eternal, uncreated God is that foundation. If the uncreated God is not the foundation of Western civilisation, there is no foundation for universal human rights. Maybe because I'm an old bloke, I have already said in another context that the contemporary social unrest, religious and political confusion, conceptual hostility, sexual muddle, and democratic decay are the consequences of rejecting the God of the Bible. The creation of God in our image will always end in tears, and those tears are very close to the surface in our time.

◆ ◆ ◆

It might be helpful to distinguish between revealed and natural religion because New Zealand's contemporary civil religion is a mishmash of secularism and natural religion. And I mean mishmash. Secularism, that Christian heresy, has a muddled understanding of natural and revealed religion. It is informed by its perception of what it rejects. Judaism and Christianity are two examples of revealed religion. God declares who he is. According to the Scriptures, God speaks directly to Moses in both religions. In Hebrew, *Ehyeh Asher Ehyeh* says, *"I Am That I Am"* or *"I shall be what I am."* God is the uncreated and eternal self-existing one. For Christians, Jesus Christ is the uncreated and eternal self-existing one who *"puts on human flesh"* to conquer sin and death. Just in passing, Judaism and Christianity depend on many similar historical events, the meaning of which is declared by revelation. For example, without God's call to Abraham and His declaration to Moses, Judaism would be without foundation, Christianity's perception of faith diminished, and its debt to Judaism undermined. If what the Bible, both Old and New Testaments, says about Jesus Christ is not true, then neither is Christianity the religion it claims to be. Indeed, the Apostle Paul points this out in his first letter to the Corinthians. Without the resurrection, Christians are *"of all men, most miserable"* (15:19 KJV). Indeed, everything I say depends on the resurrection of Jesus Christ.

Natural religions are those that human beings develop through their fear of a hostile natural world and their faltering perceptions of the sublime. They tend to be pantheistic, perhaps animistic, and primitive because they are the earliest kind of religion given content by the human imagination. The supernatural power attributed to the gods is usually experienced through the natural world, its objects, and events. The gods might be symbolic or believed to be indwelling the sacred natural world. Contemporary nature religions, such as dogmatic environmentalism and some later versions of feminism, draw on ancient traditions to lend spiritual authority. They come together in the worship of Gaia, for example.

The Bible claims that God exists beyond everything we can see. He reveals himself to his creation and is knowable by reason and faith despite the ultimate mystery of his deity. The believer admits with relief that the finite can only go so far in appreciating the infinite. Christians and Jews, however, are taught to believe that God is intimately involved in the affairs of men and women. Psalm 139:13-14 (NKJV) tells us:

> *"For you formed my inward parts,*
> *You covered me in my mother's womb.*
> *I will praise you, for I am fearfully and wonderfully made;*
> *Marvellous are your works,*
> *And that my soul knows very well."*

Among other things, God is the God of order, concerned with the welfare of His creation, and it is the human creature's privilege to learn and enjoy who He is and explore the world He created. That's why scientific method is such a big deal. Unlike the pagan gods, God is distinct from his creation and not dependent on or part of it. The God of the Bible is the source of all things and is separate from them. If we were to incinerate the whole world in nuclear folly, God would not die. Scripture is given to us to read and apply our reason, imagination, and spiritual insight guided by the Creator's Spirit. Gratitude is the Christian believers' response to the Creator of all things, visible and invisible. And, by the way, that spirit of gratitude is essential to good mental health and underpins a sense of responsibility critical to democracy.

The Parasite

New Zealand's civil religion is a parasite. Stealing its idea of dignity from Christianity, it becomes its enemy. The struggle between the parasite and the host forms the backdrop of the 'Culture War,' more accurately explained as a religious war, the battle over what it means to be human. Hence, we have all the vexatious fuss around the issue of identity. The rejection of God as the master of the universe must be replaced by the inevitable *"I am the master of the universe,"* with the pride that would mimic modesty. A culture war's aim is no different from a 'hot war' that would compel the enemy to surrender, to do the will of the victor. Kind-hearted people are the last to understand that there is a kindness that kills. They like to believe disarming the enemy without offence is possible. As desirable as that might sound, we must remember we are dealing with a parasite, unaware that when it kills the host, it will also die. The mistakes that can come from kindness can be the worst because they undermine the need to act.

I can recall another one of those dinner party debates where I was forced to try to make sense of the musings of a young PhD student (supported by his girlfriend, whom he insisted on calling his partner). And there we had it, the culture war writ small. He sat opposite me, and I can remember he had a very red face. I couldn't work out whether he had too much sun or too much booze. Anyway, he was writing something about the evils of colonialism. I can't remember much about it, but I do remember the obvious obsequiousness of the others around the table. I got into terrible trouble with the other guests by telling him he was talking nonsense. The issue was not whether I was right or wrong, but rather that I was being cruel, embarrassing a young student, and undermining his confidence. I was insensitive, but I don't think my age and experience made me grumpy. Instead, I think I was surrounded by the kindness that kills—that state of being where soft, unreflecting hearts overcome the sanity of a wisely educated mind.

The term 'culture war' originated in Germany. *"Kulturkampf"* was first used by the Prussian statesman Rudolf Virchow in 1873, who described the struggle between Otto von Bismarck and the Catholic Church. Virchow claimed that the battle was taking on the character of a great struggle in the interests of humanity. The culture war has always been, in fact, a conflict between two opposing ideologies. Understanding the battle between the Prussian State and the Catholic Church helps us come to grips with the one between Christianity and a resurgent union of secularism with paganism. It's a battle to have sovereignty over the hearts and minds of men and women.

There is always a process that modifies religion and the moral sensitivities that arise from it, sometimes evolutionary and sometimes revolutionary. However, in the post-modern West, we have a unique situation: the slow and deliberate rejection of Christianity as the spiritual and moral foundation, only to discover that nothing substantial has taken its place. And it is this 'nothing' that has left the way open for a civil religion to control the way we should think about the world. Following the 'Death of God,' the State must become the default authority. It no longer receives authority from God or the people; it is the supreme authority controlling the content of the civil religion.

Now that we have been seduced into rejecting biblical revelation, a theologically ill-educated and consequently illiberal elite convinced by multicultural doctrine would claim that none of us is responsible to God. As John Adams anticipated, when any government, still influenced by a residual Christian ethic, declares itself responsible only to the people and not God, it eventually annexes the deity's authority. Not only is the distinction between church and state lost, but the State also captures the church's role as moral guardian. The democratic state is deconstructed, and a new set of problems is created because a common ethic above the State no longer constrains it. In its quest for survival, civil religion must provide a new narrative to shape our worldview and maintain some semblance of order. By default, civil religion, to gain status, must draw its public celebratory rituals from natural religion. Sometimes, parody, deliberate or unconscious, can reveal what is happening. A recent example is the pantomime at the opening of the 2024 Paris Olympics. The organisers snatched at the hotchpotch of Pagan myth and legend, mixing it with Christian imagery in a way that looked like ridicule of Christianity. An androgynous and alien central figure surrounded by its acolytes resembled a satire of Leonardo da Vinci's *The Last Supper*. It didn't take much imagination to hear an echo of the 'goddess' briefly installed in the Cathedral of Notre Dame in 1794.

◆ ◆ ◆

Several identifiable factors, some unique, some universal, shape civil religion in New Zealand. Because recent generations fail to appreciate the source of their dignity and freedom, they are taken for granted. New Zealanders have been led to believe that faith and reason are opposites rather than complementary and that religious faith has no connection to evidence. Indeed, many of us are unsure where the evidence fits into anything. Many young people take up contemporary causes so quickly because they are driven more by ideology than evidence. Another significant difference is that, traditionally, freedom was modified by restraint and the belief that one could find the strength to do what one thought was right. The new freedom is not true freedom. The state might attempt to make the world align with human desires. But it is a fantasy. Freedom in the real world is undermined by freedom from the fantasy world.

While we're on the subject of fantasy, I remember when the Ministry of Education seemed seduced by a particular philosophy of self-actualisation. It's still lurking under the covers, luring the unsuspecting. Anyway, the idea was that a group of teachers would go away for a few days, somewhere quiet, to talk about their dreams and frustrations, perhaps even encounter a spiritual experience. Not that we had any idea what a spiritual experience might be. The process had a name, but it has slipped my mind. Ah, yes, I remember. They were called T-groups, sometimes referred to as encounter groups. We were supposed to learn more about ourselves from each other, a sharing of our vulnerability and desires. That we were indulging in some parody of Christian confession didn't come to mind. Assisted by the odd glass of wine, and the still novel ideology of sexual liberation, and if you were fortunate enough to have a compliant, attractive member of the opposite sex to confess to, slipping between the sheets for the evening was not difficult. For some, there was more to share than one's mind. Maybe that's because our first exercise in wisdom involved each participant declaring what kind of animal he or she would like to be to the group. After all, freedom is best expressed in self-actualisation. I remember the last day when some participants seemed unusually quiet, even sheepish. I don't recall anyone saying they were excited by the manufactured intimacy. Whatever the case, the therapy courses disappeared after a few years; perhaps they were too expensive to run.

Bogus Spirituality

"Lilies that fester smell far worse than weeds."
Shakespeare. *Sonnets.* 1609.

New Zealand is returning to natural religion, creating an esoteric blend of feeling and pagan intuition, which it breathlessly calls 'spirituality.' This nebulous but widespread phenomenon commits nobody to anything. Like the old Roman religions, it demands submission to ritual without offering moral guidance. A civil religion does this by not requiring an individual to be personally responsible, only obedient to the civil religion's ritual. The biblical declaration that a believer's union with God determines how we should treat each other no longer determines the health of civil society. Instead, concerns about the pervasive fragility of mental health overwhelm the practice of virtue; what we feel becomes much more important than what we believe or think. Indeed, it has become challenging to question the feelings of others in serious discussions; ideas of dignity, freedom, and identity are always fraught with an anxious complexity, like nakedness used to be.

All kinds of esoterica can be called spiritual, making rational conversation impossible. With the loss of an educated faith and the moral restraints it gave life to, it was more or less inevitable that the sexual revolution would morph into its contemporary obsession with sexual and racial identity. In the de-Christianised world, sexual proclivity and race became the two foundational markers of identity. And bubbling away in the background, the latest incarnation of Marxism has already transferred its notion of oppressor/oppressed from class to race. The entire syncretic affair becomes what it has always secretly been: a civil religion. On the one hand, we have arrived at a belief in the supreme dignity of the individual. On the other hand, the state must describe and control that dignity. It is the mirage of freedom.

A complicating factor is that the theory of biculturalism in New Zealand is compromised by multicultural doctrine. The annexation of a benign biculturalism by critical theory and its offspring from the United States, critical race theory, has given rise to the demand for co-governance. Discussions about our history, which were carried out in a reasonably civilised way, have become muddled. And in that muddle, the voice of the disenchanted gets louder. The intrusion of critical race theory into the national bi-cultural debate raises the temperature but reduces the clarity. Discussion around the Treaty of Waitangi is made all the more difficult by accusations of racism and anti-racism dogma that have their roots in critical race theory rather than any tension that might be implicit in biculturalism. With a heady mix of subjectivism and chronological snobbery, the past must be judged only by contemporary and, therefore, presumptive and enlightened ethical sensitivities. Rather than looking back without prejudice on New Zealand's history, we are encouraged to see race relations simplistically, within the already mentioned overreaching paradigm of the oppressor versus the oppressed. Without the knowledge necessary to defend tradition, even a rudimentary understanding of history, particularly empire and colonialism, and basic biblical knowledge, many young people are convinced that we live in a world where the primary moral value is to protect their perception of the oppressed against the oppressor. It is the foundation of youthful altruism and an excellent example of what a civil religion does: politics shapes morality. Well, the politics of the young, certainly.

An editorial in the *New Zealand Herald* (21/10/24), *"Māori culture—a national pride or national inconvenience?"* reflected the conflation of Treaty of Waitangi issues with a mystifying potpourri of critical theory, aggressive biculturalism, and multiculturalism. All of this is in the context of confusion surrounding the distinction between religion and culture. The editorial claims:

> *"Replete with the desire to uplift all our people . . . based on the Treaty of Waitangi, biculturalism recognises the unique partnership between Māori and the crown . . . it will enrich everyone by acknowledging the Indigenous people of Aotearoa, whose culture forms the foundation of our national identity."*

Biculturalism is not based on the Treaty of Waitangi. Biculturalism is a theory independent of the Treaty that is used to support a particular interpretation of the Treaty. The culture of Aotearoa's indigenous people cannot be the foundation of any national identity. Religion is the foundation of identity; culture is the superstructure for its expression. Whether s/he understands it or not, the writer of the *Herald* editorial means that the religion of our indigenous people forms the foundation of our national identity. But, of course, s/he can't say that because we wouldn't accept that the Māori religion is our foundation, not yet. Perhaps the writer doesn't understand the importance of making the distinction, so the issue is fudged by calling religion culture. Culture, particularly that of an indigenous people, in the context of cultural relativism, is difficult to criticise, while religion, even indigenous religion, doesn't get the same free ride.

The Herald article reveals the most delicious irony. The Treaty of Waitangi was influenced by a sympathetic understanding of Indigenous people's dignity, guided by evangelical Christianity, which was influential at the time and profoundly dependent on the Bible's explanation of human nature. However, the writer of the Herald article seems to think that the Treaty should replace the Bible as the nation's foundational religious document—not only the Treaty but also his or her particular spin on it. That is a critical issue because the Treaty's status and meaning will always depend on the time's prevailing historical and cultural sensitivities. The writer of the Herald article seems to be advocating an awkward syncretism of a revised Marxism, cultural relativism, and what looks like a manufactured mysticism.

We continue to be told *ad nauseam* that we must celebrate 'diversity' despite the ideology's clay feet. In the real world, as religious conviction changes, people pick and choose which aspects of their culture they want to keep and discard those they don't. Multiculturalism is a modern Western affectation in which people enjoy the fruits of tradition and technology while disdaining the foundation, the historical events, and the great minds that produced them. The double-mindedness intrinsic to multiculturalism has led to an unwillingness to examine the assumptions controlling much of our contemporary legislation around identity and human rights claims. Appeals to diversity and inclusion are not that at all. They are actually about exclusion and the imposition of a new religion. DIE might begin with a plea for tolerance, but will continually morph into the demand for affirmation. The celebration of diversity must always play fast and loose with history in case the cultic and parasitic nature of the ideology is discovered. Neither biculturalism nor multiculturalism possesses the necessary cement to be a foundation for anything. At best, they are theories about how we might get along. Attempts to base human rights laws on them can only lead to perceptions of increasing injustice, as they will always be captive to the frustrations of identity politics.

The refusal to accept that religion determines culture muddies political knowledge—the biblical declaration remains the only authority that sensibly declares the permanence of human dignity. The fundamental freedom has to be freedom of religious belief and expression. Some might prefer to call it freedom of thought or conscience, but that is not quite the same because freedom of thought and conscience only makes sense in the context of an already established dignity. In the West, an emphasis on culture at the expense of the biblical story turns culture into a religion that always encourages a superficial understanding of history. Marx's superficial dismissal of religion is an excellent example of how culture is disconnected from religion, only to be replaced by the presumed neutrality of secularism, which is a replacement religion. It's the religion that controls the way we think about the world and ourselves while believing we don't have one. Culture becomes a de facto religion.

In New Zealand, the critical role of missionaries in the early nineteenth century is frequently overlooked or even suppressed. The enormous impact that Christianity had on the Māori mind and spirit is misunderstood and therefore devalued. The early nineteenth-century conversion of Māori to Christianity must be one of the Gospel's remarkable success stories. Despite that, the advocates of multiculturalism and decolonisation would have Māori adopt their version of sanitised pantheism. A revised and sentimentalised religious mythology is the glue that would give civil religion prestige and ceremonial drama. All this is achieved by claiming to respect Māori culture for its own sake, despite the hypocrisy of the secular state using it to its own ends.

The encroaching version of romanticised pantheism is a godsend for those who would de-Christianise the culture and the most convenient of bedfellows for the advocates of identity politics. A sympathetic, if superficial, understanding of Māori religion and culture alone cannot lead to the radical demand for co-governance. Instead, it is sustained by the entrenchment of critical race theory, a superficial understanding of colonialism, and the conviction that all cultures are equal. It doesn't matter whether the contrived foundation for co-governance is the consequence of devious planning or simply the result of a hollowed-out Christianity giving way to pantheism's return. Either way, the result is a divided nation that the political process is expected to heal;

Rousseau revisited. This manufactured expectation of salvation by state fiat embeds civil religion even more. The loss of Christian prayer in English at public events, replaced by untranslated karakia, should be a clue. It's difficult for anyone to discern whether we are listening to a traditional recitation or a hybrid form of pantheism, whether the prayer is addressed to the biblical God or a pagan deity. The way we have come to observe Anzac Day should be a clue. It appears to be a move toward worshipping a pagan deity, with no clergyman in sight.

◆ ◆ ◆

During the 1950s, I played the bugle in my school band. With our combination of sharp uniforms, conscientiously polished instruments, and youthfulness, we were popular performers at Anzac Day ceremonies, experts on the *Last Post* and *Reveille*. A local cleric frequently acknowledged how the sacrifice of the 'Fallen' echoed Christ's sacrifice on the Cross. Encouraged to be thankful, gratitude was the prevailing mood of the day. Some of those Anzac Day speeches still reverberate in my mind nearly seventy years later. The established civil religion would have us think very differently about the *Fallen*. Sacrifice no longer carries with it that sweet perfume of the eternal.

The substitute spirituality of civil religion replaces the Christian vision of the sacred with that of a resacralised natural world. Mountains, rivers, and trees are imbued with spirits under the ubiquitous banner of inviolate indigeneity. Revelation no longer guides us, and religious sensitivities have become dependent on the increasingly authoritative psychology of feeling. So, the purloined mythical deities increase their influence over the human body, the private mind, and the public's moral imagination. DIE's triumvirate strengthens its sovereignty through identity propaganda, while pantheistic public rituals, ceremonies, and safe and sacred places are created first with government approval and then with government imposition. The religion's dogma is transmitted through the public education system from kindergarten to university. It gives rise to gods and other benefactors to maintain social order, prosperity, and widespread mental well-being. If I believed the weather reporters on TV1, *Mother Nature* now controls the weather.

We have been warned. Marxism acted like a civil religion in the Soviet Union because it was, and in China, posters of the great leader used to be everywhere. China is now a dark example of unrestrained state control and sweeping surveillance. We should not be surprised that the necessarily expansive Chinese version of civil religion is progressively trying to take control of the Chinese Church, including the thousands of underground churches. Civil religion must become the depository and purveyor of truth, at whatever stage of its development; even the United Kingdom, the cradle of parliamentary democracy, appears to be in trouble.

The *Communist Manifesto,* following Nietzsche, tells us that the Holy has been profaned. A good thing, too, Nietzsche would say: his Superman transcends Christian weakness. God is dead at last, and even better, we have killed him. Prometheus is unbound, so the energy has been released for us to embrace the new civil religion. Well, it's not new; it's just, as I've claimed, a return to the old gods. Two lines from *Delores,* a poem by the would-be Prometheus, A.C. Swinburne (1839-1909), are appropriate:

What ailed us, O gods, to desert you
For creeds that refuse and restrain?

Before the old gods could return, the seeds of identity politics had to mature. It was critical that Christianity not be considered superior. It, too, had to join the ranks of the relativised to weaken any traditional authority it might have. The *creeds that refuse and restrain* had to be levelled.

Maybe this is where I dare say that the political Left has finally left behind its Fabian-inspired version of democratic socialism. The reincarnated 'inclusive' Left and paganism have now entered into a union with all the joyless authority of a sexless marriage; it's difficult to distinguish the bride from the groom. Whatever the case, together, they would encourage the widespread acceptance of diverse religions except Christianity, which calls into question civil religion's creeping omnipresence and intimations of omnipotence. By conflating Western Civilisation and tribal cultures under the broad heading of culture, the dominance of the newlyweds' union is assured. It's now difficult to even discuss 'civilisation' because doing so might imply one's cultural superiority over others. Like the worship of an ancient deity, each culture is encouraged to consider its identity sacrosanct. A state of mind now exists that makes it challenging to claim what everyone once knew: Christianity is Western civilisation's foundation. Indeed, it's even worse that so many of us are so ignorant about our roots that we don't know where to begin any discussion. With the loss of the biblical declaration of human dignity, the Christian theology of the body is misunderstood, devalued, and then derided.

Because the secular civil religion has absorbed Māori mythology into its pantheon of spirits, it isn't easy to talk meaningfully about the human being as an embodied spirit. The spiritual and material unity of body and mind, including the Christian belief in the resurrection of the body, is denied. Secular sovereignty gains its contrived mystique from a resurgent paganism. In *sotto voce,* it would swamp us with interminable pantheistic waffle about spirituality. Those who continue to hope for a benign co-governance will be disappointed. If a sense of injustice does motivate the ideology, it will not have the wherewithal to restrain increasing state power.

The marriage between secularism and the revival of the Māori religion is a ceremonial necessity. Māori religion is given increasing status, and the secular state purloins ceremonial gravitas from its ritual. It doesn't matter whether we understand that or not. It's probably better that we don't. Indeed, we mustn't. Otherwise, the vacuousness of cultural relativism would become apparent, and the victory of paganism over Christianity would become suspect. We are not just attending to a shift in the political barometer. As a nation, we declare that we have a new vision that is not religious, despite its origins. Over 200 years of history have been an aberration, and our understanding needs serious revision. As the Herald editorial says, our roots are in the culture of Māori religion. Every public event, from university graduation ceremonies to the coronation of the Māori Queen, must be celebrated by Māori ritual. The tradition that gave rise to the concept of 'university' is ignored. We are following Nietzsche and Marx, and the 'English Flatheads' who are doing nothing more than changing one religion for another.

◆ ◆ ◆

The upstart civil religion fudges the biblical declaration of the unity of body and spirit by preaching the authority and power of self-creation while controlling just what self-creation might mean. The Christian doctrine that emphasises the oneness of body, mind, and spirit, and the resurrection of the body, is anathema to secularised pantheism. Monogamy, the gift that early Christians brought to the Roman Empire, is discarded because its foundation is denied. It suits the mishmash of civil religion to support the new sexuality as it dissolves the union of body and mind, encouraging a person to become detached from his or her body so s/he can say, "*I am trapped in the wrong body. My body is not the real me.*" Consequently, the body can be manipulated to appease the civil religion's psycho/political needs.

We need a total 'reset' that is not dissimilar from what the French revolutionaries wanted to create: a new age, a new calendar, and a new deity. Changing New Zealand's name to Aotearoa is a reasonable and natural choice. It might look like a concession to Māori when it is a revolutionary requirement of civil religion. We have seriously weakened the foundation on which any criticism of transhumanism might rest. Technology will increasingly become a master rather than a servant, because it will be controlled by that elite that C.S. Lewis warned us about. The demand for freedom will prove illusory, and some men (a self-proclaimed priesthood) will control everybody else.

So to recap, in Aotearoa, civil religion is an awkward and sometimes subconscious attempt to synthesise neo-Marxism, critical theory, critical race theory, and identity politics. Alongside that, we have a growing hostility towards our colonial past while manipulating the mythology of Māori religion by downplaying the impact of nineteenth-century Christianity. We are strongly encouraged to see Māori oppressed and united when, in fact, they are forced to fight their own religious/cultural war between those who would retain the influence of Christianity and those who would return to their pagan gods. Racism is not the issue. The charge of racism is essentially a tool to gain political ascendancy. The real battle is between two religions, two different visions of human meaning.

In the context of cultural relativism, the rising status of the pre-Christian Māori religion is opportune because it doesn't stand in the way of the state's sovereignty as Christianity does. Civil religion pretends to be an agreeable fusion of state and religious authority, with Caesar on both sides of every coin. The claim is frequently made that Aotearoa is entering into a long-awaited and just political partnership. In reality, a selective version of Māori religion is being used by activists and an overreaching bureaucracy to give the secular thinness of multicultural dogma its ceremonial solemnity. For example, the increasingly intrusive inclusion of Māori words in English texts by the Ministry of Education looks more like coercion than teaching. Furtive attempts to make a ceremonial tool of a language that most New Zealanders do not understand create a mystique that is challenging to criticise. There are several good cultural and even utilitarian reasons for learning Māori, but they are undermined by bureaucratic obfuscation, and the pervasive charge of racism is too quickly made against critics. Indeed, the language of anti-racism becomes a weapon to defend the mysteries of the civil religion. For example, public festivals and cultural markers no longer concentrate on giving thanks to an omnipotent deity. They are more about learning to accept and live in harmony with the immanent gods of nature.

The proposed new opaque standards of competence for registered nursing from the Nursing Council of New Zealand (Oct.2024, Para 1) are civil religion in action:

> *"Enrolled nurses in Aotearoa New Zealand reflect the knowledge, concepts, and worldviews of both Tangata whenua and Tangata Tiriti. They uphold and enact ngā mātāpono principles of Te Tiriti o Waitangi, based on the Kawa Whakaruruhau framework and cultural safety, promoting equity, inclusion, diversity, and the rights of Māori as Tangata Whenua. These concepts also relate to Pacific peoples and all population groups to support quality services that are culturally safe and responsive."*

Cultural relativism is the underlying ideology. What is 'cultural safety' that would promote *"equity, inclusion, diversity, and the rights of Māori as Tangata Whenua"*? Is it just the imposition of cultural relativism or something else? And with the intellectual ambition of a teenage protester, 'knowledge, concepts and world views' are put into one bag to beat us about the head. It might look like a defence of Māori culture. It is, in fact, a replacement of Christianity, which has historically informed beliefs about the nature of care for centuries, with pre-Christian Māori religion, directed by secular theory that promotes diversity, inclusion, and equity.

The Nursing Council statement can only be understood in the context of a civil religion. *Tangata whenua and Tangata Tiriti* do not hold compatible worldviews. *Tangata whenua* describes a race; more precisely, 'people of the land'. *Tangata Tiriti* is a political concept with Christian roots. Introducing Māori phrases such as *kawa whakaruruhau* and *nga matapono* is little more than a pretentious attempt to muddy the water. The Nursing Council is hiding in a shoddy syncretism it hardly understands. It suggests that a fusion of Christianity with Māori religion is compatible and fundamental to nursing. Neither of these claims is true. Pre-Christian Māori religion and Christianity are miles apart in their understanding of what it means to be human and how we should care for each other. They can only be presumed compatible by secular duplicity, which would deny both, giving duplicity a moral authority above criticism.

Another significant and revealing event that should be mentioned in the context of 'nature's gods' is the introduction of Matariki as a public holiday. One leading advisor to the government on the holiday, Dr. Rangi Matamua, sees the festival as an opportunity to renew and honour the old Māori gods. He would like to see a revival of the ancient Māori religion in post-colonial New Zealand. In 2022, the official ceremony marking the establishment of Matariki as a public holiday included karakia to the Matariki deities. Here's a small, translated example. (see *Mānawatia a Matariki* online):

> *Behold Pohutukawa*
> *Who carries the dead of the year*
> *Scatter their spirits into the cosmos*
> *You have now become stars.*

So, it's not only the 'Romancers of the Primitive' who would paganise New Zealand. A Māori constituency, perhaps small but noisy, is also on the way towards establishing a pagan narrative for Aotearoa.

The faithful believer insists on a complete rewriting. Everything has to be seen through the lens of civil religion. That Christianity might resonate more with some Māori than others is either ignored or deliberately hidden. This observer witnesses a struggle between Christian Māori and those who seek to return to the pagan gods. Only time will reveal the winner.

The substitute spirituality of civil religion must exchange the Christian vision of the sacred with that of a resacralised natural world. Sacred spaces will proliferate. In the ether of identity politics, rational criticism is silenced by attempts to create a new mythology for the emerging Aotearoa. Clarity must be kept at arm's length. One suspects that the effort to create a new mythology will be an unintentional parody imitating Virgil's attempt to give Rome its foundational mythology in the *Aeneid*. It's hard to imagine that any contemporary attempt to do so could have the poetic power and grandeur of the *Aeneid*. For example, having neither a historical nor a sensible identity, Te Pati Māori is little more than a parliamentary parody of Māori pre-Christian religion and culture.

Totalitarian Civil Religion

Under the banner of civil religion, the working dynamic between the citizen and the state is dramatically reversed. To sharpen the point, a civil religion must control how we think about the family home. When it was the last sanctuary, bringing up children was the most important thing a parent or society could do. The family was, without any doubt, the primary institution of identity and civil society. However, the state now defines the home; it is conditioned and limited by factors relating to business, technology, control

233

over how we spend our money, and state legislation. That loss of reasonable and benign autonomy should be apparent to anyone my age. However, not everyone is an octogenarian, so permit me to explain.

As the state increases its control over the people who work for it and in business by increasing regulation, parents now find themselves in the invidious position of having less and less control over their children. The state increasingly controls the morality that is taught in schools, and it tells parents what they should think about the Treaty of Waitangi and what they should say to their children about sex. As the state's moral authority increases and parental authority erodes, *"TikTok pulls the heartstrings,"* one commentator said. The old model of civil society, described either by the Protestant theory of sphere sovereignty or the Catholic notion of subsidiarity, has been eroded by state mandates (the COVID-19 fiasco, for example), media advocacy, and, most recently, commercial activism—all 'denominations' of civil religion. Civil society institutions, the family, and the Church, which once protected individuals from government overreach, have been weakened. The intergenerational family, the bulwark that protects an individual's identity and the major institution of civil society, must be undermined by civil religion.

The increasing penetration of identity politics makes it possible and even necessary for civil religion to teach the doctrine of intersectionality—the replacement of civil society by ensuring that an individual's tribal identity is not disadvantaged by sex, race, religion, gender, sexuality, disability, ethnicity, or even physical appearance. Dignity is discovered and completed only through the self-expression of tribal identity. Consequently, every identity must be given its due respect and status; failure to consider that results in unjust discrimination and privilege.

Unlike Christianity's victory over exhausted Roman paganism, civil religion is in rebellion against the democratic process and the God who gave us our dignity. Whatever one might think of Christianity today, it is a confessional faith shared by believers; it's a grassroots affair. The moral and social cohesion of that faith benefited everyone. Aotearoa's civil religion does not do that; it has two prophets: one teaches the Church to embrace identity politics, and one who teaches an elite priesthood determined to reorder reality according to ideological constraints. It involves not just the rejection of the traditional ethic but also the metaphysics, aesthetics, and, indeed, the epistemology of Western civilisation. Alongside its rejection of Christian ethics, it's even incapable of understanding the Greek philosophy of Stoic discipline that appealed to the Roman temperament. Stoicism gave the Romans and Greeks a reason to be disciplined and the courage to resist the corruption that often characterised political power.

From Virtue to Values Revisited

It should be evident that I am reinforcing what I claimed in the introduction—a profound religious and cultural evacuation has occurred in my lifetime. Recalling Himmelfarb's analysis, our confidence in distinguishing right from wrong has been eroded by replacing virtue and character, which are observable, with abstract and subjective values. Tolerance and justice, for instance, now have entirely different meanings. Tolerance now demands that we affirm everything we tolerate, while justice has evolved into social justice. Favouring children's desires and encouraging their preferences have replaced the discipline of traditional morality and character development. It's nearly sixty years since Marcuse wrote the remarkably pretentious *A Critique of Pure Tolerance.* His idea of tolerance is now the impostor's 'virtue' that sustains the entire social justice anti-discrimination paraphernalia.

To clarify the context, I have already talked about how the Christian sexual revolution in the first few centuries introduced the biblical concept of sin to the Romans and how it applied to everyone, including the paterfamilias. People began to believe more confidently that virtue was evident and observable in day-to-day human behaviour; there was a definite connection between what one considers a human being to be and personal behaviour. Without virtue describing character, we tend to collapse into the kind of banality illustrated by the school mottos already listed.

Risking the charge of sexism, indeed challenging that charge, it's worthwhile pointing out that 'virtue' comes from the Latin word *vertus,* from *vir,* the word for man, which initially meant warrior. It's not that warriors are in demand today, except perhaps on the rugby league field. Nevertheless, courage remains critical for everyone and essential to any concept of manliness and womanliness, especially to manliness. When a country is at war, both sexes will understand that very well if we don't. Like all the other virtues, it inspires and boosts perseverance. And, by the way, courageous men are essential for a free and just society. One of the best ways to encourage a young man to be courageous is to teach him about the nature of responsibility and give it to him. The contemporary tendency to extend adolescence into the mid-twenties helps no one. A young man, especially if he has children, must learn that much of his life will involve sacrifice if he is to be a man worthy of the name. He does not have the advantage of the young woman who would appear to have much of the responsibility of sacrifice built into her biology.

Echoing C.S. Lewis, the civil religion's theft of the dignity that would give us courage eats the heart out of its host's civilisation and demands that it still functions. For example, the overreaching version of human rights discrimination law would inhibit simple discernment and the courage to express it in a hostile environment. The gap between the individual's power to discern and the anti-discrimination demands of the group is ignored by a civil religion—the power of discernment described and taught by Christianity is overwhelmed by concepts of legal discrimination. The discernment required to understand each individual's dignity is negated by the primacy of tribal identity. The charge of racism is always waiting to pounce. If tribal membership is identity's foundation, the idea of legal discrimination must control the way we think about each other.

Civil religion, by nature, must be about power and social engineering. Once all the hype is dissolved, its foundation sinks into the swamp of bold assertion. Its ambition is not to have a free and just society, but one where everything must serve its dogma. Even here, there is no consistency. Rules and laws can be changed or suspended by the principles and regulations of multiculturalism's human rights theory and its criteria for redistributing those rights. Over the last decade, even the restraints and realities of biology have been questioned within the context of the new religion.

Although the new 'realities' or 'values' are impossible to defend, it's unnecessary to do so because the priesthood of the established civil religion is so confident and self-righteous that it sees no need to legitimise itself. How is it possible to rationally defend a vague value such as diversity? The consequence of turning an adjective into a noun should be obvious. We can sensibly talk about a diverse population, but when diversity becomes dogma, thinking becomes muddled. The old customs and laws regulating marriage, family life, sexual behaviour, and, indeed, what it means to be a human being are constantly demeaned, stereotyped, and silenced. The condemnation of tradition, evident in the Stanford student protest, is now fully grown. The civil religion establishes the curriculum, writes the exams, supervises progress, and grades the papers. There can be no recount.

Sin's Surrogate

Although low on any concept of forgiveness, civil religion, with its imitation of the Pharisaic priesthood, has its growing list of sins. Of course it has. The Polish writer, philosopher, and Member of the European Parliament since 2009, Ryszard Legutko, gives us a helpful list: *misogyny, sexism, racism, homophobia, transphobia, islamophobia, Eurocentrism, phallocentrism, logocentrism, ageism, binarism, populism, nationalism, xenophobia, hate speech, Euroscepticism, white supremacy, and misgendering.* Doubtless, there are more.[4]

Again, Lewis is helpful here. He points out that modern ethical innovations are merely isolated and exaggerated fragments of natural law and the virtues that arise from it. Let's examine two 'fragments' from Legutko's list: racism and sexism. Both are isolated, deconstructed wrongs or evils, stemming from the biblical source of human dignity and the commandments that tell us to love our neighbour as ourselves. The charge of racism or sexism might have some temporary corrective value, but it will prove to be limited. Because both sexism and racism are deconstructed and political versions of Christian virtue, they will have no power to influence the human heart. The state must enforce their validity. One is not encouraged to love one's neighbour but rather to fear whoever that neighbour might be. A law that dictates how to treat one's neighbour undermines the satisfying dynamic of human relationships. It's a significant step backwards because we have known for centuries that the law cannot make us good. The charge of sexism or racism will never change anyone's heart. When Christ told the rich young ruler that the first two commandments were the foundation of all morality, He was not making a suggestion.

It should be evident that the values listed above by Legutko are secular and politicised versions of biblical virtues filtered through the lens of identity politics, which has nothing to hang its categories on without the purloined biblical concept of dignity. Such deconstruction will ultimately fail to empower the private conscience. The prevention of sexism or racism, whether real or imagined, will always need government control. The primary difference between Christianity and civil religion is that civil religion will always need to devise increasingly effective mechanisms to control behaviour. Christianity will point to its roots. We should not be surprised that young university-educated students, ignorant of their heritage, frequently become DIE's fundamentalist evangelists.

With naked and unashamed hubris, Aotearoa's civil religion has its self-authenticating creedal statements: *I believe in Diversity, I believe in Inclusion, and I believe in Equity,* thereby making nearly everyone a hypocrite. Hamlet may well have thought that his conscience made him a coward. Multiculturalism is proving to be the contemporary catalyst of cowardice. A civil religion would force us to operate as though the secularised rules of primitive society and Western civilisation are reconcilable when we know they are not. Civil religion can only encourage a belief in Romantic Primitivism,[5] a state of being that never was, for a utopia that never will be. Everyone is forced to live in the chaos of ambiguous fantasy. Those who manage to find their way through the chaos must be heretics. Perhaps we should have a replacement anthem:

> *We believe in diversity*
> *We believe in inclusion*
> *We believe in equity.*
> *And we're coming for your children*
> *They can be their true selves*
> *Together, we can all fulfil our potential.*
> *Together, Together, Together, Yeh! Yeh! Yeh!*

Notes:

1. Michael Walsh. *The Devil's Pleasure Palace.* Encounter Books. 2015. Page. 39.

2. Proudhon, Pierre-Joseph. *What is Property?* Ed. Donald R Kelly and Bonnie G Smith, 1994, OUP.

3. The British historian Tom Holland makes the point that the concept of religion, as we tend to use it today, is a Western secular invention, a result of its overarching hegemony. In the ancient world, life spun around which gods were worshipped. Life was religion. Religion was life. Secular thought, assuming the primacy of reason, was able to categorise and separate culture from religion.

4. Legutko, Ryszard. *The Demon in Democracy: Totalitarian Temptations in Free Societies.* Encounter Books, 2016. p.6.

5. Sandall, Roger. *The Culture Cult: Designer tribalism and Other Essays.* Westview. 2001. Pp 47-49.

IX

Education and Civil Religion

There is something which unites magic and applied science while separating both from the wisdom of earlier ages. For the wise men of old the cardinal problem had been how to conform the soul to reality, and the solution had been knowledge, self-discipline, and virtue. For magic and applied science alike the problem is how to subdue reality to the wishes of men.

C.S. Lewis. The Abolition of Man

Education will always be plagued by ambiguity and fantasy when a civil religion matures because it must replace traditional education with propaganda. That replacement must take place because civil religion is neither natural nor revealed. Reality will be reordered to yield to the wishes of men and women, or at least some men and some women. In a declining democracy, this tendency often leads the government to vacillate between being a tyrant and a sugar daddy, adopting the latter role for as long as necessary to please the constituency and remain in power. When the democratic process becomes unworkable, it's tyranny all the way to control the increasing lawlessness. In a ludicrous anti-climax, the sugar daddy and democracy die whimpering under the tyrant's foot.

While civil religion continues to deny its Achilles' heel of subjectivism, the old culture's artistic and technological creative inventiveness slowly declines because scientific method is compromised. Only research that confirms state dogma will be funded because the priesthood of the civil religion determines value. They imitate the nineteenth-century utilitarians' fantasy, who thought that Christianity's practical value would be retained without God. Indeed, it will be worse. At least the nineteenth-century utilitarians thought they knew what they were doing. They still had some knowledge of the theology they were rejecting. So, we should not be surprised that civil religion devalues everything that has gone before. For example, denying the Sublime diminishes any chance we might have to experience awe or reverence. Ultimately, nothing is left to inhibit egotism, and everyone begins to think that he or she is the centre of the universe. It's more than reasonable to suggest that awe and reverence are essential to scientific method if it is to be applied productively.

We are condemned to live out an incoherent resurrection of a new paganism and an atheistic religion based on secular theory. A brief look at the so-called New Atheists—Sam Harris, Richard Dawkins, Daniel Dennett, and Christopher Hitchens—might be helpful. Convinced that a universally objective and secular moral standard is always open to revision, they lack the grandeur of the old atheists like Nietzsche and the poignancy of Sartre. They argue that reason does not need faith. Reason alone can discover and describe both good and evil.

Christopher Hitchens is a compelling exception because he always opposed abortion. His mother terminated a pregnancy that would have given Hitchens a sister, and that remained a 'disappointment' for him until he died. The intimacy of personal experience would seem to overwhelm the alleged power of reason, in Hitchens' case at least.

The New Atheists (not so new now) may well say they don't believe in God, but the god they don't believe in has to be the god of their creation. They might consider that atheism in Western civilisation is a justified disenchantment with the biblical God. Richard Dawkins' superficial condemnation of the story of Abraham and Isaac in Genesis 22 is a revealing example of that misleading disenchantment. He imposes his concept of a cruel God on the story, condemning Him, missing entirely the Old Testament's description of God's character, its explanation of sacrifice, and the drama of faith in a sovereign and merciful God. The provision of a ram caught in the bush not only looks forward to Christ's sacrifice but also reminds Abraham that child sacrifice, common in his day, is forbidden by God.

One cannot talk intelligently about God or deny his existence if one does not already have an idea of who a god might be or who God is. Making sense of the divine is challenging if we reject revelation as a category of knowledge. God reveals Himself to us, or we invent our own god—or, more accurately, gods. Eventually, rejecting the Biblical God encourages the drift into the new paganism, which would entrench secular universalism and lose its grip on the rational. A glimmer of the loss from that rejection might be seen in Richard Dawkins' recent admission that he considers himself a cultural Christian. He implicitly admits there is no value-neutral space rooted in reason on which a culture might be established. Although he believes Christian doctrine is nonsense, Dawkins would still much rather live in a Christian culture than one informed by Islam.[1]

Whether intentional or unintentional, schools have become instruments of propaganda. I have already considered J.S. Mill's suspicion of state education and its outcome. Children must learn that the old theme of Western civilisation, equality before the law, is not enough. The real world is saturated with glaring inequalities that must be resolved by rearranging social and legal order to achieve equality of outcome. A total reordering of what justice means is necessary. A brief examination of current primary school mottos is revealing. There is an assumption that inclusion, an essential social justice component, is a primary moral value, even a latter-day cardinal virtue. Some local primary schools display these little gems at their entrance. We have "Learning together to be the best we can be." "Growing excellence together." "Being different, belonging together." "Your bright future will start here." And the inevitable, "Believe in yourself."

Many of these schools may be good schools with excellent teachers. But why do their mottos have to reflect such a mind-numbing ersatz morality? If these mottos reflect what is happening in schools, offering children positive and confident guidance will become increasingly challenging. Conviction about right and wrong becomes embarrassing. Indeed, a fear of being excluded would make cowards of us all. The best a teacher can do is judge an action as either inappropriate or appropriate. S/he is continuously forced to check the terms that describe reality. The ground underfoot is always swampy.

◆ ◆ ◆

Freedom and justice have been foundational to Western civilisation for centuries. We have consistently recognised that glaring inequalities are caused by a range of evident and hidden factors in the real world. Realising the issue's complexity, the law did its best to be just. But that, it would seem, is not enough any longer. We now want social justice, often with great passion but little clarity. We want equity—equality of outcomes. However, the demand for equity is not a refinement of traditional justice. It is an entirely different concept and is being taught to our children in various ways. For example, to ensure equity, the Ministry of Education, under the leadership of Jacinda Ardern as Prime Minister, diligently attempted to integrate Mātauranga Māori with scientific method. The *School Curriculum Refresh*, scheduled for release in phases until 2027 by her government and still in place, is a clear example of this concerted effort to entrench social justice into a civil religion.

> *"Te Tiriti and its principles provide the vision and mandate for New Zealanders to exercise their mutual responsibilities to each other. Giving effect to Te Tiriti and its principles through a refreshed school curriculum creates an inclusive learning platform for all ākonga to participate in and enjoy an education that extends every learner's open-ended potential, produces success in multiple forms, and enables the fulfilment of lifelong ambitions and dreams. Knowing who we are, where we come from, and what makes us unique as a country will enable a more confident international outlook that extends within and beyond*

our Pacific locality to the global opportunities offered across the world. New Zealand's vision for education is grounded in New Zealanders' aspirations for education. Through giving effect to Te Tiriti and its principles, it aims to enable every New Zealander to learn and excel, to help their whānau and community thrive, and to build a productive and sustainable economy and an inclusive and caring society."[2]

If you managed to get through this torturous prose, you must have noticed the pretentious and opaque euphemism of a religious bureaucracy. It presumes that *Te Tiriti* is the foundation of human dignity. *"Te Tiriti and its principles provide the vision and mandate for New Zealanders to exercise their mutual responsibilities to each other."* No, they don't. All we have here is the theory of social justice reinforcing state sovereignty.

The Treaty has neither the depth nor the authority to sustain the writer's claim. Te Tiriti is just that, a treaty between the Crown and the Māori chiefs who signed it. The claim that its imagined principles *"can provide the vision and mandate for New Zealanders to exercise their mutual responsibility to each other"* is to turn it into a self-sustaining religious document, giving it more content and reverence than it can bear. Te Tiriti provides neither a vision nor a mandate. The only way you can find the 'vision' and 'mandate' within the Treaty is to read back into it what you think it should have said. The Treaty alone cannot be the foundation, although it is based on underlying principles. Most obviously, all human beings are equal before the law because their Creator has endowed them with dignity. That is why we have a *'mutual responsibility to each other,'* not because Te Tiriti gives it to us. It was the belief in a shared dignity and, consequently, 'mutual responsibility' that made the Treaty possible in the first place.

Like much civil religious dogma, the 'refreshing' of the *School Curriculum* is overladen with redundancy and tautology. For example, *"mutual responsibilities to each other"* and *"New Zealand's vision for education is grounded in New Zealanders' aspirations for education."* Swap "vision" and "aspiration" around; the vacuous sentence remains. Then we have, *"Through giving effect to Te Tiriti and its principles, it aims to enable every New Zealander to learn and excel, to help their whānau and community thrive, and to build a productive and sustainable economy and an inclusive and caring society."* This last opaque sentence reads back into the Treaty, a grab bag of contemporary concepts it cannot possibly bear. It seems like a mixture of ideas and words has been put into a bag, given a good shake, and poured onto the paper. It's a confused retrospective reading that would make an intelligent and honest interpretation of the Treaty almost impossible.

The 2023 change of government has yet to find a satisfactory replacement for the Refresh Curriculum. Civil religion is now so deeply embedded in government policy and bureaucratic psyche that it's difficult to know whether the Coalition Government will have the political will and depth of understanding to bring about necessary and permanent change. The Minister of Education has yet to articulate a clear vision, which would encourage confidence in the possibility of foundational change. And by foundational change, I mean a return to teachers as professional educators, not surrogate parents, and the recognition of parents as the primary protectors. Perhaps she will be encouraged by recent attempts to eliminate diversity, equity, and inclusion in the United States and the United Kingdom. Maybe the Year 7 to 13 English curriculum draft, released in April 2025, will go some way toward restoring literary and linguistic competence. But then again, perhaps not. It hasn't managed to jettison much of the educational jargon that gets in the way of clarity. All the king's soldiers are trying to put Humpty Dumpty together again. It's certainly a step in the right direction, although the English Teachers' Association doesn't seem to think so. Most recently, though, the promise of a total revamp of NCEA looks promising. We might see a return to a concentration on content rather than the current obsession with process.

◆ ◆ ◆

A brief examination of recent *Education Gazettes,* the official publication of the Ministry of Education, would encourage one to believe that the Swamp of Inclusion is getting deeper and broader. They are written with the hagiographic political enthusiasm of a Soviet poster from the 1950s; with better pictures of beautiful people doing beautiful things, they are replete with the banal language of propaganda. There is much chatter about aspiration but little about content. That, however, should not be a surprise. It is the necessary tool of every revolution to convince everyone that Utopia is just around the corner. The Gazette doesn't tell us what's happening daily in the classrooms. Developing attitudes of inclusion and skills to enforce them is the name of the game. The language of inclusion, diversity, and equity overrules. One publication (4/7/22), entitled *Advocates for Inclusion,* has:

"Akonga embrace relationships and sexuality education,
supporting sustainable hybrid learning practices and
digital citizenship in an age of disinformation."

Such pretentious political gobbledygook is indecipherable. A more recent edition of the *Gazette (10/11/24)* remains infatuated with propaganda about diversity and inclusion. Under an entirely new moral paradigm, the assumption seems to be that young people will learn the difference between right and wrong without specific guidance. Judith Butler's concept of 'performativity' hovers in the background, informing us about the real meaning of sexual identity. Under the heading of *'Keeping it relevant,'* we read this from an experienced teacher:

"We have been analysing sexuality in our community and
our society. We've been looking at consent, music and videos.
We've been looking at gaming. We went for a walk out into
the community and took photos of ads. We're looking at
pornography. We're looking at New Zealand culture and
looking at how sexuality is portrayed in those different
aspects. I'm trying to make it relevant to my students.
And what's surrounding them."

The first sentence gives the game away; the phrase *'analysing sexuality'* is loaded. It's Marcuse's *'repressive tolerance'* introduced into the classroom. Under the cover of teacher neutrality, children are learning to tolerate the intolerable and to be intolerant of their traditions. They are being taught to reorient their understanding of human nature learned in the home before it can mature. Christianity's decline has unleashed terrible new gods. All, however, might not be lost. The government's 2025 *Education and Training Amendment Bill* would make students' educational achievement the primary objective of school boards. Three other parallel objectives in the 2020 Act, which are that schools must be physically and emotionally safe environments, cater to different needs, and attend to the Treaty of Waitangi, have become secondary.

Academic Wokery, Civil Religion's Crusader

In July 2021, seven Auckland academics, including two retired professors, wrote a letter to the *New Zealand Listener* titled *In Defence of Science*. They claimed that indigenous knowledge *"falls far short of what can be defined as science itself."* The reaction of the University of Auckland's Vice-Chancellor (Dawn Freshwater) at the time was revealing. She claimed that the letter caused considerable *"hurt and dismay."* And that the views *"did not represent the views of the University of Auckland."* The academics were taking issue with the proposed changes to the Māori school curriculum, which said:

> *"Science has been used to support the dominance of Euro-centric views (among which, its use as a rationale for colonisation of Māori and the suppression of Māori knowledge), and the notion that science is a Western European invention is itself evidence of European dominance over Māori and other indigenous peoples."* [3]

The Vice-Chancellor's claim that the letter does not represent the university's views is puzzling. Does she mean that the proposed changes by the curriculum committee represent the university's views?

This raises a much more interesting question: Can a university have a view? Indeed, the language of *"hurt and dismay"* suggests it does. Indeed, it sounds more like the language of a liberal cleric than of a Vice-Chancellor.

A university used to have no prescribed view of what we should believe. Indeed, during my first year as an undergraduate, I was told ad nauseam that I was at university to learn how to think for myself. Until recently, a university was committed to free enquiry and rigorous debate. Indeed, that was its raison d'être back in the 1960s. The university was still a traditional institution that passed on what we might consider the best-accumulated knowledge. Alas, the new narrative of relativism and self-creation has consigned that to the nether regions.

The Auckland Vice-Chancellor's claim that the University has an established view on the current issue suggests that all who submit to the levelling of multicultural theory and science can somehow arrive at a permanent consensus. Neither permits open debate; they operate only by closing it down. Science, by its very nature, can never arrive at a consensus. Consensus is the language of politics and civil religion, not science. A university is not a church preaching revealed doctrine, although, in the context of civil religion, it might behave like one. It is an institution, well, it used to be, given to the support of scientific method, at the very least, in those faculties that have science in their name. The writers of the proposed curriculum, and it would seem the Vice-Chancellor too, make the grand error of the multiculturalist. They fudge the necessary distinction between the objectivity of scientific method and science as a school subject. Identifying scientific method with "Eurocentric views" is a category error; it is a constant that can be applied universally.

The condemned letter writers claim it is *"better to ensure everyone participates in the world's scientific enterprises. Indigenous knowledge may indeed help advance scientific knowledge in some ways, but it is not science."* Precisely. Science is a universal tool because it rests on the belief that the world is an ordered place, foundational to Western civilisation. Hypotheses can be imagined, experiments repeated, and the findings found to be true or false.

Māori religion before the introduction of the Christian gospel was pantheistic, even animistic; the gods were an extension of nature and not distinct from it. Without a coherent concept of the created order, there could be no foundation for establishing scientific method. Considering the road many universities now seem to be travelling down, it's ironic that they get their name from their belief in an ordered world. Would the VC have the university dominated by the cultic claim that Truth is the mere product of culture? Would she turn the traditional university into an institution, preaching the alleged truth of multicultural dogma?

◆ ◆ ◆

Auckland University continues its downward trend. No longer among the top 150 universities in the world by 2025, it has introduced a compulsory course for first-year students on the Treaty and Indigenous knowledge. It aims to *"dismantle the colonial, Eurocentric structures and knowledge systems that have historically dominated universities."* The aim is to 'decolonise' the subjects taught by the university. This represents a significant departure from the university's original purpose, which was to discover and understand the nature of truth. A compulsory course on indigenous knowledge, which is pantheistic and even animistic, would transform the university into a religious institution, like a wānanga. The university would become an institution that policed religious dogma. Its purpose will no longer be the pursuit of truth. Instead, it will become another arm of civil religion in action, teaching a religion.

When the University fails to fulfil its traditional function by ignoring its history, it becomes an institution interested only in survival, reinforcing Western civilisation's loss of confidence. Truth and, therefore, justice conform to a sliding scale determined by the evolving civil religion. The heart of the democratic process is cut out. It took a long time for the democratic nations to develop a system whereby religion and politics recognised each other's strengths and limitations. We might not have understood entirely Christ's *"Render unto Caesar the things that are Caesar's, and unto God, the things that are God's."* Nevertheless, it worked. We can only hold peaceful elections because the voters believe in a power higher than the state. It's worthwhile remembering that the working interdependence of church and state is a relatively recent invention of Western civilisation.

The university, caught up in the muddle of cultural relativism, is failing in its first duty to protect the truth, allowing civil religion to degrade, disgrace, and then destroy the memory of traditional Transcendence underpinning Western civilisation. Civil religion has no appetite for any examination of the claim that Western civilisation, sustained by Christianity, has evolved to permit government change without bloodshed. The rule of law, the institutions of civil society, the natural and intergenerational family, churches, mediating institutions, economic freedom, religious freedom, and freedom of speech, political and artistic freedom, which struggled for a long time to find their raison d'être in a historically Christian Western civilisation, are undermined.

◆ ◆ ◆

This octogenarian gets tired of hearing over and over again that Christianity is the major hindrance to progress. The truth is self-evident to anyone who takes our history seriously. Personal morality, the structures that support educational institutions, and human rights evolved from an education system informed by the Bible. Neither the Greeks nor Islam introduced science to us, as is frequently claimed. Any claim the Greeks might have had was compromised by their inability to break free from their mythology. It wasn't until Greek philosophy came into contact with the Biblical declaration that the world became a demystified, ordered place, and science became possible. Biblical knowledge fostered the belief in an ordered and rational universe, one that was open to systematic inquiry. That did not come from Islam or China. And to make a reasonable and revealing observation: the 480 million Muslims worldwide have been awarded six Nobel Prizes. Fifteen million Jews have been awarded one hundred and sixty-five. The Hebrew *Tanakh*, known to Christians as the Old Testament, must have had something to do with it. A knowledge of and respect for history and science are essential, and the ability to separate them from mythology is necessary to progress.[4]

We should not be surprised that university students, conditioned as they have been to devalue the past with their deficient historical knowledge, are convinced that colonisation, now pejoratively called colonialism, is an irredeemable moral evil rather than a recurring ancient and modern phenomenon. They cannot understand that their hatred of the British Empire is not rooted in any reasonable understanding of history. Instead, it lies in their misunderstanding of the present. They are being taught to see everything through the eyes of the prevailing and chronologically challenged civil religion.

Under the old Christian paradigm, political morality was informed by a shared public and intergenerational morality. The political process considered that traditional morality accepts that human beings are dignified, rational, and creative, yet flawed. The uniqueness of the individual was taken for granted. However, the new civil religion preaches a different understanding of human character and meaning. The human creature is not flawed; instead, s/he is a self-realising victim of one of the "isms." Social tension will be alleviated by getting rid of sexism, racism, heterosexism, and so on. The first step towards salvation is not a consequence of accepting our flawed nature. Repentance, the catalyst of humility, is superfluous. Instead, the community is saved when self-realising victims find identity in group membership. The prevailing sensitivities of civil religion determine the nature and efficacy of that identity.

While any mention of Friedrich Nietzsche in this context is likely to create problems, it is probably true that the mid-twentieth-century relativists misunderstood him when they thought he was hinting at a new and superior race with his invention of '*Übermensch*' (Overman). Indeed, Nietzsche was talking about the importance of power. It was about the power of the self to reject the prevailing Christian ethic of his time (God was dead, after all) and restore his interpretation of the ancient belief in the power of the strong over the weak. However, no matter what he thought his aspirations were, they were an exercise in vanity. To the extent that one can come to grips with it, his entire philosophy hinges on rejecting Christ's claims that He is God. Neither Nietzsche nor the new civil religion has discovered a new moral foundation. His attempt to create a new kind of human being, the Overman, for example, was not a return to the medieval pre-scientific mind but to the ancient pagan mind. Contemporary civil religion can readily be described as the fusion of Nietzsche's Luciferian hubris and the return to pantheism.

This is what subjectivism does. Rejecting the Transcendent, and in Nietzsche's case, specifically the Deity of Christ, he gave the illusion of substance to the unbelieving mind as it shaped its vision of the transcendent in its image. Horkheimer, Lukács, Gramsci, and Marcuse et al. followed on. In the end, I suppose it is all straightforward, well, it's the claim that I have been making *ad nauseam,* it might seem. One either accepts the traditional biblical God and His role in the affairs of men and women, or one doesn't. Whatever the case, we live in an either/or world. This is one of the Achilles' Heels of the rising civil religion (after all, diversity is the name of the game) because its multicultural foundation denies that we live in an either/or world. It does that by declaring self-creation real. It would turn us all into latter-day versions of Sisyphus, who the gods condemned to eternal meaninglessness. Cultural relativism would have us believe that we live in a both/and world; believing two conflicting ideas simultaneously is normal. Reality must be constantly transformed to fit its dogma.

The effect on daily life is far-reaching. Nietzsche's contribution to the shift from 'virtue' to 'values' in the modern Western vocabulary is critical to civil religion. For example, examine these two simple sentences. "Bill is courageous." "'Courage is one of Bob's values." The first sentence tells us something about Bill's character: he is courageous. The second sentence doesn't tell us much about Bob; he values courage. He might well be a coward. He might talk *ad nauseam* about his values, but that will not reveal how courageous Bob might be. Values are subjectively perceived and subjectively expressed. They are never any more than claims one makes about oneself or claims made by another. The use of values in this sense has become a religious ritual insofar as they are an exercise in appeasement made by an esoteric civil religion. Submission to the value of diversity, inclusion, and equity has nothing to say about character development.

It's already been mentioned in another context, but just to remind you, virtue is suspect; the courage of a dissenter, for example, can become bigotry. And that 'bigotry' is controlled by introducing hate speech legislation. The salvific ritual of the priesthood demands that everyone submit to its values. Civil religion has no eyes to see virtue objectively practised, objectively observed, and personally rewarded. It is blind to prudence, for example. Or, if not blind to it, it has no basis on which to value it. Any nod it might give is a half-hearted parasitic one. Instead of being the overarching vice, pride becomes the self-evident virtue that supports the conviction of self-realisation.

Such an exchange of humility for pride is inevitable because, without a vision of the sublime, how can we experience the reverence essential to humility? The King James version of Proverbs 29:18 tells us, *"Where there is no vision, the people perish, but he that keepeth the law, happy is he."* The law of the Ten Commandments, that is. And they are visionary insofar as obedience gives rise to good order and peace of mind. Reverence carries with it a satisfying, emotionally laden spiritual confidence. It encourages us to believe that our actions can be in harmony with what is right and good because the self is not the centre of our attention. It's a relief, a release from the consciousness of our failings. Reverence takes us out of ourselves as we enjoy the beauty of the sublime. One is inclined to believe that reverence is necessary for good mental health. I'm inclined to believe it has its counterfeit in the adulation of 'stardom'. I would even dare to suggest that good mental health is awakened by thinking of others, while bad mental health is evidenced by always thinking of yourself.

Civil religion replaces reverence with unsuspecting servitude. It demands a concealed obsequiousness to the faux virtue of affirming tolerance. The obsequiousness required by the civil religion makes it easy for citizens to participate in vacuous ceremonial activities that would enforce it. At the same time, doubters must be prevented from raising the reality of human duplicity. Everyone learns to live by lies, and hypocrisy prevails because people assent without believing. For example, few people think that we can change our sex or that one's chosen sexual, so-called gender identity, is so inviolate that it should be protected by law. It was the refusal of the early Christians to participate in religious festivals and related rituals that led them to become known as the "haters of mankind." Tacitus (Ann. 15.36-44) uses this phrase somewhat ambiguously when the sect known as Christians is accused by Nero of starting the fire in Rome in 64 AD. That Christians are the contemporary villains in the culture war should not be wondered at. In New Zealand, the DIE Triumvirate, Academia, MSM, and the political Left are the modern reincarnation of Caesar. Well, not quite yet, perhaps, but they would certainly like to be.

◆ ◆ ◆

The subjectivism of cultural relativism, elevated to holiness, is a dreadful master. Desire, no matter how pure one might think it to be, will always result in permanent frustration. Unrestrained desire reinforces the oppressor/oppressed model already deeply embedded in the culture. There is little chance that suffering might have a spiritual genesis or solution; everything is political. Contemporary civil religion must always claim, should it ever dare to confront the issue, that the Apostle Paul's remarks in Romans about suffering are esoteric nonsense:

> *"But we rejoice in our sufferings, knowing that suffering produces endurance, and endurance produces character, and character produces hope, and hope does not put us to shame, because God's love has been poured into our hearts through the Holy Spirit who has been given to us."*

Earlier on, I mentioned the dilution of the English curriculum in schools and the flattening of what we once called high and low culture. Insight into the subtleties of comedy, especially satire, and even tragedy, is removed from the human heart and mind by civil religion. The secularised civil religion has brought a counterfeit sublime down to earth without understanding what it's doing. Indeed, it cannot even explore the need for such an admission. The 'communicants' of civil religion cannot understand what Matthew Arnold (1822-1888) feared in his poem, *Dover Beach*.

> *The Sea of Faith . . .*
> *Was once, too, at the full, and round earth's shore . . .*

But now I only hear
Its melancholy, long, withdrawing roar.

And that, of course, is the point. Is Christianity just a *melancholy, long, withdrawing roar?* Is my concern just the whimper of a frustrated octogenarian who can't come to terms with the new civil religion? Or is something else going on?

According to the British theologian Oliver O'Donovan, the candidate for sex change has been seduced by a culture-wide mass movement bent on an understanding of freedom that would ignore natural limitations, and that it is an attack on us. Not only does it deny who we are, but it also suggests a false alternative. It hardly seems outrageous to suggest that young people are learning to despise their culture and themselves because they know nothing about either. Schools have failed to convey the historical context that would provide young people with knowledge and confidence. The mindless, youthful protest movements in major cities around the Western world confirm just that.

◆ ◆ ◆

Many readers will be too young to remember when Nobel Prize winner Alexander Solzhenitsyn came to the West after being expelled from the Soviet Union in 1974, the same year as the Stanford student protests. Embraced at first by the Western intelligentsia, he soon became their Bête noire. He didn't tell them what they expected to hear, just how superior life in the West was to that behind the Iron Curtain. In a series of lectures, he highlighted that life in the West was superficial and lacked spiritual depth. Sure, he was a grumpy old man, but he was onto something—the West's forgetfulness, even denial of its past, was the fatty tissue clogging its arteries.

All of Solzhenitsyn's speeches carry a consistent message and a dire warning. He pointed out that the tyranny he had escaped from in the *Gulag Archipelago* was the potential future for the West. Although that seems more evident every day, the Western elite is still oblivious to his warning. The dogma implanted by civil religion ensures that the rest of us fail to grasp the gravity of the situation. Traditional virtue, confidence, and respect for the law would all go. When Solzhenitsyn accused us of forgetting God, that 'Grey Lady', The New York Times, dismissed his warning. It said he was calling for a holy war.

The writer of *The New York Times* opinion piece didn't want to believe that Western Civilisation cannot survive if it rejects its spiritual foundations. And it would seem we still don't. Solzhenitsyn was not calling for a holy war. He was pointing out that Marxism, in whatever form it would take, would remain an aggressive and dark religion. "Democratic socialism" would be a smokescreen. The Stanford students look very much like they are getting their wish fulfilled; "*Western Civ*" is on the way out. We do, however, have a choice. Which religion will sustain Western Civilisation, Christianity or its parasite?

It might be that times are changing. We have good reason to be optimistic. Those with a conservative frame of mind should be encouraged. We can now say things they couldn't have said freely in public even a year or two ago. It has become increasingly challenging to portray critics of the diversity cult as reactionary. President Trump and his attempt to "*eliminate Woke*" might have been a catalyst, but it was already there. Many are beginning to accept that Christianity has, at the very least, utilitarian value, even if they cannot assume that it's about eternal salvation. Some significant writers, from Tom Holland to Richard Dawkins, are beginning to realise that Western civilisation will have difficulty surviving unless it attends to its roots. Melanie Phillips' *The Builder's Stone* is one of the more penetrating books pointing out the need for Western civilisation to rediscover its roots. The writer/philosopher Os Guinness has told us that the West is a 'cut flower' civilisation. And Douglas Murray tells us that it is time for reconstruction. At the *Alliance for Responsible Citizenship* 2025, many speakers pointed out that Western civilisation is at a watershed. The Enlightenment experiment is over. And if it's not the Enlightenment experiment, something is certainly over. The Genesis revelation of God's creation of man, male and female, in His image, needs to be re-examined. Cultural relativism has run out of puff. Indeed, puff was all it ever had. The significant historian Christopher Dawson told us last century that there has never been any unifying organisation of Western civilisation apart from that of the Christian faith. He was right. By God's grace, we might realise that and return to the claims of the Christian Gospel.

Athens or Jerusalem?

It has been claimed that Western civilisation depends on the Bible and cannot continue without it. Much of the evidence that supports that claim is the West's unique understanding of human dignity based on the Genesis creation story. It is a belief sustained by faith but not contrary to reason. In examining the status of revelation and reason's role in revelation, the challenge is to clarify without oversimplifying. There remains one fundamental issue. Did God reveal Himself to us through the Bible, and did Jesus Christ rise from the dead? It's a decision that we all have to make sooner or later. The Jews have been monotheists since Abraham, although they took some time to understand the full implications. All the civilisations around them were polytheists, including the Athens of Pericles.[5] The God of the Bible is the Creator of humanity, encompassing all things visible and invisible. The intimacy of the exchange between God and his people teaches us what He demands of his creation.

The Jews were instructed to be obedient and faithful and, therefore, to live out the practical consequences of that obedience. If the God who gave the Law to the Jews is indeed the Creator of all things visible and invisible, then the status and history of the Jews are critical to our understanding of who we are in the West. They were entrusted with the guardianship of the Great Truth of God's revelation. The Jews still wait for the fulfilment of that guardianship in the coming of the Messiah, while Christians believe that Jesus Christ is that Messiah. Christianity and Judaism are inextricably bound, and observation would suggest that history reinforces that belief. The West continues to exist under the unique belief that human beings possess intrinsic dignity. That is the first uniqueness. The second is the history of the Jews; they are the unique survivors. No other nation, race, or civilisation has existed as long as they have. And it is even more significant because they have suffered almost continuous persecution, captivity, and exile. Islam would wipe them out if it could. Indeed, many Jews have lived and continue to live outside the Western world, but for nearly two thousand years, they have shared a reverence for what Christians call the Old Testament.

Edward Gibbon may not have invented the phrase 'decline and fall,' but he certainly reinforced it in his six-volume work, *The History of the Decline and Fall of the Roman Empire*. In many people's minds, history is perceived as a recurring circular affair. It is, after all, just a matter of swings and roundabouts. The Roman goddess Fortuna, with her wheel, might not be in control, but she is somehow present in the background alongside Tyche, her Greek predecessor. Nemesis, the goddess who punished the sin of hubris, was frequently worshipped alongside Tyche. Pride, both personal and imperial, would have its comeuppance. Such was the justice of the gods. So what's the point?

Despite its philosophic complexity, Athens offers us nothing but tragedy, occasionally punctuated by satirical or bawdy comedy to relieve the terror. Certainly, the great Greek dramatists provide us with remarkable insight into human suffering and aspiration, but ultimately, they give us no hope. Gloucester in Shakespeare's *King Lear* wasn't Greek, but he captured the essential hopelessness of classical paganism: *"As flies to wanton boys are we to the gods; they kill us for their sport."* Even if the hubris of men and women assisted the gods in their 'wanton' playfulness, hopelessness prevails. One suspects that neither Sophocles' *Oedipus* nor *Antigone* would have demurred. Either one is a follower of Epicurus, like the modern self-creating progressive who will eventually fall into the cynical arms of Diogenes, but without his strength of character, or attempt to follow the abstract virtues of the Stoic.

There was, however, something quite wonderful about Athens at the height of its glory. Thucydides' rendering of Pericles' funeral oration (431 BC) in *The History of the Peloponnesian War* is a compelling eulogy praising ancestors and the freedom they have passed on. "*We have received from them a Free State.*" Being an Athenian was indeed a privilege. Pericles praises the glory of empire, declaring that the accurate measure of a man's worth is how he dies. The idea of the tragic hero was the high point of the civilisation. Although he talks of Athens as a democracy, it is a very limited one. Nevertheless, it might be that the speech was one of the best ever given by a man who couldn't have understood the declaration of human dignity in Genesis. I believe that Greek tragedy, except for the Old Testament book of Job, is literature's most harrowing and penetrating examination of human suffering, except for the suffering of the Jewish nation. The difference between the Greek dramatists and Job is critical. In Greek drama, the protagonist suffers alone. Job suffers too, but God is always in the background, ensuring justice is done. His renewed relationship with God was his reward. The enrichment of his understanding was his hope.

◆ ◆ ◆

Jews and Christians have an opportunity to understand our history differently. At the 2025 *Association for Responsible Citizenship* conference in London, Os Guinness, writer and social critic, suggested the Jews were the historical model not of 'decline and fall' but of 'exile and return.' And the most recent return is in our own time. The gods did not kill them for their sport; instead, God judged, punished, forgave, and restored. Jewish life throughout history serves as a reminder to us in the West that nations and individuals are under God's judgement. Indeed, it is difficult to see how justice could be fulfilled if God is not the final judge, for life is a messy business. The Bible, in revealing God's character to the Jews, also shows it to the whole world. The 'exile and return' concept of history that Os Guinness identifies is more encouraging than Gibbon's 'decline and fall'. Decline and fall offer us no scope for forgiveness and redemption. And by the way, that's one of the reasons why anti-Semitism is such a terrible evil. Western civilisation, permeated as it is with Christianity, recognised or unrecognised, as I have already intimated, is in debt to the Jews. To override that debt with the mindless animus of antisemitism is tragically self-destructive.

Right now, New Zealand, like the rest of the Western world, despite what the anti-colonialists might claim, is going through a 'period of exile'. It has lost its way. To quote Os Guinness again, *"It's a cut flower civilisation."* It continues to live off the Hebrew and Christian scriptures, pretending they don't exist. Athens would still enthrall the post-modern progressive mind if it knew how to be thankful. Alas, such a mind has flattened everything. There is no glory in the tragic death or weeping as *Oedipus* or *Antigone* cry out at the absurd evil that would envelop them. Despite the magnificence of its literature, Athens has nothing definitive to relieve the progressive mind's ennui, but Jerusalem does. We either return to the biblical claims of dignity and divine authority, or we continue to have the juice squeezed out of us by the unrelenting grip of secular hubris and paganism; civil religion.

Unless we live on another planet, we all know that Western education is going through a severe disruption—a state of affairs that has been bubbling away for a long time. A nation, or a civilisation, cannot deny its roots and expect life to continue as usual. The underlying malaise has finally reached the surface, encompassing foundational religious, moral, economic, and political change. It might be, I hope so, that we are going through a period when we can look around and see just what the bubbling on the surface conceals. We're confronting a deep-seated need for reassessment. One can only hope and pray that we can be a nation with the intelligence and imagination to understand that "*a cut flower civilisation*" cannot stand.

Why can't it stand? Every nation, every empire, needs a story. The Greeks had Homer, and the Romans had Virgil. The West, until recently, had Jesus Christ. The ancient Greeks or Romans toiling away in the fields might not have known much about Homer or Virgil, but they knew the stories. For nearly 1500 years, the story of Jesus Christ has held Western civilisation together. Vaguely understood by some and rejected by some, the story of sin, repentance, and forgiveness culminating in the crucifixion and resurrection was the overarching story. That story inspired most of our art, music, and literature. Now that unbelief seems to have reached what can only be called a hollow anti-climax, we have nothing to replace it. A surfeit of shallow psychological and futile therapeutic fiction will not do. Those vain, esoteric ramblings that some still call poetry will not do either. Art seems overwhelmed by a preoccupation with the disorder of the grotesque. And much modern music is all noise and no resolution. Ecstasy is all promise with no delivery. We need to cultivate our roots.

Notes:

1. See *The God Debate* on YouTube. Richard Dawkins and Ayaan Hirsi Ali. Also, see *The Poetry of Reality. Political Christian. Or truly Christian?*

2. Ministry of Education. The New Zealand curriculum online.

3. *Listener.* July 24, 2021.

4. Quoted by Joel Looper. *First Things.* 28/2/24, a collection of O'Donovan's essays called *Begotten, Not Made.*

5. I know that Plato sometimes uses God in the singular in his Phaedrus, but the biblical notion of dignity is nowhere to be found. If anyone has dignity, it is the philosopher at the top of the tree, and it takes a long time to climb. Mysticism and metaphor fuse so frequently that it becomes difficult to understand precisely what Plato says.

X

In Case You Missed It

So Jesus came out, wearing the crown of thorns and
the purple robe. Pilate said to them. "Behold the Man!"

John 19:5

In old age, accumulated knowledge is accompanied and sometimes threatened by contemporary wisdom's poignant intimations and vanity. We're all influenced by our surroundings and the passage of time, and there is always a more effective way to express something. A little knowledge is only a dangerous thing if we overvalue it. And that, as we well know, is a common human failing, although we used to call it by its proper name: pride. I like to imagine that one's perception of truth is a half-full box open to some amendment and addition. There will always be gaps in everyone's knowledge, but sooner or later, we must commit ourselves to what we believe. Life is not a game, and I will not lose heart. Nevertheless, we need to remember that Truth is permanent and eternal. If we try to make it up as we go along, the consequence can only be chaos.

In the opening chapter, titled 'The Complaint in Brief', I said *hope* seemed to fill the horizon when I was young. I don't mean something like, *"I hope it doesn't rain tomorrow."* Instead, it is a sense of trust that believes it is within the nature of God's ordered world to bring about whatever one hopes for, knowing well that such hope is open to modification. Nevertheless, it is accompanied by assurance. I'm unsure how the individual human creature would find hope convincing if he or she didn't believe in the God of the Bible. Listening to the young people around me, the horizon of their hope looks increasingly distant and uninviting. And the reason for that loss of hope is unmistakable. Most have not been taught the traditions and the truth that give life meaning. Western civilisation has not done what God told the Jews to do: tell your children that I rescued you from Egypt so you might have the freedom to worship the Lord your God. Western civilisation is not telling its children that if they are to know who they are, they must find their roots in the transcendent, in the revelation of God in Jesus Christ. If they are not told, it is difficult to see life as an exercise in serving God's purpose. They will have no touchstone to assess spiritual truth, and any political acumen they might have will suffer.

We should not be surprised that protest gives the 'anxious generation' some sense of meaning. Men or women in their maturity or youth cannot live without hope. We will seek the Sublime without having a clear idea of what we are doing. Youth need a vision. Preoccupation with the self and the belief that we can make ourselves whatever we like will not do. As usual, Saint Paul got it right: *"Now faith is the assurance of things hoped for, the conviction of things not seen"* (Hebrews 11:1). Faith, best described by trusting God, at the very least, is necessary for good mental health. And that is particularly true as mental health has now become such a wide-ranging descriptor, from snowflakery to severe mental illness. Otherwise, we lock ourselves into the darkness of loneliness.

Child-centred education intensifies the darkness because the child's imagination is impoverished when traditional stories are ignored. For example, metaphors and images from biblical stories, myths, and fairy tales that children read or heard their parents read can enhance the intensity and quality of emotional responses to stories read in adulthood. Indeed, these stories bring the generations together. Good character is given emotional and intellectual content. An understanding of our common humanity engenders a rewarding humility. If the stories that unite mind and heart are not recognised and shared, social unity is disrupted, the self is diminished, and the community is undermined. The grand biblical narrative, which provides historical insight and knowledge of the difference between good and evil, has been criticised without knowledge and forgotten. Self-declared notions of what is appropriate and inappropriate are not moral opposites by which we can live. They do not encourage us to embrace the good and flee evil. Any insightful discussion or reconciliation around the reality and anguish of human suffering becomes impossible. Life's *raison d'être* is to avoid suffering at all costs. Indeed, the exultation and triumph of desire can only encourage second-rate hedonism because it diminishes what it means to be human by turning anxiety into a neurotic art. And when I say second-rate, I mean just that. We used to believe that there was such a thing as real guilt that required forgiveness. Now, the replacement, finding a solution to mental health issues, is like being in a room where the lights are being slowly dimmed because we think guilt is merely a matter of psychology. One begins to believe that darkness is normal. The holy joy of forgiveness is not possible because no one has sinned. The contemporary ignorance or denial of human sinfulness turns the human creature into something quite different: a creature compelled always to suppress the truth of universal human vulnerability. And all that makes one vulnerable, so vulnerable that the anxious psyche failing to find relief must be guarded assiduously. Dissent is not permissible. The increasing demand for hate speech around the Western world suggests a fear of exposure to an authority other than self. It's an attempt to silence the God who, in their estimation, wounds and heals but isn't there.

I have lived long enough to notice that some allegedly critical markers of identity fade away while others take their place, not so much to describe the same thing but more to describe the changing religious and cultural perceptions. The word 'identity' is just the current frontrunner. I can't remember it ever being used in the first forty years of my life, certainly with the meaning it carries today. When we talked about 'self,' we were more likely to use the word 'soul,' which was informed by Christian Scripture, corrupted, maybe by Plato's idea of the soul trapped in the body. Perhaps our understanding of it was somewhat romanticised. Wordsworth's *Ode: Intimations of Immortality from Recollections of Early Childhood* had not yet been absorbed into the sentimental:

> *The Soul that rises with us, our life's Star*
> *Hath had elsewhere its setting,*
> *And cometh from afar . . .*
> *trailing clouds of glory do we come*
> *From God who is our home.*

The naked materialism of self-identifying pride had to shake off those *trailing clouds of glory*. Which, of course, it did.

The possession of a soul no longer identifies the self. If there is any 'soul talk,' it nearly always degenerates into waffle. The human creature is no longer an eternal embodied spirit. The idea of self has gone from soul to self-creating identity. We are all horizontal now. The old idea that one had to, sooner or later, answer to the Maker of his or her spirit has been replaced by the efficacy of the authentic self. The fulfilment of bodily desire is all; there is no resurrection of the body. One only has to go to a secular funeral, and at my age, one goes to many, to discover the poignant bleakness of most of the eulogies. The comfort of community is eroded despite a lingering desire for it. The incoherent ideology of DIE has to pretend it's the glue of social order and the lubricant of human interaction. It's just a matter of finding the right laws. Civil religion is the bubble within which we all must live. It must continuously reorder the way we think about ourselves. Words do not carry meaning; instead, we inject meaning into them. Identity is not fixed; it is fluid. Nevertheless, that fluidity is controlled by those who have the power to do so.

◆ ◆ ◆

There is a story (perhaps apocryphal) that *The Times (UK)* once sent out a questionnaire to famous writers with the question, "What's wrong with the world today?" G.K. Chesterton is credited with replying, "*Dear Sir, I am. Yours, G K Chesterton.*" So we are back to Rousseau. Either society or the human heart is the problem. When I was a young man, we were pretty sure it was the human heart, but now the villain is the multivarious Eurocentric Christian villain.

Always incognito, he'll be (mostly he) racist, sexist, homophobic, a colonialist, the corrupter and polluter of nature and climate, and most recently, transphobic, perhaps all at once. Civil religion's demand for servility must create a villain if one cannot be found. The 'patient' cannot be allowed to examine the delicately constructed collective psyche in the context of our national history. Of course, everyone wants to run away to a safe place.

Having dispensed with faith, we should not be surprised that we are losing that great Christian virtue: hope. The persistent exercise in self-justification and the accusation of the imagined villain always make it difficult to maintain any sense of hope and redemption. That hope might be a vote of confidence in God is not considered. Resentment, too quickly, gets in the way, encouraging the need for self-justification. The contemporary duopoly of the primacy of desire and oppression by the other can only bring frustration and arouse a chronic sense of anger and a bleak and clueless willingness to protest. Redemption will always flee from self-righteousness.

Because we live in a time of national and international tension, too many young idealists, compelled by their natural altruism to do something, think that protests can resolve the tension. The spiritual perversion of self-creation has seduced them; *"All peace is good and tolerance the supreme good." "Better red than dead,"* in Bertrand Russell's old Cold War language. Nevertheless, with or without Shakespeare's *Richard III,* I fear that the winter of youthful discontent will not be turned into glorious summer by the ill-met cultural and historical ignorance of civil religion turned into protest.

Now, if some find my analysis too 'religious,' let me explain it another way. Liberal democracy, based on a decaying belief in human dignity and therefore human equality, was supposed to answer our problems. That any belief in universal human dignity passed away with the death of God seems to have slipped by. Liberalism has become illiberal because it now believes that God-given human dignity is a myth and that its new notion of equality, called equity, must be enforced. After all, liberalism did not deliver what it promised. Nietzsche had already pointed out that Christianity, with its doctrine of equal dignity, was the source of liberalism. But as God was dead, liberalism had no foundation. So why not sign up to the doctrine that encourages you to join the new ruling class? Not that those signing up would see it that way, but they were claiming a new kind of knowledge, a new cultural narrative that includes everyone. So we should not be surprised when much of our language has been perverted not to offend any individual or group.

Young people have grown up in an atmosphere that would suffocate any suspicion of antinomianism. The word's too long, and the concept is too distant. And anyway, it has 'anti' in front, so it's probably a good thing. Encouraged to despise Western metaphysics, ethics, and epistemology, they cannot believe they're cutting off their blocked noses to spite their beautiful faces. The witless misunderstanding and rejection of nearly four thousand years of Jewish and Christian history, belief, and theology is the mark of a civilisation intent on self-destruction. Young people are not to blame. The baby boomers (my generation) and Generation X, as the Americans call them, are more culpable. Both generations have failed to pass on that which is their first responsibility: the truth about the past, the importance of spiritual insight, and the truth about the source of dignity. We have bred at least two generations of spiritual and theological ignoramuses who deserve a great deal better. It is indeed a tragedy brought on by terrible neglect.

We have encouraged youth for too long to believe too many lies. The one that underpins their nonsensical self-esteem might be the worst. *"I am special and maybe the most important person in the world."* And when that is accompanied by *"You can be whatever you want to be,"* you have the terrible twins of delusion. And then we have the common but superficial *"Be true to yourself,"* parroting one of Polonius' famous tautological aphorisms in *Hamlet: "To thine own self be true."* However, Polonius got nearly everything wrong; Hamlet considered him a *"tedious old fool."* His banal comments on character anticipated those of the diversity cult.

We have what I imagine to be 'The Great Rejection', fabricated by a deadly error: mistaking the fruit for the root. The social context in which we enjoy freedom and prosperity is not the product of human reason. It is the byproduct of faithfulness to the truth. Whether Trevor Mallard understood it or not, he followed Rousseau, Nietzsche, Lenin, Marx, the Frankfurt School, and others who hated the unique biblical declaration of human dignity, human sinfulness, and the need for salvation that informed Western civilisation. The State was declared the supreme power—not deliberately, perhaps, but that was the consequence. We have become conditioned to believe that the state should solve all our problems because we think it can. Wisdom has been conquered by nonsense. Democracy informed by social justice is the gateway to Heaven's storehouse.

The idealism of youth needs a vision to inform and direct its natural passion. And that idealism can only be nourished by a respect for tradition and an understanding of our history. As Western society has denied its unique roots, youthful idealism gets misdirected, and we get the social discord of mindless protest. I have lived long enough to discover that the rejection of God delivers us into a mindless inability to be discerning. If Truth is not there to act as a guide, the phenomenon of a Greta Thunberg is never far away.

One of the most prominent and recent examples of wayward passion is the way that so many young people have become enamoured by the so-called Palestinian cause. Young Westerners waving Palestinian or even the yellow Hezbollah flags as they chant from the "River to the Sea" is not just demographic and geographical obliviousness; it reflects an ignorance of the historical link between Israel and Western civilisation. In all of this, we have an excellent example of how ideology can overshadow history and manipulate youthful idealism. For instance, they are quite without any touchstone to assess the propaganda of Hezbollah or Hamas. The protesters have no idea that the birthplace of the Jewish people, where their spiritual and national identity was born over four millennia ago, is their promised land. The Jews are the indigenous people of Israel, and not the Arabs, now called Palestinians, living in the region of Palestine before Israel was restored as a nation in 1948.

It is worthwhile reminding ourselves that thirty-nine of the sixty-six books of the Bible were written by different Jews over 2,000 years ago, and only two books of the New Testament were written by a Greek, or perhaps more accurately, by a Macedonian. The cross-references that confirm the Bible's essential message are numerous and inexhaustible. Of course, that might not cut much ice unless one allows it to sink in. What the protestors don't understand is that without Judaism, there would be no Christianity, nor Western civilisation. The mindless hostility that would deny Israel's national legitimacy has the potential to turn the West into a mad dog that eats its own foot. Antisemitism is not only a great evil; it corrupts and eventually destroys its practitioner.

In a way, if one squints hard enough, their protesting is almost praiseworthy. They are, after all, protesting in sympathy for those they see as downtrodden, a virtue of Western civilisation. However, feeling sympathy is one thing; good judgment is quite another.

What the students and others don't know, because they haven't been taught, is the indisputable historical truth that the Genesis creation story makes Western civilisation different from all others, uniquely so. The full-frontal problem of our time, confusion over what it means to be a human creature, dominates because we have rejected the fundamental truth on which our civilisation is based: God's gift of dignity to men and women. This idea and its implications, grounded in the Old Testament and sustained by the New Testament, transformed the Roman Empire. Western civilisation could not have come into being without the monotheism of Israel. The ongoing desire to destroy Israel is not just an attack on the heart of Western civilisation; it is also an attempt to replace God by deifying the self. It is no accident that Israel is the only democracy in the Middle East.

The growing animosity towards Israel is the canary in the mine that should warn the rest of us. Israel is not perfect; indeed, it is far from it, just like the rest of Western civilisation. It is, nevertheless, sustained by the rule of law that teaches, both by default and by design, the sacredness of the human body and mind. It has a longer prophetic history than any other civilisation, with the means to examine its folly and the need for the human creature to come to terms with that folly. Perhaps there's an irony there somewhere; the Jews continue to wait for their liberating Messiah, Christians believe they know who He is, while the 'diversophiles' wait for Utopia.

◆ ◆ ◆

So, let me say what I believe to be a gaping deficiency of the modern mind: the loss of gratitude. Indeed, civil religion makes gratitude an impossibility. Whether one lives in New Zealand or Aotearoa, to whom and for what is one thankful? Gratitude to the abstraction of DIE is hardly sufficient as one enjoys the warm sun in the morning. Without the sustaining glow of sublime glory, how will gratitude swell our aching hearts? Few people have a deep sense of thankfulness for the comfort provided by the State as it tries to make sense of social justice. Christ meant it when he said:

> *"Come, come to me, all who labour and are heavy laden, and I will give you rest. Take my yoke upon you and learn from me, for I am gentle and lowly in heart, and you will find rest for your souls, for my yoke is easy and my burden is light."*
>
> Matthew 11:28-30

One needs the comfort of the God who put on flesh and blood, walked this Earth, and suffered alongside his creation. Without the overwhelming gratitude from the belief in the Resurrection, life is neither a gift nor a blessing. It's just a bore, one bloody thing after another. One lives through physical and emotional passions and aches for three score and ten years, maybe another ten or even twenty. Such is the contemporary context in which we experience our latest version of freedom, which tells us we are alone in the universe and the only thing we can do is live out our deepest, death-embracing desires.

◆ ◆ ◆

So, in my eighty-seven years, what have I learned for sure? The Bible offers the best foundation for understanding and practicing freedom in one's private life and the outworking of political power. It uniquely tells us how we were created and for what purpose. It explains best how men and women should treat each other. While the mystery of personal suffering remains, we are told quite clearly how suffering entered the world. We are not left without hope. And to understand it, we must ask the right person the right question. That's not an easy thing to do in a world where relativism rules. Finding a foundation on which confidence might rest is impossible.

Plato might have been the first in the Classical World to point out the importance of the right questions. Just before Socrates' trial (399 BC), Plato met a young man, Euthyphro, on the way to court, where he brought a charge of impiety against his father. Impiety might best be described as an action that offends the gods. I remember this story well because it was the most challenging text my first-year Greek class (all four of us) had to translate. Euthyphro's father had mistreated a slave, bound and left him to die in a ditch. The slave had killed a fellow worker, and apparently, that excused the father of any liability. With all the self-confidence of a young latter-day protester, Euthyphro is convinced of the righteousness of his judgement, sure that he knows what impiety is. However, Plato undermined his confidence in his definition of piety by getting him to question his motivation and knowledge. To cut a long story short, the debate about the nature of piety became one of whether something is pious because the gods approve of it or whether the gods approve of it because it is pious. The dialogue does not reach a satisfactory conclusion. That is hardly surprising because the only way we might know the answer to the question is for the gods to tell us. They told neither Plato nor Euthyphro.

Western civilisation has rested on and wrestled with this question for nearly two millennia. Jesus Christ declared Himself "*The Way, The Truth, and The Life,*" which short-circuits Plato's problem of piety and the gods. God has come to us and told us. So there is only one question left. It's always been the question, hidden in the context of every great debate and igniting the fire of every revolution in Western civilisation, sometimes forbidden, sometimes ignored, sometimes hated, sometimes embarrassing, and occasionally celebrated: *What's so special about Jesus?* Why can we discuss Buddha, Muhammad, Moses, or any other religious leader with equanimity? What is it about Jesus that always raises the temperature? Have a look at this story from the Gospel of Luke:

> "*On another Sabbath, he entered the synagogue and was teaching, and a man was there whose right hand was withered. And the scribes and the Pharisees watched him to see whether he would heal on the Sabbath, so that they might find a reason to accuse him. But he knew their thoughts, he said to the man with the withered hand. 'Come and stand here.' And he rose and stood there. And Jesus said to them, 'I ask you is it lawful on the Sabbath to do good or to do harm, to save life or to destroy it?' And after looking around at them? All he said to him was,*

'Stretch out your hand.' And he did so, and his hand was restored. But they were filled with fury and discussed with one another what they might do to Jesus."

Luke 6:6-11 ESV

This passage raises an obvious question. Why were the scribes and Pharisees so angry? Well, at first glance, Christ has broken their law; by their strict definition, healing was work. And they stuck to their law with rigorous self-righteousness. Indeed, it was this self-righteous confidence that gave strength to their self-justification. But their hatred of Christ was even more deeply seated. Hatred is the correct word here. Christ was exposing the empty powerlessness of their self-justification. The Pharisees and scribes could not bear to look into their hearts and question the validity of their pilfered authority. And by pilfered authority, I mean that, like Adam and Eve in the Genesis story, they insist that they know the difference between right and wrong, and God does not.

Christ will not allow us to pretend he isn't here. He will not allow us to continue in the insistence of our self-righteous egos that *I alone, without divine guidance, know the difference between right and wrong.* We are left with only two options. He commands that we believe in Him and follow Him. We either obey Him or disobey Him. Most of us seem like the Pharisees who would cling to their version of the law; I know the difference between right and wrong; I don't have to be told.

It should be blindingly evident, with 'blindingly evident' being the operative phrase, that the progressive illiberal, the apostle of cultural relativism, is the contemporary Pharisee, the hypocrite who must have all opposition silenced. Failure to agree with the progressive illiberals' ideology of social justice is counted as evil, and any perpetrator who suggests otherwise must be 'cancelled' in the interests of social justice. Like the scribes and Pharisees of the New Testament, the progressive illiberals miss the point. Genuine goodness is not the consequence of legal demand. The law cannot make people good. The illiberal might claim that one earns brownie points by accepting their reconstructed definition of humanity. But rational goodness turns out to be nothing more than a fashionable ideology that would try to convince us that salvation is the outcome of believing their religious dogma. Believe what they say, think, and do what they say you should, and you will be saved. The scribes and Pharisees distorted Old Testament law, and the contemporary illiberal deconstructs and reinvents the Gospel of Jesus Christ by trying to empty it of its spiritual power. Faith, believing what God says, the source and power of traditional virtue, is undermined and replaced by political obedience, and disobedience is subject to punishment. Fortunately, the illiberal, masquerading as liberal, cannot crucify those they cannot convince. But they can silence them with increasingly harsh hate speech laws—a somewhat tatty parody of crucifixion.

Some might continue to claim that I have been too religious in my attempt to explore and explain my pilgrimage, and any authority I might claim is undermined. However, I would respond by pointing out that such a charge can only come from the deconstructed secular mind. The charge of 'religious' made by someone who claims not to be religious is the same mistake that Marx made, thinking he was getting rid of religion when he was only rejecting one and replacing it with one of his own making. Nietzsche's hubris and boldness were even more astonishing. He hated Christ because Christ loved those who were weak. He understood that without God, life on Earth is a continuous struggle for the power of one man over another. I suspect that neither Nietzsche, Marx, nor any of the Frankfurt School's members realised that power divorced from love always brings tyranny. They could not accept that the sublime union of power and love uniquely found in Christ always brings peace. It's unlikely they would enjoy the beauty of the poem below.

Love III

Love bade me welcome: yet my soul drew back,
Guilty of dust and sin.
But quick-ey'd Love, observing me grow slack,
From my first entrance in,
Drew nearer to me, sweetly questioning,
If I lack'd anything.

A guest, I answer'd, worthy to be here:
Love said, You shall be he.
I the unkind, ungrateful? Ah my dear,
I cannot look on thee.
Love took my hand, and smiling did reply,
Who made the eyes but I?

Truth Lord, but I have marr'd them: let my shame
Go where it doth deserve.
And know you not, says Love, who bore the blame?
My dear, then I will serve.
You must sit down, says Love, and tast me meat:
So I did sit and eat.

George Herbert 1593-1633

I finish with a challenge. If you reject the Christian story culminating in Jesus Christ because it is religious and, therefore, an inadequate explanation of the human predicament, what do you put in its place that is not another religion? Denial of the biblical God is no less religious than affirming the same God. Where else will you find the terror of fully realised guilt and the tyranny of death annihilated by divine sacrificial love? Or to put it another way, how will the problem of suffering and justice be ultimately solved without the Crucifixion and Resurrection of Christ? How will death be defeated without Him?

Who is this man, humiliated and killed on a Roman Cross between Heaven and Hell by the creatures he had created? Friedrich Nietzsche was right. We did kill God, but not as he said. He did not imagine, in his wildest dreams, that justice and love kissed and embraced on the Cross. And that image tells us precisely what happened. Love found a way for justice to be satisfied. The Lord God Almighty is revealing Himself to us as the Sovereign Creator, Judge, and Redeemer.

"Behold the man," said Pontius Pilate when he displayed Jesus to the hostile crowd, unaware of the dreadful irony they were living through. The only sinless man who ever lived became the scapegoat for us all. Crucified, rising the third day, He defeated the power of sin and destroyed the horror of death. Following the thief on the cross who died beside Him, those of us who recognise Him for who He is will live with Him forever. Amid the most dreadful turmoil, we can pray with the comfort of divine joy, "Hallowed be your name, Your Kingdom come, and Your will be done on earth as it is in heaven."

This is the story and the prayer that makes forgiveness meaningful and gives Western civilisation any greatness it ever had.

Books Worth Reading

Ahdar, Rex. *Worlds Colliding: Conservative Christians and the Law.* Ashgate. 2001.

Allan, R. T. *The Education of Autonomous Man.* Avebury, 1992.

Ali, Ayaan Hirsi. *Infidel.* The Free Press. 2006.

Ali, Ayaan Hirsi. *Prey.* HarperCollins. 2021.

Anderson, Digby (ed). *The Kindness that Kills: The Churches' Simplified Response to Complex Social Issues.* SPCK. 1984.

Anderson, Digby (ed). *The Loss of Virtue. Moral confusion and social disorder in Britain and America.* Social Affairs Unit. 1992.

Berger, Bridgitte, and Peter. *The war over the family. Capturing the middle ground.* Anchor Press Doubleday. 1983.

Biggar, Nigel. *Colonialism. A Moral Reckoning.* William Collins. 2023.

Bilek, Jennifer. *Transsexual Transgender Transhumanism: Dispatches from The 11th Hour.* Spinifex. 2024.

Burke, Edmund. *Reflections on the Revolution in France and other writings.* Alfred A Knopf. 2015.

Carson, D. A. *The Gagging of God: Christianity Confronts Pluralism.* Zondervan. 1996.

Desmet, Mattias. *The Psychology of Totalitarianism.* Chelsea Green Publishing. 2022.

DiAngelo, Robin. *White Fragility.* Beacon Press. 2018.

Eberstadt, Mary. *Primal Screams. How the Sexual Revolution Created Identity Politics.* Templeton Press. 2019.

Eliot, T. S. *Notes Towards the Definition of Culture.* Faber. 1962.

Finnis, John. *Natural Law and Natural Rights.* Second edition. OUP. 2011.

Fish, Stanley. *There's no such thing as Free Speech, And It's a Good Thing, Too.* OUP. 1994.

Fitzgerald, Frances. *The Evangelicals. The Struggle to Shape America.* Simon and Schuster. 2017.

Girard, René. *I See Satan Fall Like Lightning.* Orbis Books. 2023.

Glendon, Mary Ann. *A World Made New.* Random House N.Y. 2001.

Goodwin, Matthew. *Values, Voice and Virtue.* Penguin. 2023.

Goodwin, Matthew. *Bad Education: Why Our Universities are Broken and How We Can Fix Them.* Penguin. 2025.

Guinness, Os. *Unspeakable: Facing Up to Evil in an Age of Genocide and Terror.* Harper. San Francisco. 2005.

Harper, Kyle. *From Shame to Sin: The Christian Transformation of Sexual Morality in Late Antiquity.* Harvard Univ. Press. 2013.

Himmelfarb, Gertrude. *The Demoralisation of Society, From Victorian Virtues to Modern Values.* IEA. 1995.

Himmelfarb, Gertrude. *Roads to Modernity.* Vintage Books. 2004.

Holland, Tom. *Dominion: The Making of the Western Mind.* Little, Brown. 2019.

Jeffries, Stuart. *Grand Hotel Abyss: The Lives of the Frankfurt School.* Verso. 2016.

Katz, Barry. *Herbert Marcuse and the Art of Liberation.* Verso. 1982.

Kendi, Ibram X. *How to Be an Antiracist.* One World. Random House. 2019.

Kimball, Roger. *The Long March: How the Cultural Revolution of the 1960s Changed America.* Encounter Books. 2001.

King, Michael. *The Penguin History of New Zealand.* Penguin Books. 2003.

Landes, Richard. *Can the Whole World be Wrong? Lethal journalism, antisemitism, and global jihad.* Boston. 2022.

Lasch, Christopher. *The Culture of Narcissism.* W.W. Norton & Company. 1979.

Legutko, Ryszard. *The Demon in Democracy: Totalitarian Temptations in Free Societies.* Encounter Books. 2016.

Lewis, C.S. *The Abolition of Man*. Geoffrey Bles. London. 1956.

Lewis, C.S. *The Seeing Eye*. (ed. Walter Hooper) Ballantine Books. N.Y. 1967.

Lewis, Jon E. ed. *The New Rights of Man*. Robinson. London. 2003.

Lines, William J. *Romancing the Primitive*. Quadrant Books. 2024.

MacDonald, Heather. *The Diversity Delusion: How Race and Gender Pandering Corrupt the University and Undermine Our Culture*. Saint Martin's Press. 2018.

McWhorter, John. *Woke Racism: How a New Religion Has Betrayed Black America*. Portfolio Penguin. 2021.

Mansfield, Nick. *Subjectivity: Theories of the Self, from Freud to Haraway*. Allan and Unwin. 2000.

Marcuse, Herbert, Robert Paul Wolff, Barrington Moore Jr. *A Critique of Pure Tolerance*. Beacon Press. 1965, Postscript 1969.

Minogue, Kenneth. *The Servile Mind: How Democracy Erodes the Moral Life*. Encounter Books. 2010.

Morrison, Wayne. *Jurisprudence: From the Greeks to Post-Modernity*. Routledge-Cavendish Publishing. 1997.

Murray, Charles. *Coming Apart. The State of White America, 1960-2010*. Crown Forum. N.Y. 2012.

Murray, Douglas. *The Strange Death of Europe: Immigration, Identity, Islam*. Bloomsbury. 2017.

Murray, Douglas. *The War On the West*. HarperCollins. 2022.

Nietzsche, Friedrich. *The Anti-Christ. (trans. H.L. Mencken)* Blinker North. 2024.

O'Keefe, Dennis. (ed.) *The Wayward Curriculum*. The Social Affairs Unit, 1996.

Parekh, Bhikhu. *Rethinking Multiculturalism: Cultural Diversity and Political Theory*. Harvard University Press. 2000.

Perry, Michael J. *The Idea of Human Rights*. OUP. 1998.

Phillips, Melanie. *The Sex Change Society*. The Social Market Foundation. 1999.

Phillips, Melanie. *The Builders' Stone*. Post Hill. 2025.

Popper, Karl R. *The Open Society and Its Enemies*. Princeton Classics. 2020.

Rabinow, Paul. (ed.) *The Foucault Reader*. Penguin. 1991.

Rieff, Philip. *The Triumph of the Therapeutic*. University of Chicago Press. 1966.

Rindsberg, Ashley. *The Gray Lady Blinked*. Midnight Oil publishers. 2021.

Rookmaaker, H. R. *Modern Art and the Death of a Culture*. Crossway Books. 1973.

Rufo, Christopher F. *America's Cultural Revolution: How the radical left conquered everything*. Broadside Books. 2023.

Rutherford, Samuel. *Lex Rex or the Law and the Prince.* Sprinkle Publications. Harrisburg, 1982.

Sandall, Roger. *The Culture Cult: Designer Tribalism and Other Essays.* Westview. 2001.

Schwartz, Howard S. *The Revolt of the Primitive.* Praeger. 2001.

Smith, Steven D. *Pagans and Christians in the City: Culture Wars from the Tiber to the Potomac.* Eerdmans. 2018.

Sowell, Thomas. *A Conflict of Visions.* William Morrow and Company. 1987.

Sowell, Thomas. *Barbarians Inside the Gates and Other Controversial Essays.* Hoover Institution Press Publication. 1999.

Sowell, Thomas. *Intellectuals and Race.* Basic Books. 2013.

Sowell, Thomas. *Social Justice Fallacies.* Basic Books. 2023.

Stark, Rodney. *The Rise of Christianity.* Harper, San Francisco. 1997.

Trueman, Carl R. *The Rise and Triumph of the Modern Self.* Crossway. 2020.

Walsh, Michael. *The Devil's Pleasure Palace.* Encounter Books. 2015.

West, Patrick. *The Poverty of Multiculturalism.* Civitas. 2005.

Zimmerman, Carle C. *Family and Civilization.* Harper Brothers. 1947.

Glossary of Key Words and Concepts Used by the Author

Gnosticism: Emerging in the late 1st century, Gnosticism is a collection of religious ideas emphasising special spiritual knowledge (gnosis) over orthodox Christian teaching. The material world is flawed or evil, created by a lesser divine being known as the demiurge, and salvation comes through enlightenment and understanding of the true divine nature. Modern Gnosticism emphasises personal spiritual knowledge above the authority of the Jewish and Christian Scriptures. It is the syncretism derived from the ancient competition of competing religions.

Multiculturalism: Multiculturalism is a political doctrine that stems from the belief that all cultures are equal.

Natural Law: On the one hand, natural law is a philosophical theory that posits the existence of inherent laws and moral principles derived from nature, which can be discovered through reason. On the other hand, there is the belief that natural law is in harmony with the divine will. Hence the phrase, "written on our hearts."

Naturalism: Naturalism claims that the material world is all there is. Material principles best account for any explanation of nature. Sometimes the word is used interchangeably with materialism. Naturalism can be used to describe a particular genre or style in art, literature, or music.

Objective Value: Objective value is a universal value. It does not depend on history or culture. It may be discovered and explained by reason, but not invented by it. In this essay, I have attempted to explain that the doctrine of objective value is rooted in the transcendent.

Pagan: Pagan is a term with real content, but is frequently used pejoratively. It's a Christian term used to describe religions that do not worship the God of the Bible. The term 'pagan' comes from the Latin word *paganus,* meaning 'country dweller' or "rustic." Initially, 'pagan' referred to a non-Christian person living in rural areas outside the major cities of the Roman Empire. The term can now include pantheists and animists, Ancient Greeks and Romans, the tribes and nations surrounding Israel in the Bible, and even a modern vocal unbeliever in Christ.

Populism: Populism is a recent pejorative term that describes what we used to mean by the democratic idea of rule by the majority.

Progressive liberalism: Progressive liberalism endorses social justice and social services, a controlled economy, and the expansion of civil and political rights. It's a corruption of classical liberalism. Unlike classical liberalism, which understands that difference and favours limited government, progressive liberalism fudges the difference between negative and positive rights.

Romantic Primitivism: Romantic Primitivism (romancing the primitive) is a belief in the myth of the Noble Savage, a stereotype uncorrupted by civilisation. The "noble" savage symbolises the innate goodness and moral superiority of a primitive people living in harmony with nature. It's an old idea that predates Rousseau. Shakespeare satirises the myth in his play *The Tempest*.

Scientism: Scientism is exaggerated trust in scientific method and, at the same time, a distortion of it.

Sphere Sovereignty: Given systematic content by the Dutch theologian and Prime Minister of the Netherlands, William Kuyper (1837-1902), sphere sovereignty differentiates the responsibility of those institutions that Edmund Burke called the 'little platoons'. Each sphere of life, family, church, unions, and clubs, has the authority, know-how, and responsibility to determine how a society should function. Sphere sovereignty involves the idea that God is the creator of social order.

Subjectivism: Subjectivism is the doctrine that the human imagination is absolute. The conclusions of the individual mind are unquestionable.

Sublime: Sublime is given a capital letter when it refers directly to the Transcendent.

Subsidiarity: With its roots in Catholic social teaching, subsidiarity teaches that social and political issues should be dealt with at the local level. The assumption is that people share a common ethic. The Oxford English Dictionary says that subsidiarity is "the principle that a central authority should have a subsidiary function, performing only those tasks which cannot be performed at a more local level. The concept applies to the family, local government, education, law and order, and communication."

Woke: A much criticised term, but helpful shorthand to describe the social justice movement.